REBIRTH

adding the first letter of their last name after Karen—Karen B, Karen C, Karen L. A few other names, such as Dan and Michael, are designated in the same way. I apologize if this is confusing, but I couldn't bear the thought of changing any names, and I didn't want to include surnames.

Rebirth is my journey back to health. I was fortunate to live through my cancer experience; many people do not. Throughout my treatment, I didn't know whether I would survive; what I did know was that while I was still here on this earth, I was going to make each day count even when I didn't feel well. It's not easy, but attitude is everything. How you think about your situation makes all the difference in the world—not just to you, but also to those who love you.

PREFACE

I began writing this book on December 18, 2003—the day I was diagnosed with leukemia. I had been journal writing since 1992, and I knew that this would be a helpful tool for dealing with my emotions throughout chemotherapy, bone marrow transplant, and recovery. After the initial shock of the leukemia diagnosis somewhat wore off, I decided that I must do something positive with this situation. This tragedy would be the impetus for me to help others. I set out to use my journal writing to author a book that would inspire, encourage, provide information, and give hope to those battling cancer and perhaps even motivate them to write their own stories because writing is an exceptional tool for healing.

Rebirth is written in journal format to give the reader more of an insight into my daily life (both the ordinary and the extraordinary), to see how a cancer patient copes or doesn't cope, and to provide strategies for improving one's state of mind and physical well-being—at least strategies that worked for me. And while this book is written specifically from an acute lymphocytic leukemia patient's perspective and experiences, this book, at least it is my hope, will be beneficial to anyone going through a difficult period, whether it is the person experiencing the pain or family members and friends trying to figure out a way to help.

There are some notes about the writing of the book I want to share with the reader. Time references are given throughout many entries. I had my journal with me at all times in order to capture thoughts, events, and medical information—especially when I was hospitalized for chemotherapy and bone marrow transplant. These time references are also indicative of the amount of time I had to fill when I couldn't do anything except lay around at home or in the hospital. Perhaps placing the time of day in these entries wasn't necessary; but it's how I recorded events, thoughts, and information. Therefore, that's how I decided to write it.

The reader will also notice that I have many women named Karen in my life. I have designated the different Karens, with the exception of my sister, by

FOREWORD

"The scariest was hearing I had cancer. What a dreadful word. However, it is only a word, and one can view it as a death sentence or as a means to discover one's strength. I feel that I have discovered how much inner strength and resolve I possess." With these insightful words, my patient Deborah Ludwig captures the range of emotions that a patient with newly diagnosed acute leukemia experiences. Although there have been tremendous advances in the treatment of leukemia, with many patients now expected to have successful outcomes, this is not a tale of medicine but rather a triumph of spirit and courage. Through this journal, we learn of the how through faith, the aid of family and friends, the support of health care workers, and the inspiration of fellow cancer patients, one individual was able to overcome her disease. Ms. Ludwig came to New York to be an actress. I am sure that this is not the story that she wanted to tell. Yet it was the part that she was cast. I am so pleased that it has a happy ending.

Stuart Goldberg, MD
Chief, Division of Leukemia
Associate clinical professor of medicine
Hackensack University Medical Center
November 14, 2007

For Barbara and Dan

In memory of Bo and Karen L

Library of Congress Control Number: 2008910353
ISBN: Hardcover   978-1-4363-8570-1
               Softcover   978-1-4363-8569-5

Grateful acknowledgment is made to the following for permission to
reprint previously published material:

"A Bend in the Road" by Helen Steiner Rice. Used with permission of the
Helen Steiner Rice Foundation, Cincinnati, Ohio. © 1965 by the
Helen Steiner Rice Foundation. All rights reserved.

Passages from *God Calling*. John Hunt Publishing Limited, 46a West Street,
New Alresford, Hants S024 9AU, United Kingdom.

Stephen Schwartz, Grey Dog Music, for reprinting the lyrics to "Defying Gravity"
from the musical *Wicked*.

Lani Ford of STARK for reprinting the lyrics to "This Day."

This book was printed in the United States of America.

To order additional copies of this book, contact:
Xlibris Corporation
1-888-795-4274
www.Xlibris.com
Orders@Xlibris.com
53495

REBIRTH

A Leukemia Survivor's Journal
of Healing during Chemotherapy,
Bone Marrow Transplant,
and Recovery

Deborah Ludwig

PROLOGUE

December 14, Sunday

The T. Schreiber Studio holiday party is this evening. It is snowing heavily, but I am going to force myself to go because it will be good for me to get out and socialize. There is no outfit I am really psyched about wearing. Well, there was until bruises began generously decorating my legs. I've noticed more frequent bruising over the past several months and merely credited it to the aging process. However, over the past few weeks, the bruising has gotten increasingly worse—more prolonged and a greater area of coverage. It looks as if someone has been pummeling me.

I went online last night to research "excessive bruising" and was not happy with what I discovered. It was very frightening in fact. There could be something wrong with me as easily treatable as a vitamin deficiency. Blood clotting or poor clotting problems were listed as possibilities as well. But what caught my eye first were the serious ailments like leukemia and non-Hodgkins lymphoma. Breathlessness was listed as a symptom of leukemia, and I find myself out of breath often when walking up the stairs and through the subway. I have rationalized this fatigue to being out of shape and leading a sedentary lifestyle although I walk everywhere in the city. I also carry huge bags packed with all the items needed for the day because once I leave my apartment, I'm out until I return from all my appointments, errands, or classes. One would expect to be out of breath carrying bags and climbing stairs, but what is disturbing to me is the length of recovery time. Still, self-diagnosing is probably not wise.

I am glad a doctor's appointment is scheduled tomorrow afternoon so that I can ask Dr. Dizon about all the bruising. I'd planned on changing insurance carriers at the beginning of the year to obtain more affordable coverage—though the actual benefits won't be as extensive, nor will the out-of-pocket costs be as inexpensive as with my current carrier. I've always been in good health, so I figure I can get by with a lesser plan. Unfortunately, if there is a major medical problem . . .

Stop it! I am getting myself all worked up again. Stay positive, and if there is a problem, deal with it at the point of discovery. For now, I'm going to doll myself up for the party and have a good time. I may not see these people for a while because I'm taking some time off from acting class to make money. It's depressing to think I won't be in class, interacting with my fellow actors—even if only for a few months.

December 15, Monday

Dr. Dizon was concerned enough about the bruising to order additional blood tests. She also wants to see me on the twenty-ninth for a follow-up visit. She gave me her cell phone number and asked that I call her next week while I'm in Indiana (I'm leaving on the twentieth) so that she knows I'm doing all right.

I'm feeling very fragile at the moment. I've done something to my right leg. The upper thigh gives me pain; if I twist it a certain way or walk while carrying my bags, it aches terribly. Maybe living in the Northeast isn't good for me. Well, I must make it good for me. My eating habits are awful—too much junk food and coffee—and my financial situation is dismal. The problem is that I'm too soft. I'm letting little things get me down, and I didn't use to let that happen. I find myself wanting to be taken care of, and the reality of my situation is that *I* must take care of myself; no one else is going to do it. Too much time has been spent feeling sorry for myself instead of being positive about my life and proactive about my situation. And why am I not as proactive about seeing talent agents as I am temporary-employment agents? The answer is simple: temporary-employment agents are more accessible than talent agents. So how do I make talent agents more accessible to me? All this worrying is making me ill.

I don't want to be sick or worried about my health and finances, so I have to start earning money. I got myself into this mess by not seeking office employment until my unemployment compensation ran out. I was seeking acting jobs and putting 100 percent of my effort and faith into finding paying jobs in the entertainment industry. Was this irresponsible? Probably, but I didn't want to surrender my acting to office work until absolutely necessary. Unfortunately, as a result, my financial situation is precarious at the moment. It's time to come up with solutions and stop wallowing in self-pity.

Hmmm . . . I wonder when I'll hear from Dr. Dizon . . .

PART I

DIAGNOSIS AND CHEMOTHERAPY

December 21, Sunday

It is said that life is unpredictable. Well, that is an understatement. I have leukemia—cancer. Never in my life did I imagine the word "cancer" could, or would, be associated with me.

I was diagnosed with leukemia on Thursday, December 18, 2003. Prior to being diagnosed, I'd been struggling with financial woes, men issues, career obstacles, and physical-appearance neuroses—all of which seem incredibly insignificant and trivial in the face of failing health. In the absence of a major life crisis, daily worries and petty annoyances are simply awarded much greater importance and urgency than they warrant.

Before December 18, 2003, I was living the life of a struggling actor in the New York City area. Despite the challenges, I was so energized to be living my dream—finally taking the career risks that I'd postponed for eight years. I'd performed in two Off-Off-Broadway productions; booked background work on *Ed*, *Sex and the City*, and an Oxygen network movie titled *My Sexiest Mistake*; and taken classes at the T. Schreiber Studio. In addition to these projects and classes, I was starting to find administrative temporary office work to help alleviate the financial problems that had begun to plague me.

Now something more sinister was plaguing me. The events that have transpired over the past five days began on December 17.

December 17, Wednesday

Early in the morning, I rented a car and drove out to West Paterson, New Jersey, to do a testimonial for a well-known grooming product. The interviewer asked me to explain why I liked the product and why others should buy it. It was unscripted, so I was able to talk about the product using my own words.

Around noon, after arriving home from the shoot, there were two messages on my answering machine from Dr. Dizon urging me to call her cell phone number as soon as possible. The urgency in her voice made me uneasy. Two days before, I'd visited her office for a follow-up appointment for some urology tests, which were fine. I then addressed my concern about the bruises that had been appearing on my legs in increasing numbers since Thanksgiving. My legs looked as if someone had constantly beaten me up—the bruises were *everywhere.*

After examining my legs, she immediately sent me down to the lab for some blood tests; and knowing that I was going to be leaving on the twentieth for my hometown, Tell City, Indiana, for the Christmas holiday, she gave me her cell phone number in case I needed to reach her. She also scheduled a follow-up appointment for the twenty-ninth. I went to the lab, had blood drawn, and walked home. I was concerned. The night before my doctor's appointment, I'd gone online to research "excessive bruising"; and to my dismay, the first word I saw was "leukemia," which understandably sent a wave of terror crashing through my body. Going into the doctor's appointment, I was well aware of how serious this could be although I was still convinced it was innocuous—most likely a vitamin deficiency of some sort that could easily be remedied. Truth be told, I hadn't been eating very well.

After listening to Dr. Dizon's messages, I immediately called her. She told me that the results of my CBC (complete blood count) were very bad. The counts for red blood cells, white blood cells, and hemoglobin were all low; and my platelet count had dropped to fifteen thousand. (A normal platelet count is 150,000-450,000 platelets per microliter of blood.) Dr. Dizon instructed me to go to the emergency room immediately. Stunned, I hung up the phone—the emergency room? Suddenly, my entire body was shaking with fear. I was supposed to meet my brother-in-law Dan for lunch, so I called him and asked that he meet me at Jersey City Medical Center. Poor guy, I'm surprised he could understand a word of what I was saying; I was hysterical.

I attempted calling several taxi companies, and no one was answering the phones. I was crying and shaking uncontrollably yet trying to remain calm in order to think rationally. Finally, someone at Flecha Taxi and Limousines answered the phone, and I told the guy, "I need to get to the hospital right now!" He was there within five minutes and sped off to Jersey City Medical Center.

In my anxious haste to exit the cab and pay the driver, I lost all $160 I'd walked away with at the testimonial shoot. It must have fallen out of my billfold onto the floor of the cab. I discovered this loss later that day and was devastated. It is almost laughable to think of a struggling actor *finally* getting paid to do a job and then, in a frenzied state of fear, losing those earnings the very same day.

At the hospital emergency room, the aides took my vitals; then I waited to be registered. Because the doctor had made my situation sound so dire, I was getting nervous sitting there waiting to be processed, so I called Dr. Dizon again. She was angry that I was sitting in the waiting area because she'd called ahead to let them know to expect me. It seemed so surreal that not two hours before, I'd been shooting an on-camera television spot, and now I was sitting in an emergency room with an unknown diagnosis looming in front of me.

After hanging up, Dr. Dizon, via phone, facilitated my getting through registration and into the emergency room immediately. I changed into a hospital gown, and the tests began. Meanwhile, Dan had picked up my sister Barbara, and they both arrived at the ER about an hour and half later. Relief washed over me when Barbara walked into the room. Barbara is fourteen months younger than I and possesses the same small bone structure; she stands about five feet three while I measure about five feet two, and despite the fact that she has blonde hair and mine is light auburn, our physical similarity is undeniable.

She waited with me while the results were being processed. Not only did they draw blood, but they also ordered a chest x-ray and an electrocardiogram (EKG). An electrocardiogram records the electrical voltage in the heart and is used in the screening and diagnosis of cardiovascular diseases. Numerous other tests were conducted as well.

Dr. Dizon arrived around 5:30 p.m. when the emergency room lab results came back. The Jersey City Medical Center's CBC matched Dr. Dizon's CBC results, except that there didn't appear to be any blast cells. Dr. Dizon had seen blast cells on her results, and thus, she suspected leukemia. (Blast cells, per the Leukemia & Lymphoma Society's informational booklet about acute lymphocytic leukemia, refer to the earliest marrow cells identified by the light microscope. Blasts represent about 1 percent of normally developing marrow cells. In acute leukemia, blast cells, similar in appearance to normal blast cells, accumulate in large numbers, perhaps up to 80 percent of all marrow cells.)

Dr. Dizon was not comfortable with my being tested for leukemia at Jersey City Medical Center; so following my insurance company's instructions, she referred me to Hackensack University Medical Center (HUMC), which is located in Hackensack, New Jersey. HUMC's Adult Blood and Marrow Stem Cell Transplantation Program is the sixth largest and one of the most prominent stem cell-transplantation programs in the United States. Over two hundred stem cell transplants are performed each year.

I was discharged at 6:30 p.m., and Dan drove Barbara and me to HUMC. On the way there, I received a call on my cell phone from my friend Lynn, who is a nurse and lives in Rockport, Indiana. A few days earlier, I'd sent her an e-mail message in which I mentioned the bruising. Lynn was calling to check on me. I explained the situation to her, told her we didn't know anything conclusive yet, and asked her not to say anything to anyone because my parents had no idea what was transpiring at the moment. After I hung up, Dan was compelled to inject a bit of levity into the situation by remarking, "Boy, some people will do anything to get attention!" We all laughed. As an actor, many times in the past, I would kid around with people about how I loved getting attention and how "it was all about me." Unfortunately, this time, it was all about me; and I didn't like it one bit.

Once at HUMC's emergency room, I underwent the same barrage of tests that I had just completed that afternoon. I have never felt so poked, prodded, pricked, and x-rayed before in my life. It was a very long, frustrating, and scary day.

Looking back over the day's ordeal, I feel that God guided me in choosing Dr. Dizon as my primary care physician. When I first moved to the area, I knew no doctors, nor did I have a referral from a friend or family member. I merely selected her from the physician directory based on her location and gender. I am so impressed with the attention she gave me and the initiative she took with my care that afternoon—working with the staff at Jersey City Medical Center and my insurance company while simultaneously tending to the patients at her office. She is a very special lady—my guardian angel.

Dr. Dizon wanted the on-call physician at HUMC to admit me that night because she was afraid I could start spontaneously bleeding due to my low platelet count, which to me is an absolutely terrifying thought. The last thing I wanted to happen was to be sent home, start hemorrhaging, and bleed to death; I was determined to be admitted.

Barbara and Dan left around 1:00 a.m., and two hours later, I was finally transferred to a private room on the ninth floor of the Pavilion where I eventually fell asleep.

December 18, Thursday

This morning, Dr. Robert Alter, a hematologist (a medical doctor who specializes in the diagnosis and treatment of diseases of the blood and blood system, such as anemia, blood-clotting disorders, and leukemia), came in to my room to review the emergency room results with me. I was adamant that I was not leaving the hospital without being tested for leukemia. He told me that if it were just a platelet issue, he'd send me home, and we'd work on an outpatient basis; however, with the white blood cell count being low, it could be indicative of leukemia, so he wanted to conduct further tests. To test for leukemia, a bone marrow aspiration had to be performed and a bone sample retrieved for a biopsy.

The bone marrow aspiration was not a painful experience but rather an uncomfortable one, especially since the doctor was working so diligently to retrieve marrow that had essentially dried up. Healthy bone marrow should flow freely from the bone.

To begin the process, I had to roll over on my side. The nurse sterilized the area of skin where the back of my hip bone is located on the right side, and a shot was given to numb the area. A needle was then stuck into my bone. There was no pain, just a lot of pressure. Dr. Alter had difficulty retrieving marrow. He made several attempts, pushing and working the needle into the bone, which later resulted in extreme soreness. I tried to relax, breathing slowly and deeply while tears welled up in my eyes, not due to the pain, but because what was happening to me seemed unbelievable. In the end, he cut a piece of bone and sent the sample to the lab without any marrow. The bone alone would confirm whether I had leukemia.

Barbara had returned early in the day to be with me. All day, I was dreading the results and trying to stay positive. Barbara was, and has continued to be, a great source of support and comfort to me. She allows me to talk incessantly about my situation and gives me needed hugs. When I first moved to New Jersey in the fall of 2002, she and Dan let me crash at their home for three months until I found an apartment. It was at Dan's encouragement that I made the move because he had told me that I was welcome to stay with them for a while. Opening their home to me made my transition much easier. I'm very lucky to have such a loving family.

At about 5:30 p.m., Dr. Alter entered my room, and I knew immediately the news was going to be life changing. He sat down and informed me that the bone biopsy came back positive for leukemia. A jolt of panic surged through my entire body. I took a deep breath, pursed my lips together, and tried to hold back the tears. I parted my lips slightly and released my breath slowly. I glanced at Barbara, and clearly, she was upset. I had suspected as much, but actually hearing it was shocking. Dr. Alter informed me that Dr. Stuart Goldberg, my oncologist, would be in later to talk to me more in depth about what I was facing and the treatment options available. He also said that another bone marrow extraction would be performed the following day because the marrow is needed to determine the type of leukemia I have as there are several varieties.

He left the room, and I started sobbing. How could I tell all my friends and, most of all, my parents and other sister, Karen? This news would devastate my parents. Barbara said that she would call the family, but she wanted to wait until after we talked to Dr. Goldberg so that she could provide them with more specific information. I agreed.

About forty minutes later, Dr. Goldberg arrived. I put on a brave face and listened intently to what he was saying. I'm surprised I remembered as much information as I did, but it was good that Barbara was there because she retained more than I. He explained to us the composition of blood, how leukemia develops, and the treatment options.

First, he gave a very simplified version of what blood is composed of and how leukemia develops. Blood is made up of red blood cells, white blood cells, and platelets. When blast cells (usually immature white blood cells, myeloblasts or lymphoblasts, but can also be immature red blood cells, erythroblasts) take over, this causes a disruption in the production of healthy cells and platelets. He likened this to weeds in a garden. The weeds, if not contained, will eventually take over and kill the vegetables or flowers (the "good stuff") in the garden. Blood cells start out large and as they mature, get smaller. These "immature" blood cells, or blast cells, in essence refuse to grow up, remain large, and thus crowd out and destroy healthy cells.

He then enumerated the side effects of chemotherapy, all of which can be dreadful and some even permanent. Side effects include the following: anemia (when the level of healthy red blood cells [RBCs] in the body becomes too low), bowel obstruction, diarrhea, fatigue, infections (where, in some cases, complications from infections can result in death), hair loss, mouth sores, nausea, neuropathy (the deterioration of the peripheral nerves, which can cause tingling, itching, and burning sensations in the fingers and toes), sleep problems, appetite loss, and infertility.

For years now, I've been contemplating adoption over biologically having a child, so I was surprised that I was upset about discovering that chemotherapy could render me infertile. Merely knowing that the option to potentially conceive a child could be taken away from me was heartbreaking.

Before Dr. Goldberg left the room, the actor in me mustered up the courage to face the situation head-on, and I exclaimed, "Okay, let's kick the shit out of this thing!" But as soon as he departed, my brave exterior crumbled. I got up out of bed, took a few steps, covered my face with my hands, and started sobbing. My first words were an anguished yet quiet and understated declaration of "I'm so screwed." (Except I didn't use the word screwed.) My sister hugged me tightly.

We released our hold on each other, and Barbara picked up the phone to call our parents and sister. I ended up talking to Karen because I wanted her to call some of my girlfriends—I didn't want them to hear this news via e-mail. I gave her the phone numbers for my closest Cincinnati friends: Karen B, Lisa, Natalie, Robin, and Yvonne. Earlier, I had spoken to Lynn, who then called Cindy and Maria (both lifelong friends like Lynn) to give them a heads-up about what might be happening.

While Barbara spoke with Mom and Dad, I remained in a daze—completely shocked. How could this happen? I'm only thirty-seven years old. My future held such promise. How, how, how could this happen?

Barbara had been asking the same question. She has been so strong the past couple of days despite her fears. We've cried a lot together. I found out that last night when she went to my apartment to pick up some clothing, my journal, and my computer for me, she had a meltdown. She needed some time away from me to cry, grieve, and come to terms with this situation herself. Right now, she is my rock; I know that whatever I need, she will provide. I've written the following statement numerous times throughout my years of journaling, but I'll write it again: I am so blessed to have the family and friends that I do. I am not fighting this disease alone; there are many people fighting with me and giving me an enormous amount of strength.

After making the phone calls, Barbara left for her home to get some rest and see her baby boy, Aidan. A nurse came in to inform me that I was being moved from the ninth floor to the Benito and Carmen Lopez Stem Cell Transplantation Center, located in HUMC's Medical Plaza, on the eighth floor of Pavilion East (8PE). I gathered my belongings and was wheeled down to my new room. It was very nice—a private room with a thirty-seven-inch plasma-screen TV, Internet hookup, and twenty-four-hour room service from the kitchen. If one had to be in the hospital, this was the place to be. This center was designed for immunosuppressed patients, and therefore, no air from other parts of the hospital enters the unit's air ducts. There are nineteen private rooms and two isolation rooms.

I was immediately placed on a low-microbial diet and instructed that due to the bacteria and dirt found in fresh flowers or plants, I was not to have these in my room. This was the nursing staff's subtle way of telling me that friends and family should not send flowers or plants to me.

The low-microbial diet, in a nutshell, prohibits fresh fruits, unpasteurized dairy products or juices, "moldy" cheeses—blue, Roquefort, gorgonzola—(all of which I love), and all raw vegetables. Meat and fish must be cooked to well-done. Eating from salad bars and selecting food out of open containers are off-limits. There are many other guidelines, but these were the ones that particularly caught my attention. Given all these precautions, I was quickly discovering that my immune system had become extremely vulnerable to infections.

December 19, Friday

Dr. Goldberg attempted to extract bone marrow again—this time, from the left hip bone—and managed to retrieve a small amount. There is a genetic component that has to be tested for as well, which will determine if I have the Philadelphia chromosome. Dr. Goldberg defined this as an abnormality of chromosome 22 in which part of chromosome 9 is transferred to it. There is usually a reciprocal break in chromosome 22 that attaches to chromosome 9. This chromosomal abnormality places leukemia patients in the high-risk category and makes treating the disease much more difficult.

The results came back later in the day, and it appeared I most likely have acute lymphocytic leukemia (ALL), which is the most common form of leukemia found in children. Of course, like any childhood disease (e.g., chicken pox) in adults, ALL is more problematic in adults. If the Philadelphia chromosome is present, then I will definitely have to have a bone marrow transplant because, in this instance, adult ALL cannot be cured with chemotherapy alone. It will be several days until we have results regarding the Philadelphia chromosome because the cells being tested must grow before any conclusion can be made.

December 20, Saturday

This ordeal is just beginning, yet so many people have already reached out to me. Today, I had visits from Eleonore and Russ (Dan's parents) and later Bob and Donna, who are very good friends of Dan's parents; Donna is like a second mom to Dan. Barbara showed up later. Nelson, a Cincinnati friend who now lives in New York, has offered his frequent flyer miles to my family so that they can visit me as often as they like. Michael D, a dear friend from Cincinnati and an excellent dance partner, is watching Karen's dog, Dante (a black lab/husky), so that she and her husband, Jeff, can travel here from Cincinnati; they could not find a kennel at this late date. People are offering so much help, and I am on prayer lists all over the country. The power of prayer is a very potent ally—I truly believe that.

Throughout all of this, Barbara and Dan have been amazing. Since Dan has a cold and pinkeye, Barbara has kept him away from me. However, he is doing so much from a distance—helping with household chores, working to install wireless capability on my computer, and paying bills. They paid off my credit cards, which was no small amount of money. I feel badly that they did it, but Barbara said she didn't want to worry about paying a bill for me every month; plus she added, "You'll be debt free when you are well again." Of course, contemplating all the inevitable medical expenses is pretty daunting; however, I know, and everyone tells me, the financial aspect of this situation is the last thing I should be worrying about at the moment. They're right. My focus has to be on getting well.

I had a CT (computed tomography) scan this morning. CT scans use advanced x-ray technology to take pictures of cross sections of the body. These machines can see inside the brain and other parts of the body and into areas that cannot be seen on regular x-ray examinations.

After the scan, I became very flushed. This was a result of the dye injected into me prior to the procedure. I felt quite feverish and became fearful that I was getting sicker. Inevitably, I know that I will get sicker before I get better. Once chemotherapy commences, my whole immune system will be destroyed.

I was feeling discouraged when one of the pastoral care ministers, Pat, came into the room to talk with me. She let me cry and asked me questions about my acting career. She is also a Reiki specialist. (Per the International Center for Reiki

Training Web site, Reiki is defined as "a Japanese technique for stress reduction and relaxation that also promotes healing." It is administered by "laying on hands" and is based on the idea that an unseen "life force energy" flows through us and is what causes us to be alive.)

After we talked, Pat performed Reiki on me. When she was done, I felt lighter and calmer, and the flushed feeling had disappeared. I am definitely going to continue with energy work. Before leaving, Pat recited to me Helen Steiner Rice's poem "A Bend in the Road." It was so inspirational, beautiful, and moving that I shed tears.

This leukemia diagnosis is the scariest, most daunting obstacle I've faced in my life. When I make it past this "bend," I will be a changed person—at least I hope so. I no longer intend to take anything, or anyone, for granted. I intend to be fearless, and I intend to make a difference in peoples' lives.

December 22, Monday
8:30 a.m.

Yesterday, I had a more positive attitude than in the past couple of days. I'm trying to be strong, and at some point, trying will turn into being.

My cousin Mike called Saturday night. He fought esophageal cancer this past spring and summer. He was the first person with whom I've spoken that I did not shed tears. Perhaps that's because of our shared experience with cancer. He revealed his feelings of fear, anger, and hope throughout his struggle enduring chemotherapy and surgery. Even at present, in remission, he admitted that living from doctor's visit to doctor's visit—now at three-month intervals—is an agonizing exercise. Mike told me that he always thought he'd die of a heart attack as an old man while pushing a lawn mower. I agreed with him that I never thought I'd get sick this young. He also encouraged me to find the strength within myself because no matter how much support I have from family and friends, I am the only one physically going through it. He added, "At eleven o'clock, when they shut off the lights, you're the only one there."

So I must gather the strength and courage from within myself. Of course, allowing my loved ones to support me however they feel necessary for their own peace of mind is important too. Mike's reaching out to me made me feel ashamed that I did not call him when I found out about his cancer diagnosis. Of course, he was always in my prayers, but I failed to contact him. This was a huge lesson for me: don't delay reaching out to people in need. His effort meant the world to me, and I intend to do the same for others when they're in a crisis. Mike and I ended our conversation with a pact to keep each other in our prayers.

I have experienced a myriad of emotions over the past few days: sadness, fear, determination, hope, and even a little rage. I have yet to express that rage though.

Natalie and Nelson both told me, "But that's not in your nature." Actually, it is very much in my nature, but I do tend to dwell more in the emotions of sadness and fear when in a crisis. When I allow myself to really think about the situation, I am furious—furious about losing my health and fighting for my life at age thirty-seven, furious about the disruption of my fledgling acting career in New York City, and furious about the timing of it all (being Christmas)! Unfortunately, there are many people of all ages in this world feeling despair, and I am no more important or special than anyone else to think that tragedy could never touch me. I have been lucky up to this point in my life. The most major losses I've dealt with were my grandmothers' deaths, which were bad enough. Now my family has to deal with my illness, which will not be easy for them.

I've had a thought, and I hate to even write it down. But this is my journal, and I need to be as open as possible. Over the past year, there were two times when I felt very depressed and life seemed so tough that I thought if I died, no one would have to worry about me anymore. I have to wonder, did my subconscious somehow conjure this cancer into being? I'd choose life over death any day now that I'm looking my mortality directly in the face.

I would rather struggle through life's difficulties than die. I was feeling sorry for myself. So many people in this world are in much worse financial or personal turmoil than I am. I feel I've been so self-centered over the past years though friends and family refute that notion. I have this skewed vision of how I see myself—at least that's what I've been told by friends and my sister Karen. I have rarely felt that I am "enough," and I don't give myself credit for my accomplishments or my abilities. I scrutinize my shortcomings, especially the physical, and I don't recognize the kind things I do for people and how those kind gestures positively affect them. I don't value myself. I've picked myself apart for so long that I don't have a clue what I truly appreciate and love about myself.

11:15 a.m.

I've taken a shower and feel much better. I sent out e-mail messages to let people know what is going on with me and am quite overwhelmed by the outpouring of love and support I've received. Cindy and Lynn were calling as early as last Wednesday. Friday, Lisa, one of my dearest friends and a cofounder of Ovation Theatre Company, called and asked, "You will do anything to get me to come visit you, won't you?" That question made me laugh.

So many emotions . . . My mind wandered again to Thursday night when Dr. Goldberg informed me that at my age, with the chemotherapy, it would be very unlikely that I would ever bear children. I've held the idea of adoption in my mind for so long that I didn't expect to feel so distraught about not being able to have a child. I guess that in the far recesses of my psyche, I had held out the hope of having a biological child. That option is now out of the question because I would never expose a fetus to my body after going through the ravages of chemotherapy. The loss of my reproductive ability is a loss with which I must come to terms.

I not only have to come to terms with the possibility of infertility and early menopause, but I also have many personal issues to work through. One of those issues is to stop trying to do everything on my own and recognize when to ask for help. I believe now that my refusal to ask for financial help over the past six months contributed to my failing health—maybe not leukemia, but definitely my compromised immune system.

Barbara scolded me on Saturday, "You always ask for help if you need it—that's what families are for." She added, fighting back tears, "It broke my heart when I walked into your apartment Thursday night, and you had no food. I felt like a bad sister." She went on to say that when she looked around my apartment, she felt guilty that I was living in such a small place and wondered if she had been so wrapped up in her own life that she hadn't realized how unhappy I was. Should she have helped me more emotionally and financially?

Barbara's confession made me realize that by shutting her out and trying to protect her from my troubles, I was hurting her. She is the last person I'd intentionally hurt because I love her, and words are inadequate to describe how deeply that love extends.

10:35 p.m.

Dad arrived today. Dan dropped him off at the hospital. Mom stayed away because she has a cold; I'm not supposed to be around anyone who is sick.

Dr. Scott Rowley, chief of the Division of Stem Cell Transplantation, came in around 6:00 p.m. and informed me that they have definitively concluded that I have ALL. I shouldn't be so negative, but I am assuming the genetics will be bad because I'm not a child; in fact, for an ALL patient, thirty-seven is old. Most likely, after chemotherapy is completed, I will have to have a bone marrow transplant.

Usually, at this time of year, I review the past twelve months and write about my goals that were and were not achieved. This year, I'm going to reassess my emotional state and how I ended up in this situation instead. I somehow feel that I contributed to my illness no matter how irrational that may sound. Was I so stressed out and unhappy that I unconsciously willed myself to get sick so that I wouldn't have to hold myself accountable should I fail to achieve my goal of being an actor? Did I compromise my health by drinking, eating poorly, avoiding financial issues, wallowing alone in my depression, and depriving myself of sleep? These are unhealthy actions in which I repeatedly engaged.

The positive aspect of this is that if I *did* contribute to my illness, then I can *undo* it; the mind is a powerful instrument. There are studies that show we can, and do, contribute to our own illnesses; and because we can make ourselves sick, we also possess the power to make ourselves well.

I've always felt that God had a big plan for me—something important and/or inspirational. I still believe that—so what is it? That is one of the major questions to which I will be searching for an answer. There is so much self-exploration to do. In essence, I must chart a map of the changes I want to make in order to live a more fulfilling life.

Donna gave me the book *The Power of Full Engagement* by Jim Loehr and Tony Schwartz. Eleonore gave me *Head First: The Biology of Hope* by Norman Cousins; *The Creation of Health* by Caroline Myss, PhD, and C. Norman Shealy, MD; and *Living Through Personal Crisis* by Ann Kaiser Stearns. I have much reading to do and am hoping these books will be enlightening and inspirational. A positive attitude throughout this process is going to be essential to my healing.

There are several changes I want to make. First is to live each day fully, to be in the moment. I thought I was already doing that; however, in reality, I was always in the planning phases, looking toward the future. Planning is good, but I'm obsessive about it. I need to enjoy the here and now. Second is to be fearless. After facing my mortality, casting directors and agents will seem completely nonthreatening, or so I hope. Is this a chance for me to begin an acting career anew without the fear and trepidation I have felt in the past? Is this the chance to develop a meaningful new career in life—maybe writing or outreach? This all needs to be explored.

This huge obstacle I've been given to overcome may be one of the greatest gifts I've ever received because it has, and will continue to, put life into perspective for me. And when I am well again, perhaps my purpose in life will be much clearer. *I want to be healthy again! I must have a second chance at life! I must live!*

December 23, Tuesday

My first thoughts today were about Aidan. At his baptism, as his godmother, I made a promise to be there for him throughout his life; I plan to honor that promise. It is one of the most important commitments I've made. He is so precious to me, and I will not abandon him.

It's been an emotional roller-coaster ride today. When I'm scared, I cry yet try to be brave, but it's difficult. I must trust the faith I always cling to during challenging moments—knowing that God is on my side gives me courage. Every time I receive chemo, I have to hold on to all the love, support, and prayers of my family and friends and believe that God is there watching over me. It's going to be a tough fight, but I'm going to make it. I'll be damned if I'm going to let everyone live thirty to forty years without me.

I'm starting to consider my treatment options. Tomorrow, I will make my decision to either enter the ECOG study or undergo the Hyper-CVAD protocol. Either way, chemotherapy will commence soon. It is difficult to ponder that at some point in the near future I could be dead, but I am conquering that fear because death is not an option. I am banishing death from my mind and am focusing on life—life that I love and treasure. I always felt that I valued life; but until this happened, I didn't truly realize how much I cherished it, even in all its messiness. This is the fight of my life. I'm going to face it with every bit of determination, energy, and positive thinking I can muster. This is my "renaissance." This cancer diagnosis literally splits my life into two parts—the first half of my life before cancer and the second half of my life after cancer. I plan to make the second half spectacular.

Karen and Jeff arrived today, which gave Barbara a much-needed break from driving to and from the hospital. Dad spent the night in my room with me last night because he didn't want me to be alone. It's comforting having them all here.

December 24, Christmas Eve

Around 1:00 a.m., I began experiencing intense pain in my pelvis and legs. The pain started in my thighs and slowly progressed downward. Painkillers and even a small dose of morphine did not alleviate the ache. At one point, in the very-early-morning hours, my nurse sat down with me, held my hand, and let me talk about my fears and sadness. She even held me for a while as I cried. I will never forget that moment, and she will never know what her concern and attentiveness meant to me. To take the time out of her busy schedule to sit with me was a truly compassionate act.

Still, I was up all night—moving around, stretching, crying, and hoping that I'd gotten myself all worked up over nothing and that the pain was merely muscle tension. I walked around the ward this morning and did some of the vibration exercises I had learned in my body dynamics class this past fall, but the throbbing persisted.

Kathleen came in to do some Reiki on me, which calmed my mind and eased some of the pain. Later, Dr. Rowley informed me that what I was experiencing was not muscle pain but most likely bone pain from the leukemia. That information terrified me and made me think that chemo should start today because this was the first day I had experienced any pain associated with the leukemia. I knew I had to talk to Dr. Goldberg again before I decided which treatment option to pursue.

A researcher had stopped by to discuss the ECOG (Eastern Cooperative Oncology Group) study with me. Karen and Jeff were with me during this discussion, and Karen posed many questions that I would never have thought of asking, such as, "Does she have T-cell, B-cell, or pre-B cell leukemia?" Pre-B cell was the answer. Since finding out about my diagnosis, Karen has been doing a great deal of research on leukemia, and she confessed later that much of what she was learning scared the hell out of her.

The ECOG study consent form that I was given to review contained the following information:

This study involves the use of chemotherapy to obtain remission, followed by either conventional treatment with more chemotherapy or either autologous bone marrow transplant or allogeneic transplant if a suitable donor is available. The purpose of this study is to: 1.) slow or stop the growth of your leukemia; 2.) gain information about your disease; and 3.) evaluate the safety and effectiveness of drugs and procedures which have shown to be effective in other patients with this disease.

Chemotherapy drugs will be administered for 28 days, followed by more chemotherapy or bone marrow transplant.[1]

The study, of course, was extremely detailed with regard to chemotherapy drugs, the number of times each would be administered throughout the first twenty-eight days, and a list of variables that would determine whether the patient received an allogeneic or autologous bone marrow transplant or continued on with a two-year chemotherapy protocol. It all made my head swim. And the thought of being pummeled with chemotherapy drugs for twenty-eight days straight was repugnant to me. I needed to speak with Dr. Goldberg.

After the researcher left, I had a grueling pulmonary test in which I performed several different tests, breathing into a tube while my nostrils were clipped shut. This was not an easy task for someone challenged in the hemoglobin department. Upon returning to my room, the onset of nausea caused me to vomit. I felt awful, and I was scared and crying. I could tell that my father was distressed and felt helpless as he begged the nurses to do something to assuage my discomfort.

Finally, Dr. Goldberg arrived, and he explained the Hyper-CVAD protocol to me again. I decided to go down that route as opposed to the ECOG study because the ECOG path seemed much harsher. I needed a gentler treatment protocol, even if it was drawn out over a longer period of time. However, Hyper-CVAD is not all that gentle due to the amount of chemo received during each cycle. There are four A cycles alternating with four B cycles. Each cycle requires admission to the hospital for four to five days, every two to three weeks.

I decided that for me, spending time with my family and rejuvenating my spirit between treatments was more important than being battered with chemicals for a month straight, which I feared would break my spirit. I told Dr. Goldberg that I longed to hold on to some quality of life, to which he responded, "Unfortunately, you won't have quality of life—not for a long time." Well, we'll see . . . I may not have my usual quality of life, but I can definitely make the most of each and every moment of each and every day, and that I plan to do.

Unfortunately, right now, my spirit is weakened. I received many phone calls today, but as the day progressed, I was unable to take them because of my fragile physical and mental states. It was a very distressing afternoon and evening. At 8:00 p.m., I began chemotherapy, and morphine alleviated my pain. This was a welcome and much-needed reprieve from the constant bone pain. Drifting in and out of consciousness and then sinking into morphine-induced delirium, I finally found repose.

December 25, Christmas Day

Christmas has always been an exciting time of year for my family. The few weeks between Thanksgiving and Christmas are filled with numerous preparations—the decorating, shopping, and cooking. My parents always made the holiday season special—Dad with his love of Christmas recordings and holiday movies and Mom with all her baking and decorating. When we were in grade school, my sisters and I would write out several revisions of a list detailing how we would spend Christmas Eve day (we opened our gifts on Christmas Eve evening). Christmas 2003 was going to be more of the same, minus the childhood lists. We were all planning to gather in my parents' new home that they'd moved into mid-September, right before Karen and Jeff's wedding.

My parents, Bill and Nancy, are about as opposite as two people can be; yet somehow, they managed to hold their marriage together all these years. They both grew up in Tell City. My dad was a small-town boy while my mother was a farm girl. Mother was valedictorian of her high school class and was a very prim, proper young woman. (She remains prim and proper to this day.) On the other hand, my father was probably close to the bottom of his class, not because he lacked intelligence—he just didn't care (a fact he grew to be ashamed of as he matured). He was also a hell-raiser, pulling practical jokes and drinking with his buddies. Yet somehow, they connected after being introduced by Bob, a friend of Dad's, who was dating Mom's sister Ruth Ann. Bob and Ruth Ann eventually married. (My cousin and friend Cindy is their only child.)

My mother has brown hair and is small in stature like Barbara and me though she stands a little taller at five feet four. Dad is about five feet ten and was a redhead in his younger days. The red hair is now white, which looks distinguished on him. He actually resembles CNN's Wolf Blitzer—same haircut, hair color, beard, and glasses.

My mother works for the *Perry County News* as a bookkeeper/office manager. My father is a case manager at Branchville Training Center, a minimum-security prison located twenty miles north of Tell City, off Highway 37. He is the supervisor of the F dormitory and is the case manager of the arrival and orientation unit.

I'm glad my parents are here, but I had so been looking forward to getting out of the northeastern rat race for a week or more and celebrating the holiday with my family. Everyone was to be there—Barbara, Dan, Aidan, Karen, Jeff, and me. Dad's wish of having a house with a fireplace had finally come true, and I'd planned on spending much time warming myself and relaxing in front of that fireplace. However, the Christmas that I'd envisioned was not to be. Instead, this holiday, everyone flew to New Jersey to be with me.

I'm feeling much better today than yesterday. It is my second day of chemotherapy. A few days earlier, Dr. Klein had inserted a temporary indwelling catheter into my chest area in order to access a larger vein as opposed to the tiny one in my right arm they'd been using. This catheter—which is used to give blood and platelet transfusions, to administer chemotherapy and other medications, and to retrieve blood samples—was tunneled under the skin of my chest to keep it in place.

Mom and Dad are with me now; they both stayed the night at the hospital. Mom and I went for a walk around the leukemia unit this morning, but the workout had to be cut short due to the incessant beeping of my dose-rate calculator. This machine regulates the volume and the speed at which chemotherapy, blood products, and fluids are pumped into the body. These machines beep all the time, and because they are so sensitive, as little as a tiny air bubble in one of the lines will set them off. The nurses must get so frustrated because they are constantly running from room to room, adjusting them for all the patients.

The dose-rate calculator is attached to the IV pole, which is next to my bed. The dose-rate calculator, which is also battery-operated, can be detached from the electrical power cord attached to the wall so that I am able to move around. The IV pole and dose-rate calculator go with me everywhere—to the bathroom, the shower—anywhere I am able to venture. I call it my dance partner.

After returning from my brief sojourn around the ward, Sally,* from the pastoral care office, came to my room to do some guided imagery and Reiki work with me. Mom and Dad participated too. All of us concentrated on the imagery that Sally was verbalizing while laying their hands on me.

After Sally left, a nurse informed me that I would be receiving a platelet transfusion because my platelet level had dropped to nine thousand. However, there was some good news. The preliminary tests show that I may not have the

Philadelphia chromosome. Dr. Goldberg is having some additional detailed testing done to further confirm these results. What a great Christmas gift! Karen was ecstatic. She had been doing so much research and, of course, being the information guru that she is, had collected all the facts—the good, the bad, and the ugly. So she was very pleased to hear this positive news.

Karen is the youngest of us three girls—ten months younger than Barbara. Despite being the youngest, she ended up the tallest, measuring about five feet seven, has a muscular build, and possesses gorgeous long curly dark brown hair. She and I shared an apartment for nine years in Cincinnati—and we still like each other.

Karen is working toward her PhD in political science in the areas of public opinion, research methods, and elections. When she and Jeff started dating in November 2001, she was employed as a research assistant at the Institute for Policy Research. She is now employed at the Evaluation Services Center at the University of Cincinnati as a research associate. Jeff is employed at Kroger as a senior analyst.

I was friends with Jeff for several years before he and Karen started dating although they knew each other. In the fall of 2001, Jeff bought a condo in Anderson Township and shortly thereafter, threw a housewarming one Friday night. Natalie, Karen, and I were planning to attend together. However, at the last minute, I decided against going because I didn't feel very well. Karen was disappointed. I told her to go without me, that I was sure Natalie would welcome her company. So she called Natalie, and they drove to the party together. Apparently, Karen and Jeff spent a great deal of time talking that evening. Jeff asked her out a few days later, and the rest is history.

I received more calls from friends. Carol, my body dynamics instructor, left a voice message on my cell phone, telling me to "heal the child in you that has the acute lymphocytic leukemia (ALL) since ALL is the type of leukemia most often found in children." I plan to explore this thoroughly. She also mentioned that she detected an urgent quality in my voice on my voice mail outgoing message. I've always known I've carried a lot of tension in my body, which is probably due to a low level of anxiety that resides within me. She could hear that anxiety in my voice. She suggested that I read *Healing Visualizations: Creating Health Through Imagery* by Gerald Epstein, MD. Eleonore then proceeded to go out and purchase this book for me.

Robin, a Cincinnati friend, called shortly after I'd retrieved Carol's message. I think she felt much better after talking with me. I explained all that was going on—the tests, the blood and platelet transfusions, leukemia, the components that make up blood, and my treatments. She said, "You are the only person I know who could make this interesting and put a good spin on it."

"I don't know about that," I chuckled. "But I am trying to turn this dismal episode into something positive."

This Christmas was void of all the usual holiday frills and merriment, but with family surrounding me, it truly affirmed for me that this holiday is for celebrating love—the birth of Jesus and the precious gift of family. Never in our wildest dreams did my family think we'd experience a Christmas that held such gloom. Regardless of how dire this situation is, my family is here by my side, and thoughts and prayers from all over the country are pouring in. How beautiful is that? I feel so loved and safe, even though I am extremely scared. I thank God for my family and friends.

I also thank God for health care workers (in fact, all employees who work on holidays). The staff at HUMC is amazing—kind, empathetic, knowledgeable, and loving. I feel secure in the hands of these doctors, nurses, and aides.

* Name change

December 26, Friday
10:50 a.m.

Dr. Goldberg performed my first intrathecal therapy procedure this morning to see if any leukemia cells are present in my spinal fluid. If cancer cells are in the spinal fluid, they could seep into my brain. The intrathecal therapy procedure is as follows: The doctor inserts a needle into a space between the vertebrae in the lower back until it enters the space that contains the spinal fluid (this is referred to as a lumbar puncture or a spinal tap) and then extracts spinal fluid to be tested for the presence of leukemia cells. After retrieving this fluid, he injected chemo—in this case, methotrexate—into the area to destroy any cancer cells that might be present or to prevent cancer cells from developing. It didn't hurt except that the numbing of my lower back burned, but other than that, it was mostly just uncomfortable—quite uncomfortable, actually—and very similar to a bone marrow aspiration.

Karen held my hand throughout the procedure. I had to sit up and lean forward over a bedside table so that the doctor had clear and easy access to my lower back in order to manipulate the spinal region. The thought of what was happening was worse than the actual procedure, and afterward, I was quite emotional. I was instructed to lie flat on my back for an hour to prevent a severe headache.

I was so glad that Karen was there holding my hand. I cried because I was feeling sorry for myself. Spinal taps, bone marrow aspirations, CT scans, pulmonary tests, heart MUGA scans, needles, IVs—all of this was becoming incredibly overwhelming. How much can one little 108-pound body endure?

Karen stayed by my side, letting me talk and cry, and then she read to me the healing affirmation Dad had copied out of a book and sent to me. Calmly and slowly, she read it over and over. At first, every muscle in my body was tense, but the gentle melody of her voice helped my body to relax; and I eventually opened up my arms with palms facing up, uncrossed my ankles, and allowed the positive energy to flow through and over me like a loving stream of warm water that both strengthened and soothed me. I must tap into that same feeling of renewal each time I experience a harsh procedure, a distressing emotion, or anything upsetting to my sense of security and balance. That's how I must approach this whole process.

This is my struggle, my journey; and though it's terrifying, I'm trying so hard to approach it with grace and aplomb. I must allow myself to experience all emotions. If I want to cry, then I cry; if I want to scream, then I scream; if I want to curse, then I curse; if I want to laugh, then I laugh. It doesn't matter; what matters is to experience these emotions truthfully and fully.

I'm alone now. Jeff has picked Karen up at the hospital, and they are driving to West New York to help Dad and Dan move my belongings out of the apartment. I am going to relax and enjoy my solitude until my family returns tonight. A smile curls my lips as I think of them.

2:20 p.m.

Nelson and Beckie called. They've been keeping very good tabs on me, almost daily, from Puerto Rico. And the poem "A Bend in the Road" that Pat recited to me last Saturday, Nelson found it online and e-mailed it to me. Here it is:

A Bend in the Road
by Helen Steiner Rice

When we feel we have nothing left to give
And we are sure that the song has ended,
When our day seems over and the shadows fall
And the darkness of night has descended,
Where can we go to find the strength
To valiantly keep on trying?
Where can we find the hand that will dry
The tears that the heart is crying?

There's but one place to go and that is to God,
And dropping all pretense and pride,
We can pour out our problems without restraint
And gain strength with Him at our side.

And together we stand at life's crossroads.
And view what we think is the end,
But God has a much bigger vision,
And He tells us it's only a bend.

For the road goes on and is smoother,
And the pause in the song is a rest,
And that part that's unsung and unfinished
Is the sweetest and richest and best.

So rest and relax and grow stronger . . .
Let go and let God share your load,
Your work is not finished or ended . . .
You've just come to a bend in the road.[2]

5:30 p.m.

Karen and Jeff have returned to the hospital. They lost Dan and Dad on the return drive from West New York to Basking Ridge, and since they only knew how to get back to the hospital, that's where they came. My apartment is empty; its contents now are being stored in the basement of Barbara and Dan's home. I feel a deep sense of loss, especially of my independence. That basement studio wasn't good for me, but it was affordable. It was maybe 210 square feet, no sunlight ever shone in, and there were definitely environmental issues. There were two or three occurrences, within eleven months, of sewage creeping up from the shower drain and too many times to count when water was leaking down the walls in the kitchen area, coming from the water pipes in the apartment above mine. In the end, moving out was for the best.

One of the social workers just popped back in the room to provide me with information about adult ALL and an application for financial assistance from the Leukemia & Lymphoma Society. I may be eligible to receive up to $500 in reimbursements for the cost of medications and transportation to and from my outpatient doctor's visits.

Karen and Jeff stayed until 11:00 p.m., which was when my fifth chemo treatment ended. They fly back to Cincinnati tomorrow morning. I'll miss them. Karen and I cried when she told me how much of a void there would be in her life if I didn't make it. I try not to think of that, but it is a possibility—none of us is guaranteed tomorrow. I promised her that if I needed her, I would reach out any time of the day or night.

December 27, Saturday

The sixth chemo transfusion is done. I am supposed to be released tomorrow in time to celebrate Aidan's first birthday. I cannot wait to hold him in my arms. I haven't seen him since Thanksgiving weekend. On the table next to my bed is an adorable framed picture of him wearing his little brown bomber jacket and sitting on Santa Claus's lap. Barbara brought this picture to me my second day in the hospital, and it makes me smile every time I look at it.

Oh, the doctor just informed me that I'll be going home tonight! However, I'm scheduled to return to the Cancer Center, which I also refer to as the clinic, for an outpatient visit Monday morning.

2:00 p.m.

I'm having lunch. It's about three hours after my chemo, and I'm feeling a bit nauseous, so I'm hoping the food will settle my stomach. I have two chemo injections scheduled for 3:00 p.m., and then when the family gets here, I can pack up and go home for the next three weeks.

Speaking of food, I remain on a low-microbial diet. I have been on this diet since they moved me to the Stem Cell Transplantation Center. This is the diet that forbids raw fruits and vegetables, sushi, rare meat, moldy cheeses, pepper (pepper is heavily contaminated with a fungus known as aspergillus although cooking kills this fungus), and a whole list of other restrictions. Any food that carries bacteria or fungi can potentially cause serious infections in a body that is immunosuppressed. Therefore, neutropenic patients are told to avoid certain foods and are given instructions for food preparation in order to eliminate or reduce the presence of bacteria and fungi. I am being sent home with a detailed packet outlining these strict dietary guidelines to ensure that I don't eat anything I'm not supposed to. (Neutropenia refers to a situation in which the number of neutrophils in the blood is too low; thus, someone who has a low-neutrophil count is considered neutropenic. Neutrolphils are white blood cells that surround and destroy bacteria in the body.)

The spinal fluid sample came back negative for any leukemia cells, which is excellent news. Dr. Klein will remove my temporary catheter before I am discharged this evening. When I return to the hospital for my next round of chemotherapy, she will install a permanent catheter, which will remain in my chest for as long as it is needed.

December 28, Sunday

I'm at Barbara and Dan's home with my parents. It is Aidan's first birthday. Today, I haven't felt very well—quite lethargic, easily winded. Merely walking short distances such as to and from the bathroom makes my heart race. Nausea is also a problem. Perhaps a bowl of soup and a bit of ginger ale will calm my stomach.

Donna, Bob, Eleonore, and Russ came over this afternoon to celebrate Aidan's birthday. Eleonore wore a mask because she's recovering from a cold, but she was sneezing a lot and occasionally removed her mask, so I decided to retreat to the confines of my bedroom. I don't blame her for taking the mask off because I know from experience how uncomfortable it is to have it covering one's mouth and nose. I didn't feel much like celebrating anyway.

December 29, Monday

It was an exasperating day. I woke up feeling very tired, weak, and winded and experienced a small amount of indigestion—I never have indigestion. I was miserable by the time I arrived at the clinic for my first outpatient visit at 9:00 a.m.

The entire clinic visit was a nightmare. I was released over the weekend from the hospital, so my appointment for this morning had not been scheduled. As a result, getting vitals taken and blood drawn took longer than it would have had I been on the schedule. I was aggravated with both the check-in process and the front-desk personnel. I snapped a couple of times at staff members, then immediately apologized. They were very understanding because they knew I was frustrated and not feeling well. When we arrived at the clinic, the man at the front desk asked if I had an appointment. Leaning on the counter, mask covering my face and breathing heavily, I growled, "Well, I better have an appointment! I feel like crap!"

Mom told me later that the guy at the desk had been making a phone call in my behalf to expedite getting me in to see Dr. Goldberg and told someone, "Well, she said she better have an appointment because she feels like crap."

I had to laugh. It sounds rather comical when someone else says it. It was rather bitchy of me yet in a way, in the midst of all my agony, kind of funny too. Well, at least the staff worked to get me processed as quickly as possible. Sometimes, you have to make a few waves to get things accomplished. I just had to muster what little bit of attitude I could in my weakened state to help move the process along.

Actually, the guy at the front desk did as much as possible to facilitate my registration, labs, and vitals. I discovered that he is a bone marrow transplant survivor of three years, and January 19 is his transplant anniversary. One piece of advice he gave me was to keep my mask on when I'm out in the waiting room area and when I go out in public, especially when my immune system is compromised. Good advice. No wonder he is so patient; he has experienced this situation himself. Compassion is a beautiful thing.

Once I was settled into a blue reclining chair in the chemo room, I was given fluids. Dehydration was what was making me so fatigued—well, that on top of a low-hemoglobin count. I must start drinking more fluids because I am no longer receiving them intravenously, and staying hydrated is so important, especially when you're ill.

I received a Neulasta shot while there. It's a drug I'm supposed to take after each chemo treatment, which aids in increasing my white blood cell count. Phyllis, a nurse who works closely with Dr. Goldberg, had prescriptions written for me for acyclovir (antiviral), Diflucan (antifungal), Cipro (antibacterial), and allopurinol (lowers blood uric acid levels to prevent kidney stones).

When I arrived home, there was a message from Terry, my acting teacher. He, Joseph, and Cristina (Joseph and Cristina were in Terry's class with me) were calling to check on me. Karen B, one of my closest friends in Cincinnati, had left a message also. I will call them all when I feel stronger.

There is some good news—Barbara told me today that she is pregnant. I am so happy for her and Dan. I hate that this has been such a stressful time for her. I don't want her to be overly burdened or anxious because of my health crisis. She's been so worried the past week, going through this ordeal with me, knowing she was pregnant, sharing this fact with the doctor but not with me because she didn't want me to have more to worry about.

As happy as I am for her, I can't help feeling sorry for myself. While a new life is being celebrated, I am fighting for mine. It seems so unfair, but then, whoever said life was fair? And I feel wretched being consumed with this self-pity because I will love this little baby as much as I love Aidan. I'm frightened and sad, but I'm going to think of this as a time of birth for both of us—the fetus arriving into the world in August as a beautiful baby and me emerging cancer free at the end of chemotherapy, which may be around July or August too. This will be our journey together, this new nephew or niece of mine—his or her birth and my rebirth.

[Four years later, I would discover the agony Barbara went through during this time period. Since a bone marrow transplant might be necessary down the road, she wanted to find out if it were possible for her to be a donor, being pregnant. She was troubled that the pregnancy might interfere with saving my life, so she looked for an opportunity to get my oncologist alone. One evening, during my initial hospital stay, she made an excuse to follow Dr. Goldberg out of the room. She told him that she was pregnant and asked if she could still be a donor if necessary. Dr. Goldberg congratulated her on the pregnancy, then said that she could be a donor if the time came for that. He did not tell her at the time that bone marrow donation during pregnancy was very rare; she would discover that information later.]

December 30, Tuesday

Dan has been so supportive throughout my convalescence. He needed a hug tonight, and I was more than happy to oblige. Dan is three years younger than Barbara. They met in Cincinnati and began dating in 1995. Soon afterward, Barbara took a yearlong assignment in Frankfurt, Germany, with Procter & Gamble, the company with whom she was employed at the time. Dan moved back to New Jersey shortly thereafter.

He too was a Procter & Gamble employee though he worked in a different area of the company. Barbara worked at the Winton Hill facility as a senior engineer in the paper science division. She was working on Bounty when she left the company. Dan wrote software for the sales force and worked in the downtown offices. He was still employed with Procter & Gamble as a systems manager when he moved back to New Jersey but eventually left the company to work for his father's business, which, at that time, built software to run warehouses.

Barbara and Dan endured a long-distance relationship for about a year, and then Barbara decided to make the move to New Jersey. She found employment with Johnson & Johnson, working as a group leader in the feminine hygiene division. Finally, October 7, 2000, Barbara and Dan were married. Barbara eventually moved over to ETHICON, another division of Johnson & Johnson, as patient and professional marketing director.

Though younger than Barbara, Dan has started getting gray hair; like my father, it's attractive on him. He also has a fourteen-year-old daughter, Alyssa. She's absolutely beautiful with long brown hair, brown eyes, and fair skin. She resembles both Dan and her mother, Amy. I don't consider her my stepniece, but rather my niece because she is part of my family, and I love her.

December 31, Wednesday

I never imagined that I'd be spending New Year's Eve in an outpatient clinic, receiving chemotherapy. But I'm determined to make the most of today. I'm sitting here in my chair, writing in my journal, contemplating my situation, and waiting for the platelets to arrive from the pharmacy downstairs. The doctor doesn't order platelets or blood until he sees the CBC results. If blood products are needed, an order is faxed to the pharmacy and then delivered to the chemo room. This whole process can take a while. After I get platelets, I see Dr. Goldberg for an intrathecal injection.

Mom and Dad left to grab some lunch; then Mom is going to the Shoppe on Fifth, located on the fifth floor of the clinic, to look at some wigs. She's going to bring a couple down for me to try on. I still have all my hair, but it will soon fall out. Wigs aren't really my style as I prefer hats and scarves. However, one never knows when a wig may be necessary or preferable.

The platelet transfusion was done by 3:30 p.m., at which time, Dr. Goldberg did the lumbar puncture to collect spinal fluid, then proceeded to do the intrathecal injection. Afterward, like the last time, I had to lie flat on my back for an hour to prevent a painful headache from occurring.

We left the clinic at around 5:00 p.m.; we'd arrived at 10:00 a.m. The drive home was grueling. I was irritated and impatient with Mom's driving and then felt awful about being critical of her. She gets nervous because she isn't used to driving in this kind of traffic. Plus she had difficulty seeing in the dark because there was a glare on her eyeglasses from all the headlights, which I didn't realize. I should've cut her some slack. Before going home, we had to stop at the pharmacy to drop off a prescription. I felt so weak and silently fought back tears because I didn't want my parents to know I was crying.

Once home, a wave of nausea suddenly washed over me, and I threw up and continued to do so four more times within the next three hours. This was the first time chemo hit me this hard. It was painful to vomit, and my stomach muscles ached from the spasms. Mom stayed with me in my bedroom that night because I didn't want to be alone. I felt like a little girl, but I felt safe. What a way to ring in 2004.

January 1, Thursday

Last night's nausea was the worst reaction I've had so far to the chemo. I had hoped to at least have a quiet evening at home with my parents, eating pizza and watching the New Year's countdown. However, I couldn't swallow any food or beverages due to the impulse to retch; and eventually, my stomach muscles were in a great deal of pain from the stress of throwing up nothing—dry heaves are horrendous.

I remain shell-shocked by everything that's transpired over the past two weeks. I'm doing everything I can to stay positive, but the diagnosis is still so fresh, and I must allow myself to grieve. I feel like an old lady right now, with my strength and energy so depleted. I even have an idea how Grandma Lucy (Dad's mother) must've felt as she tried to get around the last couple of years of her life as her emphysema worsened, and she was on oxygen.

A huge howling cry of grief and fury has yet to erupt from me, and at some point, I'm sure it will. And damn it, I'm allowed to feel sorrow and anger. I'm supposed to be following a dream, meeting new people, living my life to the fullest, and feeling good. Instead, I've been sidelined, and it's torturing me emotionally. How will I get back into the acting arena? Will my body ever again handle running, dancing, or any other physical activity? Will I look haggard after all the chemo? How many people will forget about me? There are so many unknowns. I should be more enlightened and spiritual about it. However, the anger and grief have to be dealt with before I can move forward. Then I can figure out how to make this the most constructive, growth-oriented period of my life.

Barbara just cut fives inches off my hair. This is one of many ways to empower myself during this crisis. Marleney, the saleswoman at the Shoppe on Fifth, suggested that it might be less traumatic for me if I cut several inches off my hair before strands of it begin falling out in long clumps. The thought of losing my long light auburn mane is not a pleasant one, but one I will inevitably face.

January 2, Friday

This is my life for at least the next six months, but I must make it work for me: three days a week for three weeks in the clinic and then four to five days in the hospital for seven rotations of chemotherapy (three A cycles, four B cycles—I've already had the first A cycle). Today, I received an injection of vincristine and two units of red blood cells. When I arrived at the clinic, I was extremely fatigued because my hemoglobin level had dropped to 6.4. The normal hemoglobin range for adult women is twelve to fifteen grams per deciliter; a significant anemia occurs when the hemoglobin drops below ten grams per deciliter. Hemoglobin binds with oxygen within the red blood cells, which then allows the red blood cells to transport oxygen throughout the body. So naturally, after receiving my two units of blood, I felt better.

I need to accept the fact that these outpatient visits can be all-day affairs and find a way to make the most of the time I am spending here. The last thing I want to do is sit here for eight hours feeling sorry for myself and being bored stiff. So to occupy my time, I will write in my journal, read, listen to music, and make lists. I love making lists, and more than making lists, I get immense satisfaction crossing items off those lists.

Yet I'm not doing these things; but rather, I find myself observing the other patients and their interactions with family members, nurses, and doctors. There's much suffering in this room, but there's much grace and elegance in that suffering too. The strength of the sick, the support of their families, and the compassion of the medical staff are inspiring to me. There is a resignation in pain—a certain amount of it is going to remain with you regardless of the medications given to alleviate it. For me, positive thinking, prayer, and meditative visualizations help manage the pain; music is soothing too. The headache I've had for two days is gone, probably because of the increase in red blood cells that are moving oxygen through my body. (It's amazing how this all works!) Hopefully, soon, my body will start replenishing these red blood cells on its own. I'm learning so much about blood—unfortunately, it took getting leukemia to obtain this education.

As I watch the blood drip through the line and into the vein in my arm, my thoughts turn to all those people who donate blood. The blood I'm receiving was donated in order to save my life. The blood of others is coursing through my veins, sustaining my life—how extraordinary! I've never given the gift of blood, and now I will probably never be able to donate blood because of the poisons being pumped into my system, not to mention the cancer.

Strangers and friends alike have given generously to me, and before long, it will be my turn to give back. My contribution could be working with children and adults who have blood cancers, advocacy, and fund-raising. I'm pretty sure some of my future work will include helping to find cures for blood cancers, which is now a very personal mission.

January 3, Saturday

The headaches are coming and going, but at least I have energy. What I accomplished today was significant—at least I think so. I mailed all the prescriptions to Tel-Drug, started completing the online Social Security Disability application, updated my Simply Audiobooks account (a gift from Natalie), and played with Aidan. This was my second day of taking dexamethasone (two more days to go). I have to take ten dexamethasone pills for four days. They're very tiny pills, thank goodness, and will be taken after every A cycle. Dexamethasone is a hormone that, when taken in large doses, can kill leukemia cells.

This evening, Mom, Dad, and I were discussing the day I was diagnosed. I discovered that Dan and Barbara had alerted them to my being in the hospital on December 17. (I was under the impression my parents didn't know anything until the eighteenth.) My parents had been in Evansville earlier that day to do some Christmas shopping. They had just returned home when they got the news of my emergency room visits. According to Dad, it was a major downer because everything had been good that day. Mom said from that moment on and into the next day, she was anxious and fearful.

The evening of the eighteenth, Mom's cell phone rang as she was heading down the driveway on her way to Grandpa's home to take him the dinner she'd prepared for him. It was Barbara informing her of the leukemia diagnosis. Feeling angry, upset, and helpless and because Dad was not home at the moment, she drove on out to Grandpa's. When she returned home, she broke the shocking news to Dad. Upset and distraught, they discussed plans to travel to New Jersey to be with me. A day later, Barbara helped coordinate their flight to Newark. Dad spent the next couple of days taking down all the indoor and outdoor Christmas decorations. His holiday spirit had died.

January 4, Sunday

Yesterday, Dad read an excerpt to me from a newsletter or a book (I don't recall which one) about a link between smoking, birth control pills, and leukemia. That's the first I'd ever heard of a connection between smoking and leukemia. I'd always heard that women, especially those over thirty-five, who take oral contraceptives and smoke have a higher risk of heart attacks, stroke, and blood clots—but leukemia? That information has been haunting me. I have been on birth control pills since the age of twenty-five, and I have smoked on and off for the past twelve years—never a lot, but at times, definitely more than I should have. No amount of carcinogens is a good amount of carcinogens, right?

I have to wonder how much of a contributing factor that has been to my illness. I won't dwell on it because it's in the past, but I can definitely change my future behaviors. There are probably numerous factors that have contributed to my illness, but then again, maybe none of them did—it was just a fluke. Who knows? I'm trying to explore all the possibilities that could have contributed to my getting leukemia so that I can make changes; I want to be a healthier, happier person.

Dad leaves for Tell City this afternoon. He's been a wonderful source of support and inspiration. He's leaving me with Catherine Ponder's books on healing as well as a list of affirmations on which to meditate. I love him so much. He would trade places with me in a heartbeat. I don't think he would ever get over it if any of his daughters died. "Children are supposed to bury their parents," he says. Of all my family members, my father, in my estimation, would least be able to deal with my death; so I have to make sure he doesn't have to deal with it. Plus I'm not ready to leave this world because there is too much to do and accomplish. There would be a great void in the world if I were gone. (I have to be a little egotistical sometimes and retain a sense of humor.)

Today is an anniversary of sorts. I started my period twenty-four years ago today. I know, it's funny, but I remember this date every year. *Are You There, God? It's Me, Margaret* by Judy Blume was a book that had a huge influence on my adolescent journey to womanhood. When I finally got my period at age thirteen, it was a huge deal, and I was definitely well prepared for it. It was so exciting—I was a woman! (Or so I thought.) Thanks, Judy.

January 5, Monday

Before we left for the hospital this morning, I called my insurance company to check on my conversion option. I'm currently on COBRA and need to change to an individual plan on March 1. I'm eligible to switch plans with my current carrier because I am enrolled in an HMO. Had I been in a PPO, I would have been ineligible. I would've had to find a new insurance carrier, and who is going to insure someone newly diagnosed with cancer? However, here in New Jersey, by law, they cannot turn you down; and if you've been covered under a previous plan with no more than a sixty-three-day lapse in coverage, the preexisting condition limitation is waived—this is considered continuity of coverage. At least, that is my understanding. What a pain to have to worry about insurance coverage when going through a major illness. Anyway, my insurer is sending me information describing the plans from which I can choose.

I'm more winded today than I was over the weekend, but I managed to prepare my own breakfast—a bagel with cream cheese, orange juice, and coffee. Afterward, I bathed and did my hair and makeup. When I feel good, or at least relatively well, I want to look attractive because it lifts my spirits and makes me feel normal again.

1:30 p.m.

The blood work is processed. The doctor does not need to see me, so now we're waiting for Dan. He drove Mom and me this morning and after dropping us off, left the clinic for a meeting near the hospital. I can't reach him on his cell phone—bummer.

2:30 p.m.

I called Dan again, but still no answer, so I left another message . . . it's been an hour. I'm trying to be patient, but I have this irritating mask covering my mouth and nose, which makes it difficult to breathe. Dan probably won't check his messages until 3:00 because that is the time I'd estimated my appointment would end, but we finished extremely early. I'm hungry, I'm tired, and I want to go home. My ears are clogged, so that is making me even more ill-tempered. Mom keeps telling me to be patient. I'm trying to stay positive, but I'm failing miserably.

To pass the time, I have been reading through the Social Security Disability information. Many financial documents need to be gathered and submitted with the application. I have been pretty thorough, I think. I'd like to have the paperwork completed and the supporting documentation organized tonight so that I can mail it tomorrow.

Finally, Dan's here!

January 7, Wednesday

I woke up this morning experiencing awful mouth pain. Not pain from mouth sores, but from a tooth infection. Because of my low-platelet counts, I haven't been able to use a toothbrush. Instead, I have been using these pink sponges attached to small sticks (maybe four inches long). They are completely inadequate for cleaning teeth, and as a result, food has gotten trapped beneath the flap of skin over my wisdom tooth on the right side of my mouth. I can't chew or swallow easily, and the gland where my chin and ear meet on the right side of my face is swollen; it really hurts. To further compound my agony, I also have a bit of a headache and am experiencing indigestion; and due to constipation, my stomach is upset. I rarely have headaches and never indigestion. Despite the discomfort, I'm attempting to maintain a positive attitude—at least I'm not nauseous and vomiting.

At the clinic today, I received platelets and red blood cells. I had several questions about medications, side effects, and the Hyper-CVAD protocol. Dr. Goldberg gave me some additional information about Hyper-CVAD: The study was conducted on 204 adult ALL patients between 1992 and January 1998. Overall, 185 patients (91 percent) achieved complete remission, and twelve (6 percent) died during induction therapy. Estimated five-year survival and five-year complete remission rates were 39 percent and 38 percent respectively (not encouraging numbers in my opinion). The conclusion drawn reads "Hyper-CVAD therapy is superior to our previous regimens and should be compared with established regimens in adult ALL."[3]

However, I had some good news. My white blood cell counts are coming up, and the more-detailed genetics test results revealed no sign of that nasty Philadelphia chromosome!

January 8, Thursday

My hair is dropping like leaves from trees in late autumn. I have to laugh, or I'll cry. It is freaking me out a bit because I'm really not ready for it to happen. Maybe I can get a stylist to come to the house and shave my head. Hair loss is not my only issue at the moment; my mouth is in agony too.

My mouth is very sore, which makes it extremely difficult to eat. I've taken some oxycodone (pain medication), which has lessened the mouth pain but has made me jittery and light-headed.

I'm sorting through the Social Security Disability supporting documents to be submitted with the application. I want this done by the end of the week. I'm having trouble signing my name to these forms because my hand is so unsteady—my signature is completely illegible. This shakiness is from all the chemo and numerous medications my body is trying to process. It is truly a nuisance not feeling well and having to take care of so many details concerning finances, insurance, and disability. I don't want to have to think about all of it.

Okay, enough about me. Mike has a follow-up appointment today with his doctor in Cleveland. I hope all goes well. I plan to call him this weekend and inquire how he is doing. He's called me twice since I was diagnosed, and it helps me to talk with someone who can identify with what I'm going through—different types of cancer, but cancer all the same.

Tonight, I was reading *Healing Visualizations*. There is one imagery exercise specifically for leukemia that I'm going to try. I need to commit the exercise to memory and then start putting it to use.

A week ago, I created my own visualization: on the inhalation, white healing light penetrated my body; on the exhalation, the light pushed out the black malignant cells. I think it has been helping because my white blood cell counts are up. I plan to use guided imagery often throughout the healing process.

January 9, Friday

Russ drove Mom and me to the clinic today. We stopped for Dunkin' Donuts' coffee on the way home. This was the first day I've felt like drinking coffee since I was hospitalized.

After talking with Dr. Goldberg today, I am feeling very positive. We may be able to fight this cancer with chemotherapy only. With chemotherapy, positive thinking, prayer, and lifestyle changes, I plan to have a long, healthy life. I will spend the next however many months nurturing myself. So regardless of my hair loss, weight loss, and shedding skin inside my mouth, I am going to stay focused on the goal of healing.

My mouth is feeling a little better, but soft foods are still all I can chew. I just devoured an entire box of macaroni and cheese. Well, I needed the 1,200-plus calories. I love to be able to eat this much and not worry about it. I'm 101 pounds right now with clothing and shoes, so chow down.

January 10, Saturday

I was greeted this morning by the sun filtering through the white shades and casting a golden hue throughout the room. This warm light seemed to emanate from vibrant shades of blue, gold, and purple lingering near the window. I lay there captivated by the stunning, soothing array of colors surrounding me. I want to become more aware of everything around me, more conscious of utilizing my senses, more alive in the present moment.

Barbara drove Mom to the airport this morning. I'm sure Dad will be glad to have her home. She has been such an amazing caregiver. She slept in my bed with me the past three nights, and last night, we even said some prayers together. As I watched her sleep, an overwhelming love for her consumed me. She has dedicated her life to her family, and this experience has shaken her world, but she is strong.

My energy level has definitely decreased since yesterday. It is more of an effort to do things, so I'm going to relax today.

I received a card from Michele, a grade school and high school friend. Michele's card included a few senior-prom photos and a prayer card. Those photos made me cringe and then laugh. I weighed about 120 pounds at that time. The cut of my tea-length baby blue satin dress was unflattering and made me look incredibly busty, and my hair was so eighties looking—curled with hot rollers and highlighted with Sun-In. At the time, I thought I looked pretty hot. It was nice to hear from Michele. The last time we spoke was at our fifteen-year high school class reunion. This summer, we'll celebrate our twenty-year class reunion—unbelievable.

Lani visited this evening for over three hours. She brought with her a huge goodie bag of books, games, and note cards. Her friend Liz even sent a couple of items—a decorative flower pin and a miniature glass owl. We munched on pizza and chips and chatted all evening. Dan and Barbara liked her very much. This was a wonderful opportunity for Lani and me to reconnect.

After she left, I realized that I had decided to abandon our friendship too soon last summer. I was frustrated with my own life, and I had started sensing negative energy when I was in her presence. She probably really needed me at that time, but I just couldn't bother trying to sustain this friendship because of my own issues, so I distanced myself from her. I regret that decision now because she was going through a very difficult period, especially with Peaches, her beloved little bulldog, who was very sick and eventually died. Peaches was such a sweet animal. Lani gave me two adorable photos of me and Peaches in Central Park in which I am holding a water bottle to her mouth so that she can take a drink.

If I ever doubted Lani's sincerity as a friend, that doubt has been eliminated. She has called often since she heard of my illness and is my first visitor of all my friends. Lani drove out to Basking Ridge from Manhattan in a car she borrowed from a friend. Lani's actions are an example of the kind of friend I want to be, and her visit meant the world to me. Plus it was a nice change to talk about her life and not just mine, which is all I've been talking about for the past two weeks.

She and STARK (her band) are going into the studio this week to start recording a CD. Good for her—it's about time. I hope that 2004 brings success to her in her music career; she's worked so hard and been up against many obstacles—it is her turn to succeed.

I learned two lessons tonight: one, don't take friendships for granted; and two, don't be too hasty in discarding a friendship that could turn out to be very precious.

January 11, Sunday

Geralynn, a college friend, called this afternoon to see how I was doing. I discovered that she'd been dealing with her own health issues. She was diagnosed with Bell's palsy the day she gave birth to her daughter, Rachel. (Bell's palsy is sudden weakness or paralysis of the muscles on one side of the face due to malfunction of cranial nerve VII [facial nerve], which stimulates the facial muscles.)[4]

She said at first she thought she was having a stroke because she could not feel the left side of her face. Once she knew this was not a stroke but rather Bell's palsy, her relief quickly turned to aggravation as the physical debilitation affected simple actions like drinking and speaking. However, the emotional toll was the most difficult part of the experience because the facial distortion made her hyper-self-conscious, and she dreaded venturing out in public. She admitted that this facial disfigurement made her very aware of her own vanity. Her Bell's palsy eventually disappeared, but she still experiences residual tingling on the left side of her face and an occasional twitch above her eyebrow or cheek.

She belittled her health issues in comparison with mine. I rebuffed her, saying, "There are always degrees of illness, and I can find people much worse off than I. The bottom line is that our health is important, and when we aren't feeling well, it's a big deal. Ill health affects our quality of life, so don't *ever* diminish your health problems."

January 12, Monday

Russ drove me to the clinic, my labs were processed, my vitals taken, and then Phyllis spoke with me briefly. My white blood cell count is up, so I have an immune system, and my platelets have doubled since Friday to 128,000. Phyllis also told me I have no more doctor visits this week and that I can stop taking my meds—Diflucan, Cipro, and acyclovir. She is scheduling me for the OR on January 19 to have my indwelling catheter inserted, and after the OR, I'll be admitted for my second round of chemo. Phyllis encouraged me to use this six-day window to enjoy myself—go to the movies or out to dinner. However, I am still going to be cautious about where I venture and what I do. More than anything else, I am going to treasure every moment of the next week.

When I returned home, I had a lovely phone conversation with Joseph. He is currently working on a play, *Landscape of the Body*, at the T. Schreiber Studio, which Terry is directing. Terry had called me back for the role of Betty, but I didn't get cast, which obviously was for the best. Terry told me that I kept looking younger and younger as the callbacks went on that day. Betty is in her thirties (as I am) and is the mother of a teenage boy (I could be). I think my long hair and small stature tend to make me look younger, particularly at a distance. Plus I would venture to guess that the actor they cast as Betty's son looked too old to realistically be mine.

Joseph has been in rehearsal for at least a month. I know he would've liked to have worked with me, and I would've enjoyed working with him again. In November, we worked on a scene in Terry's class from Lanford Wilson's *Burn This*. It was during this time that we developed a friendship. I am hoping that I feel well enough to see *Landscape of the Body* during its run. He is trying to put together a care package for me. I think he misses me; I definitely miss him.

Finally, the Social Security Disability application is done. It goes in the mail tomorrow.

January 13, Tuesday

I've had many realizations lately, one of which is how much I enjoy being me, especially when reflecting on all the amazing people in my life. No matter how awful this situation is, one of the gifts I've received from it is self-worth. There is also renewed appreciation for family and friends, for good health, for not taking life so seriously, and for being open to all experiences and possibilities. Reevaluation of my priorities and values is one way to get my life back on track.

January 14, Wednesday

I am trying to view this experience as a gift. That may sound bizarre, but shouldn't we remain open to the gifts that suffering may present? Cancer has been the instrument by which I've come to acknowledge the value of my life and the value it has to others. There has been an awakening of my spirit that desires an even better, more enriching life—or perhaps, more accurately, a more contented and balanced life. The details of this more enriching, contented life have yet to be tweaked, but I am working on them.

Karen B sent a gorgeous faith box to me yesterday. It is stunning—a small ceramic bowl painted sage green with silver décor and a lid that covers the bowl. On the lid is written Faith Is the Substance of Things Hoped For (Hebrews 11:1). To use this faith box, you write a prayer on a small piece of paper, put it in the bowl, and let God's work unfold. What a beautiful concept. I showed the faith box to Barbara last night, and she said, "Karen B's taken good care of you, hasn't she?"

"Yes, she has," I replied.

January 15, Thursday

It snowed last night, and the accumulation totaled about seven inches. It looked gorgeous today—the clear blue sky and sunlight glistening on the powdery blanket of snow. However, it was a bone-cold seventeen degrees outside, and I was glad I had nowhere to go.

I spent the day reading Catherine Ponder's book *The Dynamic Laws of Healing*. It's a faith-based book filled with inspiring and empowering affirmations. When I'm done with this one, I will read her book *Healing Secrets of the Ages*. Dad left both books with me. He's had them since I was a child, and these are the sources for some of the affirmations he wrote down for me.

Speaking of inspiring, Natalie called. I love talking to her; she is so wise and always says something that sparks contemplation. She and I are very much alike in the way we think, live our lives, and utilize our spirituality to navigate through difficult times. She has seen her share of hard times too. Our situations have paralleled over the past year. Just as she was getting ready to embark on a career-changing move to Boston, her father died. Throughout this period of grief and loss, she remained in Cincinnati to settle her father's estate. She is now considering a move to Cleveland to be closer to the rest of her family. She seems to be doing well—she's teaching a video-production class at Raymond Walters College, and she's securing freelance producing jobs. I admire her resolve and tenacity in shaping her life to correspond with how she envisions it. She inspires me to approach my future in the same way.

Today's mail call included a gorgeous photo from Karen B of herself, Nelson, Lori, Natalie, and me that was taken at J. Alexander's restaurant in Cincinnati. The photo was taken shortly after 9/11 when we all attended a show in which Natalie was performing. It was our first outing together after that devastating event. Karen B had written under the photo, "In the words of Nelson—what affects one of us affects us all. We are in this together. Friends forever." And she signed all their names.

January 16, Friday

I phoned Phyllis this morning and left a message on her voice mail because the leucovorin (a faster-acting and more potent form of folic acid) prescription wasn't ready, nor did the pharmacy have a record of anything being called in last night. I haven't heard from her yet. I must have those vitamins before my next hospital stay. During my next round of chemotherapy, I will receive a twenty-four-hour methotrexate drip. The leucovorin is supposed to help fight stomach and mouth sores as well as reduce any other toxic side effects. Methotrexate blocks an enzyme needed by cells to live. This interferes with the growth of cancer cells, which are then eventually destroyed by the body.

After the phone call, I read several more chapters in *The Dynamic Laws of Healing*. It is an inspirational book and offers many strategies for self-healing. Some of my favorite strategies include using the occult law of healing (shaping your destiny by the things you attach to the words "I *am*,"[5] for example, "I *am* healed, or I *am* prosperous"), imaging,[6] and using the "Yes" law of healing (affirmations).[7] Some affirmations I particularly like are from Ponder's *The Healing Secrets of the Ages*:

I PRONOUNCE EVERY ATOM AND CELL OF MY BODY GOOD, LIFE-FILLED.[8]

LIGHT, LIGHT, LIGHT. LET THERE BE LIGHT. THE HEALING LIGHT OF THE CHRIST MIND PENETRATES AND BANISHES ALL DARKNESS FROM MY MIND AND BODY. I AM THE LIGHT OF MY WORLD.[9]

I LET GO AND TRUST.[10]

LIFE CHARGES MY MIND, FLOWS THROUGH MY VEINS, PERMEATES MY TISSUES, NERVES, MUSCLES, CELLS, MY EYES SHINE, MY SKIN GLOWS, MY WHOLE BODY RADIATES HEALTH.[11]

I wonder if my hemoglobin level is up—I have so much energy. I realize that I am still sick, but it is quite encouraging to have a week of feeling normal. Maybe all the prayers and positive thoughts are hastening my recovery? Wouldn't that be something? It could be a miracle!

January 17, Saturday

I checked the messages on my cell phone, and there was one I should've retrieved days ago. The producer of the testimonial I did the day before I was diagnosed with leukemia called to inform me that I was going to be in the infomercial. He needed to verify the spelling of my name, which of course, he spelled as "Debra." I immediately called and left a message with the correct spelling. It might be too late for the correction because they are testing the infomercial this weekend. Oh well, it's just a spelling error, right? It's so awesome that I made the cut into the spot. It will probably only air regionally, but one never knows—maybe it'll be shown nationally. It would be great if people in Cincinnati and Tell City could see it. Mom and Dad would be quite excited.

I was thinking about Joseph this morning. I received a cute card from my acting class yesterday. Several people had signed it; Joseph signed it twice. The second time, he wrote, "Okay, knucklehead [he called me a knucklehead!], and you thought you didn't make an impact."

He told me in one of our conversations recently that he had cut his hair. I know that I had something to do with this because when we were working on the scene from *Burn This* in Terry's class in November, I had told him that I thought he should think about cutting his hair. We were sitting in the dressing room after our scene was over and another one was in progress. I told him that I felt it would make him more marketable, and with his leading-man good looks, casting directors and audiences want to see his face. His longer hair was gorgeous, but was always in his eyes. Anyway, he has cut it, and I can't wait to see what it looks like.

Barbara, Dan, and I went out for dinner this evening—my first nonclinic outing. We went to an Italian restaurant, Ciao, around 5:00 p.m. We decided to go early so that there would be fewer people in the restaurant. I donned black pants (which used to fit snugly but are quite loose now) and a dark crimson sweater set. I tied a scarf gypsy style around my head and allowed the ends to drape over my shoulder. The crimson, brown, black, and gold colors in the scarf coordinated nicely with my clothing. I applied makeup too because I wanted to feel pretty, and I actually did. Barbara thought I looked quite elegant.

At my last doctor's visit, Phyllis told me that it would be all right if I had an occasional glass of wine, so I had two glasses at dinner. I ate almost all of my pasta—a delectable dish with eggplant, tomatoes, parmesan cheese, and tomato sauce. It was wonderful to get out of the house. It was a very good day indeed.

January 18, Sunday

It's snowing again. The gray skies, the white ground, and the falling snow create a serene landscape. I am rather mesmerized by the wintry scene outside my bedroom window.

This afternoon, anxiety arose as I gazed into the mirror to scrutinize my impending baldness. The last of my hair is clinging tightly to my scalp. I try combing it repeatedly and even pulling on it, but it remains stubbornly attached. I could shave it off, but for some reason, I'm resisting that action. Sometimes, I look at myself in the mirror and long to cry. Yet when the tears well up, I find myself fighting them back because I know this is only a temporary situation—my hair will grow back. I have to remind myself that the chemo is working to make me well. Even though I may be sick at first from the toxins, the process is going to restore my health and cure me.

I had an interesting conversation with Katie this afternoon. (I met Katie in Cincinnati in 1994. She now lives in Alexandria, Virginia, with her husband, Kevin.) She admitted that she'd been worried about me when we last spoke, which was about a month before my illness was discovered. At that time, I had been telling her of my financial woes, how I was surviving on one meal a day, and scrambling to get acting and temp jobs. I was very stressed out, and she knew it. She admitted that although she was devastated to learn of my leukemia diagnosis, she was actually relieved to know that I was hospitalized because at least I was being taken care of and eating regularly. I confessed to her that there had been several times over the past few months that I'd almost wished something would happen to me—actually, that I might die—so that people wouldn't worry about me or so that I wouldn't be a burden on anyone.

Did this happen because I willed it? My rational mind refuses to accept this, but in working with the affirmations in *The Healing Secrets of the Ages*, there is an affirmation that addresses change and how "all change in my life is perfectly timed."[12] Was this illness, this life change, perfectly timed for my physical, mental, and spiritual well-being? Perhaps in a way it was. Fear and anxiety about my career and finances were consuming me. I was heading down a dangerous path and could have easily found myself fighting alcoholism. I was drinking too much and too often by myself. I was depressed, and this depression may have served as the fuel to alcohol dependency, or maybe not. Maybe I would've pulled myself together eventually. One never knows. However, I do know that the timing of all this was like a swift kick in the behind, telling me to wake up and halt these destructive behaviors before it was too late.

Still, in all fairness to me, I *was* beginning to address the financial problems by working temporary assignments; and more temp assignments would've been available to me. After I was hospitalized in December, both of my temp agencies called me to do longer-term jobs with the National Football League and Dolby Labs where I'd worked one day each. I've always been able to garner positive responses from employers because I have a strong work ethic and a friendly personality, and people seem to like me.

So maybe this leukemia was the universe's way of slowing me down and making me take a closer look at how I had been living my life. I was harmful to myself—eating junk food, drinking way too much, crying a lot, and ignoring my financial problems. Yes, looking back, I guess I did need a good kick in the rear. I was being self-destructive, and God just wasn't going to allow it. Not that I believe God gave me this disease, but . . . I'm not sure what I'm thinking at the moment. All I know is that when I think about how horribly I treated myself, it makes me sad—I'm crying right now. I must make everything right with myself. Healing is my first priority—healing my body, my mind, and my soul.

January 20, Tuesday

I'm in the hospital again. There is a Hickman catheter protruding from my chest and not a port-a-cath, which is what I was hoping for because it is smaller and would be discreetly hidden beneath the skin in my chest area. Dr. Klein explained that a Hickman is the catheter that must be used due to the large quantity of fluids and chemicals to be pumped into me. The Hickman catheter can handle much larger quantities than a port-a-cath. Of course, that makes sense, but it's going to limit what I can wear.

Not only am I disturbed that I have these long tubes dangling from my chest, but I am also disappointed that I'm on the fifth-floor oncology unit and not in the Stem Cell Transplantation Center like in December. And to my chagrin, I have a roommate. Fortunately, she's very sweet; however, my expectations were that I'd be on 8PE again, and well, this just is not the transplant unit. I know—I'm a spoiled brat. I did have a small diva moment when leaving the OR.

I was awake and being rolled upstairs when the transport person informed me that I was going to the fifth-floor oncology unit. I declared abruptly, "I'm supposed to be on eight—I'm a leukemia patient."

She checked the orders and replied, "Well, your doctor has you assigned to fifth-floor oncology. You'll have to talk to him." I was quite miffed by this unexpected turn of events but resigned myself to waiting for Dr. Goldberg to discuss this *obvious* mistake.

As of 1:45 p.m., Dr. Goldberg still hadn't checked in on me, and I didn't know when I was supposed to take the leucovorin (for the methotrexate). Barbara left right before lunch, and then I watched some soap operas.

The Creation of Health is the book I am now reading. Pages 131-135 in particular have made an impression on me. These pages include the sections titled "Cure versus Transformation" and "Ego Pain versus Soul Pain."

In "Cure versus Transformation," Ms. Myss writes,

> The holistic model of treatment has brought to light the need to help a person heal the stresses in his or her life as an integral part of healing the body. In order to do this, a person must be willing and able to look at all the pieces of his or her life, including emotional injuries (both given and received), unfulfilled emotional needs, disappointments in relationships, broken promises, unfulfilled ambitions, disappointments in oneself, and other patterns of unfinished business that form a person's inner grief.[13]

She further states,

> Self-analysis is certainly a part of the answer, but it is the goal of analysis that is healing and that goal is *completion* and *validation*.
>
> Completion is the opportunity to understand and bring to a close—literally and figuratively—the open wounds of your life.
>
> Validation is the deeply healing process of sharing your pain with another, not so that the other person can make it go away, but because no one can bear the inner weight of suffering alone.[14]

In the section "Ego Pain versus Soul Pain," she writes,

> Soul pain is the processing of that which we cannot change, avoid or
> otherwise remove from our lives; it has a purpose and a depth to it that
> is not present in ego pain.

> Suffering that involves the soul teaches us about ourselves—our dark
> sides, our inner strengths and our capacity to rise beyond our previous
> limitations.[15]

I need to look at those parts of myself that are incomplete, unfulfilled, and unhealed so that the wounds can mend. I must find the courage to confront the demons that have tortured me for years. I have commenced this personal exploration, but I have much more investigating to do, so I will continue to study my history in order to discover the issues that need to be resolved.

At 5:50 p.m., my first chemotherapy, Rituxan, was administered. A large bottle of clear liquid was hooked up to my IV. Tomorrow begins the twenty-four-hour methotrexate drip, and then Thursday through Saturday, I will receive cytarabine—four to five bags at twelve-hour intervals. (Cytarabine works by blocking a natural enzyme needed by the cancer cell to build RNA and DNA. The damaged cells are then destroyed by the body.) I'll be pumped full of poison again.

I have no dietary restrictions right now. Dr. Goldberg has ordered a regular diet for this evening, but tomorrow, it will change to a low-microbial one. I had a small salad that was merely iceberg lettuce and carrot shavings with French dressing, but it tasted delicious and refreshing.

Bobbi, a New York friend, called to let me know she will be visiting tomorrow. Mom phoned three times—morning, afternoon, and evening—and in the evening, I spoke with Dad who tried to come up with many topics to entertain me and prevent me from feeling lonely. Karen called to let me know that she'll be flying in Sunday. Nelson is letting her use some of his frequent flyer miles.

Beckie and Nelson were here from 8:00-10:30 p.m. They always put a smile on my face. I am so lucky to be friends with them. They brought me gifts: many magazines, *The Hours* DVD, and the *Insight Meditation Kit: A Step-by-Step Course on How to Meditate* (includes book, CD, and meditation cards) by Joseph Goldstein and Sharon Salzberg.

Oh, my hopes for a single room on 8PE have been dashed. Dr. Goldberg told me that from now on, I will be in the oncology unit for chemotherapy. I was in the Stem Cell Transplantation Center in December because I was initially being diagnosed and treated, so they wanted to keep me in a contained environment. Alas, no mistake was made in my room assignment—drat!

January 21, Wednesday

I introduced myself to my roommate this morning. Her name is Jamie;* she's twenty-four and has two children, ages eight and two. She has been diagnosed with breast cancer. Her mother died of breast cancer back in 2000. She shared with me that her mom had put off seeing a doctor for years. By the time she finally sought medical care, the cancer was so advanced, there was nothing to be done. Jamie is only at stage 2, so there is so much hope for her. I will keep her in my prayers. We've talked a lot, and I think it helps both of us to share our stories and concerns. Helping and encouraging one another is so important, and if I can make someone smile or feel better, that's what I'm going to do.

* Name change

January 22, Thursday

I am feeling more tired than usual and battling indigestion. I need more Mylanta. The methotrexate drip ended at 11:00 a.m., and the level of it in my system was at 7. If it were 20 or higher, Dr. Goldberg would start my "rescue" (the leucovorin) immediately; but since the level is low, he'll start it tomorrow. The cytarabine is now being administered at twelve-hour intervals, and I am using prescription eyedrops every six hours.

My appetite is diminishing again. However, with all the fluids being pumped into my body, I'm still weighing in at 108.

Dan, my sole visitor today, dropped off my computer and stayed only a short while. I'm lonely and depressed; I feel like crying . . .

January 23, Friday

I am very fatigued and a little emotional today. Shelley, my only visitor, was a welcome sight. The final cytarabine drip is tonight, and since my methotrexate levels are going down nicely, I will be released tomorrow. The leucovorin is to be taken four more times. I am to continue using the eyedrops because my eyes are dried out from the methotrexate, but the eyedrops have blurred my vision, which is really annoying.

January 24, Saturday

Jamie has been released. Her family was very kind, and they are keeping me in their prayers.

I just took some more Maalox because the indigestion is getting worse. I can't stand all the belching—it's really disgusting; at least there is no acid reflux.

A home health care nurse will be visiting me some time this week to demonstrate how I should take care of my indwelling catheter. She'll also be delivering supplies for flushing the lines, sterilizing the incision area, and disposing of the biowaste. Improper care of the catheter and the incision area can lead to serious infections, and so vigilant attention to catheter maintenance is essential.

I'm so tired yet hoping to organize most of my belongings before Barbara arrives. I may need her help packing everything—books, gifts, clothes, and toiletries. It's cold outside and may even snow. I hope Karen arrives safely tomorrow without any flight delays.

8:00 p.m.

Dan picked me up because Barbara was not feeling well. I'm home now but am depressed. I feel weak, the indigestion is terrible, and I need a good night's sleep. However, I have to take leucovorin at 11:00 p.m. and use my eyedrops at 12:00 a.m., then both again at 5:00 a.m. and 6:00 a.m. respectively. How am I expected to sleep when I have to stay on a schedule like this? I haven't slept well since this whole ordeal began.

Before I left the hospital, I was given a copy of my CBC results. The results read as follows: white blood cell count, 4.6 (4 to 11 is the normal range, meaning four thousand to eleven thousand white blood cells in a drop [microliter] of blood); hemoglobin, 7.7;[16] red blood cell count, 2.37 (normal range is 4.2 to 5.4 million red blood cells in a microliter of blood); and platelets, 317,000.[17] At least the white blood cells and platelets are in the normal ranges although they'll plummet soon too.

I had a very brief phone conversation with Mom because I didn't feel well. I don't think she comprehends that each time I get hit with chemotherapy, it's going to be tough for a while; I won't bounce back immediately. It's a brutal process, and my body is being invaded by toxins. I know she wants me to be chipper and upbeat, but I'm not going to be right now. I'm not going to pretend I feel fine.

No matter how many people are around me or contact me, I still feel so alone. I need a hug. I need you, God. I need strength—carry me.

January 26, Monday

Karen is a godsend. I knew she'd be a wonderful caregiver. She immediately cleaned out the bathtub for me, washed my sheets, made phone calls, and kept me fed and hydrated. I was extremely dizzy this morning every time I stood up. The indigestion is still terrible, and now I have gas too. My bowel movements have an odd consistency (not diarrhea, but soft), I have shortness of breath, and my white blood counts are decreasing, which is normal.

At the clinic, I received a Neulasta shot, which will help increase the white blood cells. One of the side effects of Neulasta is bone pain. (I haven't experienced bone pain since Christmas Eve.) They also gave me fluids intravenously to prevent dehydration.

Upon returning home, I had received a box of Godiva chocolates from Lynn M, producing artistic director at Ensemble Theatre of Cincinnati. Also, my cousin Mike sent a couple of books: *It's Not About the Bike* by Lance Armstrong (who, as of 2003, has won the Tour de France five times) and *Man's Search for Meaning* by Viktor Frankl. Lynn M's gift would satisfy my sweet tooth and put a little weight back on me, and Mike's gift would provide inspiration.

On a different note, Karen C, another actor friend in New York, called yesterday. It's been a while since I spoke with her, so we had a long conversation. In fact, she's one of the last people I saw before being diagnosed. Monday, December 15, after my appointment with Dr. Dizon, I went into the city to meet Karen C for dinner. That night, I confided in her that I suspected I had a serious health issue.

Karen C told me that she admires my strength and the way I've handled my situation. I am trying so hard to live through this cancer battle with as much dignity, strength, and compassion as I can muster. It's not always easy to do though.

January 27, Tuesday

Karen made several phone calls on my behalf today to Social Security to follow up on my disability, to my insurance company regarding my conversion application (also a follow-up call), and to the post office because I've not yet received any forwarded mail.

I called about the Neulasta prescription. It will cost me $85 through Tel-Drug; but if I went through a pharmacy, it would cost $2,500, and that's with 50 percent coinsurance. Unbelievable! Once I no longer have my current coverage, who knows how much it will cost?

My stomach is still upset, and when I blow my nose, there is blood. I took a long hot bath, exfoliated, and rubbed lotion all over my body. My skin is so dry. Before getting dressed, I taped my catheter to my stomach so that the tubes wouldn't dangle around beneath my shirt.

January 29, Thursday

The producer of the testimonial I did the day before I was diagnosed with leukemia called today to tell me that they were definitely using me in the infomercial. He said it's going to air all over the country starting in a couple of weeks. How exciting! He also shared with me that his wife had just received an all clear on her colon cancer, which she'd been diagnosed with last summer. Her cancer had been in stage 4 at the time of diagnosis. He encouraged me to maintain a positive attitude and said if I needed or wanted to talk to let him know. The kindness of so many people is very heartwarming.

January 30, Friday

I'm back at the clinic. Blood has been drawn, and I'm awaiting the results. My vitals are pretty much the same as they usually are—temperature is 98.6 °F, relatively low blood pressure, and 105 pounds.

I feel good today except for being a little jittery from the two cups of coffee I drank earlier this morning, but I ate some cereal too, so it's not like my stomach is empty. I'm sure much of the shakiness is a side effect from all the medications. We'll see if I get any blood products today. I bet they wait until Monday.

I was right—no blood products today. Dr. Goldberg is sending me home, but I really have to monitor my temperature because my white blood count is 0.4. The last time, it was 0.8; so basically, it went from 0 to 0 as the doctor said. Right now, my body is lacking an immune system, and my platelets have dropped to forty-five thousand. If I get a temperature, Dr. Goldberg instructed me to pack a bag, call him, and head to the hospital.

2:45 p.m.

Once again, Karen has been doing follow-up work for me—Social Security Disability, forwarded mail issues, insurance. What a pain. I really appreciate my sister's help. At the moment, Karen is upstairs transcribing her focus group recording. (She has to do a little bit of work while she's out of the office.) I'm relaxing on the couch, watching TV, and trying to stay warm—it's always cold here.

I need to record some of the guided meditations in the *Insight Meditation* book. My concentration is better when I hear the words and follow along as opposed to trying to remember the words without the recording. I want to begin meditating this weekend.

I have arranged the meditation area in my room. A small cardboard box about twelve by eight inches is situated on the floor beneath the windowsill, which will enable me to gaze out the window (should I wish) while I meditate. A taupe silk scarf decorated with a black-and-red Oriental pattern is draped over the box. On the surface of the box are placed a miniature crystal owl (given to me by a friend of Lani's), the faith box (Karen B bought me), a small white vanilla-scented candle, a tiny white ceramic bowl with blue flowers painted on it and filled with an assortment of rocks (Bobbi's contribution), and a four-inch square wooden box that holds my rosary and two gold Mary medallions. I have treasured this tiny wooden box since the summer of 1994 when Tina, a *Godspell* cast mate, gave it to me. Tina, a gifted artist, painted the box. The figure of a woman—or an angel, perhaps—is on the lid. She resembles Edvard Munch's women in his paintings, *Puberty* or *The Dance of Life*, only Tina's rendering is much prettier. I will always remember Tina's strength and character, especially having endured the loss of her only child shortly before I made her acquaintance.

On the floor to the left of the box are two mass cards Mom sent to me; on the right side of the box are my list of affirmations, the *Insight Meditation* kit, and three books: *The Miracle of Mindfulness*, *God Calling*, and *365 Tao*. It's an inspirational spiritual area adorned with items that are significant to me. It sounds cluttered, but the items are displayed in an organized fashion. I'm very excited about using it. I'd start today, but I'm tired. (I know—excuses, excuses . . .)

Lisa and Tim will be driving here today from Cincinnati. I miss Lisa so much. I saw her last when I was in Cincinnati for a couple of days in April 2003.

January 31, Saturday

Dan told me this morning that his friend Baron saw my infomercial in Houston. I guess it will air all over the country. Too bad I'm not receiving residuals. Oh well, at least it is exposure.

I called Karen B this morning to inquire about her plans for visiting but had to leave a message. I left her an out by saying that if this trip was causing her financial stress (she's unemployed) or time stress (being away from Cincinnati) that I would not be upset if she decided not to visit. Karen B is so wonderful for wanting to come, but the real help is needed transporting me to and from the clinic. Other than that, there's really not a lot to do unless I'm feeling ill.

Karen left for the airport this morning, about fifteen minutes ago, and I miss her already. She and I have such great conversations. Last night, we were discussing meditation. I told her that through my meditation practice, I am hoping to discover the presence and mindfulness that will allow me to listen closely to my inner voice, to relax and let go, and to trust that I will know the next right move to make on this chessboard that is my life. I'm sitting here on my bed and writing. Perhaps I should put down the pen and allow myself "to be"—good idea . . . pen is being put down. (Pause)

Karen B called. She is arriving Tuesday and is staying until the following Monday. Monique called to tell me that she just saw my infomercial in Cincinnati. She said that she had the TV on and that suddenly, she heard this familiar voice; she looked up, and there I was on the screen. How funny.

Lisa, Tim, and Joshua visited today and stayed for dinner. Joshua is so cute. He's about two months older than Aidan and has blond hair. Joshua and Aidan played together very well. Aidan found a new appreciation for some of his toys, which was rather amusing because he'd lost interest in many of them until he saw Joshua enjoying them.

I met Lisa in 1995 when I directed her in *The Diary of Anne Frank*. She portrayed Mrs. Frank with grace and strength. What a performance! As her director, I was so proud. Needless to say, she and I became best of friends very quickly. She went on to direct me as the Witch in *Into the Woods*, I directed her again in *The Nerd*, and both of us were two of the five founding members of Ovation Theatre Company in Cincinnati. We've definitely been through a lot together when it comes to theater, but we've also been through much together personally, and I had the honor of being a bridesmaid when she wed Tim on November 13, 1999. Lisa is still one of the people running Ovation, which is in its fifth season.

I am still so moved that they would drive all the way here to see me. Lisa told us that when Karen called to tell her that I had leukemia, she cried for half an hour, and Tim asked, "Okay, when are we going to visit her?" She also told me that one of her first thoughts upon waking the next morning was, "Deborah can't die in Hackensack!" This made me laugh. I guess Hackensack sounded like a dreadful place to her. I love her and Tim so much.

Lisa brought a gift bag from her and Tim, a bag from Joe (another Ovation Theatre Company cofounder and Cincinnati friend), and one from Vickie and Jon. (I met Vickie and Jon while doing community theater in Cincinnati.) Lisa's bag contained body bath products that also came with a jazz CD, a bath pillow, hand and foot mitts, a black knit cap and matching gloves, and a deluxe nail file.

Joe's bag was filled with chocolates, a President Bush (Mis)speak calendar, *The Blue Day Book*, a candle, and a framed photo of our *Crimes of the Heart* cast. In the picture, we're all surrounding the table on the set, readying ourselves with open mouths to voraciously attack the chocolate cake, which was used in the last scene to celebrate Lennie's birthday. I relished performing that scene because at the end, Corrine (Babe), Amie (Lennie), and I (Meg) would indulge ourselves by eating giant pieces of cake.

Vickie and Jon's gift bag contained a puzzle book, two novels, a burgundy knit cap, pages of sagas Jon had written about himself (I'm sure they're hysterical—he has a great sense of humor), and a photo of Jon and Vickie (she's lost 107 pounds and looks amazing!).

Receiving all of these gifts is somewhat overwhelming. Don't get me wrong—I love receiving them. Someone told me recently that although I'm the one who's sick, I've affected so many people because my illness makes them think about their own mortality—that if this can happen to Deborah, it can happen to anyone. Hopefully, it will help them reflect upon their own lives. It is so interesting how one life touches so many others, and if I've touched so many lives in my own small way without having known it, what could I accomplish if I really set out to make a difference?

February 1, Sunday

I feel centered and present after having completed my first meditation lesson. My mind wandered often throughout the twenty-minute session, but I conquered these distractions by gently returning my focus to the breath. I think I did all right for the first time, especially for someone whose mind is like a freight train chugging along the tracks, never slowing down or stopping. The goal is to practice daily and increase my sessions to sixty minutes.

February 2, Monday

Russ and I arrived at the Cancer Center around noon, and now I'm in the waiting room, hoping that a chair will open up soon in the chemo room. A medical assistant just informed me that they are waiting for the blood products to arrive, and as soon as they are here, I'll be assigned a chair. Russ left to get food and water for me—I'm starving.

5:05 p.m.

The first unit of blood is almost gone. That was so fast! I'll be getting a second unit shortly. The last time I received blood, it took four hours for the red blood cells to transfuse because it was being pumped through a vein in my arm. To prevent pain (and at first, I experienced excruciating, burning pain in my arm) as the blood flowed into my vein, it had to be transfused very slowly and with saline solution. This time, however, because the Hickman catheter is inserted into a much larger vein in my chest area, the blood products were administered in about half the time. I still need to get platelets, so I estimate all blood products will be administered by 8:00 p.m.

February 3, Tuesday

Yesterday, I received a card from Sister Bernardine Ludwig, my father's cousin, whom I've never met. Sister Bernardine's letter reads,

Dear Deborah,

Your Aunt Addie wrote to me to tell me of your sickness. Even though you don't know me, I am your dad's first cousin. His dad and my dad were brothers, so that makes us second cousins.

I just want you to know that you are in my daily prayers. I have you on our prayer list so the sixty-one sisters I live with are praying for you also. I know how hard it is to be sick. Thirty-one years ago I had cancer and after a few rough years, I was good as new. How I pray you will be so blessed.

Keep your chin up and do trust in God and His loving Mother—miracles happen every day. If you feel up to it I would love hearing from you.

May God bless you and give you peace.

My love and prayers,
Sister Bernardine Ludwig

This letter meant so much to me. Her having dealt with cancer thirty-one years ago and still living to tell me about it is amazing. Talk about inspirational. I hope to meet her someday.

Also, Aunt Nellie (Mom's oldest sister), her husband, Richard, and their children's families sent a card with a $200 cashier's check. This will help me pay some bills.

Interestingly enough, there are events happening around the country and the world other than my cancer battle. Since this is a presidential election year, there are Democratic primaries today in South Carolina, Delaware, Oklahoma, Arizona, New Mexico, Missouri, and North Dakota. North Dakota and New Mexico actually have caucuses rather than primaries. I'll be watching the results. This is an important election year.

12:15 p.m.

I just finished twenty minutes of meditation. I'm surprised my mind doesn't wander more than it does during these sessions. Of course, it does wander, but not as much as I would expect it to—knowing me. Meditation reinforces the importance of awareness. I have already caught myself twice in the past week being mean or nasty to someone—and that's not how I want to be. I want to be patient and kind even when I feel the other person doesn't deserve kindness. These reactions are about me, not the offender—although I guess it is about the offender too because we should value all life, not just our own. But I have learned and must remember that other people's bad behavior stems from their own suffering.

2:20 p.m.

The nurse from Chartwell was knowledgeable and kind. Her instructions were quite thorough, and I now feel comfortable flushing the catheter lines by myself.

On a different note—a news note—ricin was found in the Capitol Building in Senator Frist's mailroom. At the present time, three Senate buildings have been evacuated. It is frightening that someone can hate so deeply that they're driven to endanger others' lives. Forty people are being put through a complete decontamination process. They must be terrified.

People who have so little regard for human life make me furious. You may not like your government representatives or the decisions they make, but that does not justify harming them. And usually, it's staffers and mailroom employees, not policy makers, who end up being the victims. Everyone deserves to be safe, regardless of their political views—that includes the president and all members of Congress.

On a happier note, the Leukemia & Lymphoma Society approved my transportation and drug reimbursement grant application for $500. I have to utilize these funds by June 2004, which is the end of their fiscal year. However, that shouldn't be a problem because the first reimbursement I submit will be over $100.

February 4, Wednesday

Karen B and I met at a party the summer of 2000, and it only took twenty minutes of talking to this woman to know that she would become a dear friend. We had an immediate connection. She is taller than me and has blonde hair and beautiful big kind eyes. She and Nelson developed a friendship while working for Procter & Gamble. I knew Nelson through his ex-girlfriend before I knew Karen B, but he was more of an acquaintance at that time. After Karen B and I met, suddenly, we were all hanging out together. We had some great times in Cincinnati—especially the salsa and swing dancing, two to three times a week. Natalie and Lori were part of our group too, Nelson and his women.

Karen B arrived at 10:20 p.m. last night. We were up until midnight talking while watching the primary results. John Kerry won North Dakota, Arizona, Missouri, Delaware, and New Mexico while John Edwards took South Carolina.

General Wesley Clark barely beat out Edwards in Oklahoma. Interesting . . . Kerry is doing really well so far though Clark is my preference.

Karen B drove me to the clinic today. My blood counts and platelets are way up, so I do not have to go back to HUMC until I return there on the sixteenth for my next round of chemo. I am experiencing some bone pain, but it is bearable.

We arrived home around 1:30 p.m. and had lunch. Then I opened my friendship box that she'd brought with her on the plane, which was no small feat either by the size of it. A gorgeous round hat box with gold, beige, and yellow flowers on it was filled with gifts from many generous people. On the inside of the lid was written, "Deborah's 'Friendship Box'—You are a treasure to so many people. We love you dearly! Love, Karen B and Dena D."

This was Dena D's idea, and she doesn't even know me; she's a dear friend of Karen B's. I am so touched by all the lovely items and notes. How extraordinary to have all of these people in my life! There are even folks I don't know sending gifts, messages, and prayers.

February 5, Thursday

By 7:30 a.m., I had already done healing visualizations and worked with some affirmations. I am having difficulty sleeping through the night, so by the time the sun starts rising over the horizon, I am ready to get up and face the day.

Dr. Goldberg instructed me to stop taking my meds—even the Ovral (a high-dose oral contraceptive) because he wants me to have a period in order to get me on their schedule for chemo. Previously, my doctors did not want me to have a period due to my low-platelet count.

At the moment, I feel mostly peaceful. Only the insurance conversion information, mail yet to be forwarded to me, and my Bank One credit card statement (which I haven't received yet) are making me a little anxious. This anxiety needs to be transferred to a constructive place. Recently, I've come to the realization that I have lived with a low level of anxiety most of my thirty-seven years, and I long to eliminate it completely. I'm hoping that my meditation practice will help. I also need to stop assigning such importance to those things that cause me stress, but sometimes, it's so difficult not to worry. For example, the whole health insurance-conversion situation stresses me out because health insurance is so vital to me at the moment. Coverage cannot lapse, and the transition must be seamless. However, I should not let these concerns nag at me and consume my thoughts. That obsession is what leads to anxiety, which causes tension to creep into my body, and tension is not good. Relax and let go (as one of my affirmations reads)—oh, and breathe.

Two packages arrived today. Maria sent two Origins face creams that emit an orange scent. One is for use at night, and the other is for day. Also in the package was a photo of Maria's parents with her children: Olivia, Eliza, and Nathan. Olivia and Eliza colored some pictures for me. Olivia, Maria's eldest child, colored a page that had two elephants on it—a mother elephant and a child elephant. There were flowers surrounding them. Olivia had colored them beautifully, using the appropriate color palette and staying well inside the lines. She also drew six horses around the edges of a blank sheet of paper. These horses were drawn using a stencil. At the top of the page, she wrote, "I'm sorry you are sick. Love, Olivia."

Her younger sister, Eliza, colored a woman (who I assume is supposed to be a teacher), Snow White, and a dog—all from a coloring book—and then cut out the pictures. All of Olivia's and Eliza's pictures are taped on my bedroom wall.

The other package was from Mom—two hats, a blue blouse, one pair of white Keds (I'd specifically told her I needed the Keds), stamps, and holy water from Lourdes (Dad's contribution, which I immediately placed on the meditation box).

February 6, Friday

I was saddened to hear they found the body of Carlie Brucia. The eleven-year-old girl was abducted near her home in Sarasota, Florida, on February 1. She was walking by a car wash on her way home from a friend's house, and a surveillance camera caught her abduction on tape. She was raped and murdered, and her body was buried behind a church. Her body was found behind that church after Joseph Smith, her killer, told his brother where he had hidden the body.

This disgusts and angers me. I had been praying for her, but obviously, hers was not to be a happy ending. My hope is that she didn't suffer too much. It infuriates me that there are people in this world who value human life so little—I don't, and I'll never comprehend that. I guess some people are not wired for compassion, empathy, and respect for human life—or any life for that matter (like the ricin incident in DC earlier this week—it all makes my blood boil).

On a different note, I'm very concerned about my health insurance. The conversion information that I've previously requested still hasn't arrived, and March 1 is rapidly approaching. I'm trying so hard not to let all these things anger me or bother me, but obviously, I'm failing miserably (I wrote about this yesterday). Maybe I need anger management? No, silly, just breathe and meditate.

So I meditated . . . Will there ever be a time when my thoughts don't wander? I know meditation is a discipline that takes time and practice, but I want the focus and discipline now. Okay, that's my impatience surfacing. The goal: continue to meditate and be compassionate toward my inability to concentrate for even short periods of time. I know this practice will be beneficial to me emotionally, physically, and spiritually. By cultivating awareness, I will be more grounded in the present and more tuned into my life. It may also prove beneficial to the larger world as I become a more serene and compassionate individual, passing serenity and compassion on to others.

February 8, Sunday

Nelson and Beckie were here yesterday from noon until 9:30 p.m. Donna and Bob showed up too, so it was a big afternoon party with Aidan as the entertainment. Aidan loved Beckie. I think he was particularly attracted to the lilting tone of her British accent.

My friend Dan G had sent five seasons of *Sex and the City* on DVD for my viewing pleasure. So after Bob and Donna headed home and Barbara and Dan departed for their date, we popped the first season into the DVD player and devoured the carryout entrees we had ordered from an Italian restaurant.

I have definitely gained back all the weight I lost, so now I need to cut down on the sweets. I don't want my weight to get out of control; I still care about how I look.

This week, I'm going to start working with my Pilates and yoga tapes to give my body a little bit of a workout. My muscles need the exercise. Lying and sitting around for the past eight weeks has become my modus operandi. The exercise will get my blood circulating, increase my respiratory capacity, and strengthen my muscles. I really do not enjoy being so sluglike.

Karen B inquired last night about my getting back into acting when this ordeal is over. I think I want to, but I'm not certain of it. I haven't had doubts about acting in years; however, at this point, I don't know what else I'd like to do—maybe write, lecture, or teach. Teach yoga or something to do with spirituality? What I am sure of is that I want to work in a creative field. There are so many questions to answer, and I'm not prepared to answer them yet.

February 9, Monday

I return to the hospital next Monday, so I'm going to make the most of this week—enjoying every moment of every day is the plan. I feel good despite having a slight cold.

Karen B and I went for a thirty-minute walk. It felt amazing to be out moving my body, working my muscles, and breathing in the cool, crisp winter air.

Unfortunately, this feeling of well-being didn't last long as I found myself later that afternoon fretting over the cost of converting my COBRA coverage to an individual health plan. (I finally received the information packet today.) I started crying, thinking of the cost of everything—it will be exorbitant. Karen B told me that money is the last thing I should be worrying about and that I need to trust that everything will be fine. She's right, but it's so scary and overwhelming to think about all the medical costs involved—not only chemotherapy and hospital stays, but also insurance premiums and medications. I'm trying to be brave, but—no excuses—I will be brave.

Lynn called this evening. Bo, her mother, had chemo today. Her chemo treatments are very different from mine. She actually has an apparatus, which Lynn tells me resembles a grenade, that she carries in the pocket of her clothing. This apparatus allows her to dispense the chemo into her port-a-cath. When it is empty, it flattens out so she knows the chemotherapy infusion is complete. Bo does this on an outpatient basis. Lynn says her mother has not lost her hair although it has thinned some. My last strands are clinging to my scalp for dear life—I can't even yank them out. I want them gone. Maybe the next round of chemo will complete the balding process. I am considering buying an electric razor to shave my head.

It's almost midnight, and though I should go to sleep, part of me feels like reading, and another part feels like praying a rosary. I think I'll pray the rosary. My family, friends, and I all need prayers. Amen.

February 10, Tuesday

Karen B and I spent a quiet day at home reading, writing, checking e-mails, and talking. I have loved the time we've been able to spend together—chatting, contemplating life, crying, laughing. We share so much of our lives. As much as she's helped me, I think I've helped her too. That's what friends are for. She's so supportive, and I've opened up to her more than I have in the past—especially about my childhood. It's easier for me to listen to others than allow them to listen to me. I'm more comfortable in the role of counselor or advisor, but I'm learning to let others help me.

I drove Karen B to the airport around 6:00 p.m. and afterward, spent the evening in my room, sorting through the friendship box. I found Lori's inspiration cards—there are four small boxes. Each box has a different theme: Bliss, Hero, Dream, and Believe. I chose a Bliss card:

It is not the years in your life, but the life in your years that counts.

—Adlai Stevenson

On the back of the card, there are blank lines to write notes. So I wrote, "I'm going to make my years count. From now on, no more taking my days for granted. Work to achieve the goals I set, help others, and live in the present."

February 11, Wednesday

Today is the Feast of Our Lady of Lourdes. Mom enrolled me in a special Healing Novena of Masses from February 5 through 11. I said a prayer to Our Lady of Lourdes to rid me of the leukemia so that I may go on to live a long, healthy, productive, and wonderful life. I also blessed myself with the holy water Dad sent. My parents definitely believe in the power of prayer, and so do I.

I also added to my faith box the following request: "Dear Lord, please let my insurance change transition smoothly and let me stop worrying about it—let me trust that you will take care of it. All will be well. Amen."

Before saying and writing these prayers, I meditated. I am finding more and more enjoyment from my meditation practice. Afterward, I reviewed lesson 1 in *Insight Meditation* and read chapter 3 in *The Miracle of Mindfulness*. Chapter 3 discusses the benefit of setting aside one day a week as a "mindfulness day." I would like to try that, but I have trouble being mindful for an hour—who am I kidding? I have difficulty being mindful for five minutes! Still, it is a discipline well worth attempting.

Today, I am trying to use mindfulness as much as possible by being conscious of all the nuances of my actions as well as staying present in the moment. For instance, the attention paid to the details of making and drinking a cup of tea resulted in a very different tea-making experience than it normally is. By performing the task slowly and methodically, the nuances of each action created a deeper awareness of the process and my mind-body connection to it. To begin, I was conscious of the feel of the mug—it's cool ceramic hardness and the weight of it in my hands. I examined the colors of the mug, its various shades of brown, dark blue, and cream. I listened to the dribble of water leaving the spigot in the refrigerator as it filled the mug. Next, I followed the movement of my arms as the left one opened the microwave door and the other placed the mug into it. The slamming door and the whirr of rays heating the water broke the silence.

Next, I opened the tea packet, exploring the feel of the paper and the scent of the tea as the bag was pulled from the wrapper. The beeping of the microwave signaled the water was ready. I retrieved the mug, observing the steam rising from it and sensing the heat of the cup in the palms of my hands, and then gingerly placed the tea bag in the bubbling water. This three-minute process was executed with precision and careful attention. Not only did I make the tea in mindfulness, but I also drank the tea in mindfulness—savoring the taste, smell, and warmth of the libation as it traveled down my throat into my belly. It is interesting how enjoyable making and drinking a cup of tea can be when attention is paid to the details.

I want to make this type of awareness a consistent part of my life. Somehow, I will find a way to live in peace, free of anxiety. We don't have to hurry through life, nor do I want to anymore—been there, done that—and it is exhausting. I want the rest of my life to be balanced and calm, even when I am struggling through difficult times. Realistically, I know this isn't always possible; but I can try, right?

Donna called, and we talked for a while. She told me something that I've heard before but never really hit home with me until now: fear and faith cannot coexist. She's right. When we're afraid, we aren't having faith, so we need to learn to let go and put our trust in God or whatever higher power it is we believe in. Easier said than done, but that's one of the goals to strive for in order to reach a higher level of faith and self-empowerment.

Update on election 2004: John Kerry won yesterday's primaries in Tennessee and Virginia while John Edwards came in second in both states. General Wesley Clark has bowed out of the race—officially withdrawing today. (He was my first choice for the Democratic presidential nominee.)

February 12, Thursday

Morning is the time I reserve for meditation, prayer, and writing. It's very tranquil here on weekday mornings. Once I'm back out in the workforce, I'll most likely not have my mornings free. I hate nine-to-five jobs. I long to make a living working in a creative field where I can more or less set my own schedule. Of course, if I'm in a play or on a set, I have to abide by the producer's schedule. This I can deal with because it's work that I love. Okay, time to make phone calls . . .

Well, I won't lose insurance coverage for leukemia treatments because I am going from one plan to another within the same insurance company—what a relief! I'll also still use the Tel-Drug service, but the cost of my Neulasta is going to be outrageous. I need to figure out what to do about this because I cannot afford to pay $2,500 to $3,000 for each injection. I estimate that I will need five more injections after this upcoming round of chemo.

Trust that all will be well; fear and faith cannot coexist. This is what I must remember.

5:30 p.m.

Barbara and I spent the afternoon together. She took off from work, so we had lunch at McCormick & Schmick's, a seafood restaurant in the mall. Afterward, we did some shopping. Barbara bought Valentine's Day gifts for Dan and Aidan, and she even got me a small collapsible map of Manhattan, which includes a subway map. I need to purchase a little something for her and Dan as a thank-you for everything they've done for me.

All the inspirational books and quotes that I've been reading have made me want to reflect more on life, its meaning, and my journey throughout the years. So today, I reflect on the journey of life: The stages of life are simple—we're born, we grow, we live, and we die. The journey of life is complicated, intricate, and fascinating. In between being born and dying, it's what we accomplish and how we live that's important.

We are always planting the seeds of our lives and waiting for them to grow—from family plans to career plans and anything else we deem worthwhile. The seeds of hopes and dreams are planted and nourished, and we wait to watch them blossom—even when they seem to wither. It is when these hopes and dreams seem to elude us that we must trust the journey, trust that our world will be as it is meant to be. Our job is to keep nurturing the hopes and dreams, especially if we truly believe in them.

And lastly, when it is our time to exit this earth, we must trust that what we were put here to accomplish has been fulfilled (even though we may not have accomplished the goals we set for ourselves). The journey of our lives is finished; now we're in God's hands.

February 13, Friday

I have been eating so much lately; what a porker! I have gained probably eight to ten pounds in the past two and a half weeks. I'll be better about watching my caloric intake after the next round of chemo. Not that I need to diet because a little extra weight right now isn't a bad thing, but I can't let my eating get out of control. The last thing I want to do is gain a lot of weight I can't easily shed.

Barbara found out today that the baby is a boy. His due date is August 18. I was watching Barbara with Aidan tonight—she is so good with him and very attentive, playing with him and teaching him. No wonder he's so smart.

Today's reflection is on the vicissitudes of life and how these incessant ups and downs can be positive forces: I try to flow with the vicissitudes of life, but that openness to flowing with them has definitely been tested over the past eight to nine weeks. One might ask, "How can this leukemia be a good or positive experience?"

1. It is good because it forced me to take a break, to examine my life and my history, and to begin implementing changes for the better.
2. It is positive because it has opened my eyes to the value of me and to be more willing to ask for help when I need it.
3. It's positive in that I'm working hard toward trusting that problems and/or concerns I obsess about will be fine—letting go of fear and having faith.
4. It's given me a new appreciation for life and health. I want to be a whole, healthy person again; in that wholeness and healthiness, I intend to make some real contributions to the world.
5. To live in the moment, to treasure each minute, to be mindful; the present moment is all we have—embrace it!
6. I believe that out of this experience, I will be a more enlightened, peaceful, loving, and fearless human being.

I still have a long way to go, but I am working on improving the quality of my life every day—some days more than others, but at least a smidgeon of self-improvement work is attempted daily. I am using affirmations and meditations from many sources to spark my thought process. I think it will prove helpful to explore how I feel and connect to various inspirational writings. Perhaps some inner clarity will arise out of all my musings because I never know what thoughts are going to pop out of my head or flow from my pen. It is interesting to examine these sayings and words and discover the meaning and insights they have for me. Here are two sentences from a meditation in *365 Tao*:

Stretching
Stretching—both literally and metaphorically—is a necessary part of life.

Metaphorical stretching leads to expansion and flexibility in personal growth.[18]

When we stretch our boundaries, we grow, we learn, and we discover that we can achieve goals we never thought possible. It is important to stretch ourselves. Physically stretching to keep our bodies flexible and healthy is as important as metaphorically stretching our minds. When we stretch past (what we believe to be) our limits and succeed, we feel great satisfaction and accomplishment. And if we don't succeed, at least we tried. What a rush! Life is about taking risks—without risk, one never knows what she/he is capable of achieving. So stretch—stretch to the moon. As Les Brown said, "Even if you miss it, you will land among the stars."

Tonight, after everyone had retired for the evening, I found myself alone in my room and still struggling to wrap my head around this cancer diagnosis. Earlier in the evening, I had noticed fog creeping into the neighborhood. I love fog at night, the way the light disperses through the haze, obscuring reality and conjuring a mystical, almost-haunting atmosphere.

I needed to explore my feelings, and somehow, gazing into the deep mist calmed me. I lit the candle on the meditation box, put on some soothing lyrical Celtic music, extinguished the bedside lamp, opened the shades, and sat down cross-legged in front of the window, staring out into the darkness and searching for I'm not sure what—answers, assurances, enlightenment?

This was my time to discourse with God, and I reached out for strength and guidance. I sat there for an hour, tears streaming down my face, talking to God about the future and how I knew my work here on earth was incomplete. It's not that I think I'm more special than anyone else, but I've always believed that God wanted me to accomplish wonderful things, and I still believe that. I was just beginning my "new life" living in the New York City area, and to have it come to an abrupt end seemed like a cruel twist of fate. It couldn't all be over at age thirty-seven. I poured my heart out and adamantly affirmed that I was not ready to die. I suppose that is arrogance—having the audacity to tell God when you're ready to leave this world. For the most part, I've been one who speaks her mind, and I wanted God to hear me loud and clear.

I eventually calmed down, blew out the candle, turned off the music, and climbed into bed. This conversation with God had been cathartic, allowing me to fall asleep in peace.

February 14, Saturday

Today, Mom called with some Web sites for me to check out regarding Neulasta. One is http://www.drugstore.com and the other is http://www. freemedicinefoundation.com.[19] I'll research these and other options for purchasing drugs at a discount. This injection is extremely expensive, and because I can't afford to pay even half the original price, an alternate supplier is essential.

Barbara set up a spreadsheet to calculate which plan under my new insurance coverage would be the most cost-effective. It appears that initially, at least for this year, the $10 copay and $656-per-month premium plan will be the least expensive. Imagine, $656—that's more than I paid a month for rent!

On a happier note: Aidan got his first official haircut today. It's adorable, and he looks like a little boy, not a baby.

Today's reflections/thoughts turn to my future: At present, my thoughts are creating my future. Everything I write down on paper is a possibility for the life I long to lead and how I plan to accomplish goals. As much as I am trying to live in the present, the future is a huge part of my daily thoughts because I want a future of good health, creativity, and accomplishment. I want my life back—only more fulfilling, more balanced, and more daring. I believe that our thoughts shape who we are destined to become. Our thoughts arise from our deepest desires and strongest beliefs, even though sometimes these thoughts are not so beautiful or good but are downright ugly.

I also want to begin thinking in unlimited ways. I thought I had been, but reviewing past attitudes, I've always accepted a certain mediocre level of attainment or success regarding income or career. Maybe I am afraid of this type of success or lack the confidence in my ability to attain it. Too many people, including myself, place limits on themselves; limits prevent us from moving forward and from discovering what we can achieve. My advice to myself is to think in limitless terms and see what amazing possibilities can become reality. Of course, we have to work for our dreams and goals; success and fulfillment won't materialize out of nothing. But as I have written many times in past journals, you have to be able to dream or conceive of something before you can ever make it a reality. If you can't dream it or visualize it, it can't happen because you haven't set the dream or idea into motion.

I have so many dreams and wishes . . . The most important wish right now is that I want to be cured of leukemia; I want it blasted out of my body, *never* to return so that I can go on to live the life I'm envisioning for myself.

February 15, Sunday

Today's reflections/thoughts turn to my "being enough." "Being enough" means knowing who I am and what values I cherish and being comfortable in my own skin. "Being enough" means I don't and shouldn't have to prove my worth. I must stand strong in acknowledging who I am and not allow outside influences to degrade my self-worth or make me doubt my intelligence, talent, or appearance. Life is too short to be concerned about how I measure up. And I measure up fine. Now to live it, believe it, know it. Keep repeating it: I am enough.

What a great day! I took the train into the city, and my first stop was the Tomato Restaurant in Chelsea to meet Karen C for brunch. I got to the restaurant first, so I grabbed a table, and she arrived soon afterward. She thought I looked mysterious with my scarf tied gypsy style—she didn't think I looked like a cancer patient at all, but rather like a very stylish woman. We talked about the acting business, her new manager, and, of course, my leukemia.

Thankfully, we had plenty of time because it took forever to get our food. I dared not even ask our server for the side of mayo I so desperately wanted because

I knew I wouldn't get it before we left. The restaurant was crowded. Our waiter, I'm sure, was very inexperienced; however, there is a bar to be set for customer service. (I waited tables one summer in college, so I am just as critical of, as I am sympathetic toward, wait staff.) Still, in the end, we were generous with the tip.

Karen C is such a lovely woman. It was so relaxing to sit and talk; it felt like old times. After lunch, I headed to the T. Schreiber Studio to attend a matinee performance of *Landscape of the Body*.

The excitement was mounting as I approached the studio building. I hadn't seen any of these people in two months and was looking forward to the show. After making a stop in the ladies' room to freshen up, I entered the studio, and my beloved teacher was the first person I encountered. We gave each other a big hug, and he introduced me to his daughter. He asked how I was, welcomed me, and told me that he had posted my thank-you card on the bulletin board for everyone to read. I then ran into Peter, Peter's mom, and Todd (Todd and Peter were in class with me). We all sat together during the performance. I saw Sarah who works in the office. Sarah said, "You are the talk of the dressing rooms—well, at least the men's."

The show was wonderful. Every time Cristina, Joseph, or Erica was on stage, I had this big goofy grin on my face. I felt like a proud mother—and of course, at every funny stage bit they performed, a cackle of delight erupted from me.

We remained inside the theater after the performance. Little by little, the cast emerged from backstage. Cristina was out first, and we yelled to get her attention. She gave me a huge hug and excused herself for a minute (she had to quickly see a friend); then Joseph came out—beelined for me—and we hugged tightly. We looked into each other's eyes, smiling, and he gave me a kiss on the mouth. Sarah was standing next to us, so when I looked at her, she gave me a look like "Is there something going on between you two?" I shook my head no, reinforcing that we were just very good friends.

I have to admit, though, I loved the way he held me, the way he looked at me, and the way he kissed me. It wasn't a long romantic kiss, but a solid right-on-the-mouth-I-care-about-you kiss. His hair has grown out since he got it cut, but I could tell it was shorter than two months ago, and he did look handsome. I know that I am reading too much into his attentions, but he makes me feel safe, and I enjoy that feeling, so I'm going to cling to it for a while (even though desire and clinging hinder following the "middle way," which is taught in mediation practice).

My classmates and some of the cast members went to the Black Door, a bar a few buildings from the studio, for drinks afterward. I joined them and even had a glass of wine—only one, though, and with my doctor's permission. I enjoyed being with my friends and feeling like all was normal again, even if only for a couple of hours, knowing all the while I'd be back in the hospital tomorrow.

Cristina talked to me about her liver disease when she was in high school—she was really sick. Cristina and Erica told me that it meant so much to them that

I was there to see the show. Everyone thought I looked great and that my eyes retained their sparkle.

We left the restaurant before 7:00 p.m. because I wanted to catch the 7:21 train to Morristown, New Jersey. On the train ride home, I couldn't focus enough to read, so I merely sat and reflected on my perfect day—and it was a perfect day. I enjoyed every moment of it. Well, every moment except maybe the five-and-a-half-block walk from the restaurant to the studio (it was so cold that my nose was dripping—yuck). So thank you, God, for such a splendid day—it was a gift. I needed to see these people, be in their company again, and talk to them. They nourish my spirit and encourage me. I really love them.

February 16, Monday

I'm back in the hospital. My roommate's name is Karen (going forward, she will be designated Karen L). She was diagnosed with lymphoma on December 22—four days after my diagnosis. Dr. Goldberg had told her about me, so when I introduced myself, she asked, "Are you Deborah Ludwig?" I was bit surprised. Barbara and I were joking later about her knowing my name. I laughed, saying, "She must've seen my infomercial, or maybe she saw me on *Ed* or *Sex and the City*." This is funny because I was a background actor on these TV shows. So if you blinked, you would miss me, and that is if I was even visible in the scenes at all. No one would even recognize me except those people who actually know what I look like and knew to look for me in a particular scene.

Once Barbara left, I requested lunch. While eating, I made a list for the nurse of items missing from my bedside. (Once you've been here a couple times, you get used to having certain objects readily available and within reach.) The list included tissues, the nurse-call mechanism, a small pitcher of water with ice, cups, urine bowls for the bathroom, and extra pillows. I then activated my phone and TV. It's a very busy admission day, so the staff is running a bit behind schedule.

6:00 p.m.

My dinner had to be reordered because they obviously did not receive the initial menu I completed. The kitchen totally screwed up my order by sending carrots, bread, fruit, hot tea, and vegetable soup—gross. They did manage to get the chicken and wild rice right, but you should get what you order. I'm going to request another meal be sent yet remain calm and be as kind as possible—practice patience.

7:30 p.m.

Now I'm really not happy. Where is my food? All my chemo is here except the one I need first. My nurses aren't as efficient as my roommate's nurses—she's got really good ones. I hate to be critical, and I understand it's been a crazy day, but I don't like Monday admissions. I think from now on, I'll shoot for Tuesday admission, which I'm sure will be less chaotic. The whole admission process can be quite tedious from checking into the room, to completing the admission questionnaire (answering the same questions every time I'm admitted, which seems to me a colossal waste of time and resources; why isn't this computerized?), to settling in with all the needed extras as mentioned previously—extra pillows, nurse-call button, ice.

The nursing shift changed at 7:00 p.m., and my night nurse hasn't been in to see me yet. I'm not getting the attention my roommate is, and that angers me. I hate being ignored.

7:35 p.m.

Unbelievable! The kitchen sent the wrong order *again*! So Karen L's nurse, Maureen, took my order and called it in. Who knows what they'll send next? Are they totally clueless?

It's now almost 7:50 p.m., and I still have no food, but my chemo has arrived though Dr. Goldberg wants to do the Cytoxan drip first and then the Rituxan. It's been a rough day, and I'm trying to remain patient—but oh, it's difficult. This would definitely be a good exercise in patience for me if I weren't failing so miserably.

8:00 p.m.

My day nurse is gone, and I still haven't seen my night nurse. I feel like I'm being ignored, and aside from rudeness, being ignored is one of my biggest pet peeves. Stay positive, Deb. It doesn't do you any good to be angry or upset, but I'm hungry, and I want my dinner!

9:05 p.m.

Finally, dinner arrived. It was mostly correct, but there were still items I hadn't ordered such as apple juice and carrots (for the third time—they really wanted me to have those carrots).

My roommate, Karen L, and I talked for a while; I discovered that she has non-Hodgkins lymphoma. She is married and has two daughters—Claire is six, and Brooke is two. Larry is her husband. I admire her strength going through this with two little girls to take care of and worry about.

I told her, "All I have to worry about is me."

To which she responded, "That's a big thing to worry about—don't you discount that."

We talked about how we first knew something was wrong, how we reacted after being diagnosed, and what our experiences have been during treatment. Karen L is a great roommate. She, as well as her family, will be added to my prayer list.

9:30 p.m.

Mom called. She received my photo and the wording for the article the Society section editor may put in the *Perry County News* (my hometown newspaper) about my infomercial. We'll see what ends up in the paper.

Mom didn't want the film *My Sexiest Mistake* mentioned in the article under my list of film credits. This prudery goes back to her concern with "appearances" and is a bit ridiculous because, in this film, I worked background as a bookstore patron—nothing at all risqué. Well, that's her hang-up, not mine. I'm not ashamed of any acting jobs I've ever taken, and she shouldn't be either. It did make me a bit perturbed at her; however, I soon let my annoyance go, realizing this is her issue, not mine. So be it. I've been very agitated today . . . gotta calm down . . . breathe . . .

February 17, Tuesday
12:30 a.m.

I just spent two hours talking with Karen L. She and I are so much alike. We discovered that we are both control freaks and that we are both very spiritual (though she's more religious than I). We have placed inspirational and prayer items next to our beds and have both received an overwhelming outpouring of love and support from friends and family. We are encouraging each other to stay strong and have hope.

Right now, I'm receiving Rituxan. The remaining Cytoxan drips are scheduled at twelve-hour intervals beginning today and ending on Thursday at 10:00 a.m. Each Cytoxan drip is administered over a two-hour period.

10:00 a.m.

The second bag of Cytoxan is now being administered. I've already done some healing visualizations, one for cleansing and another for leukemia; then I prayed a rosary.

Today's thoughts/reflections are about letting go of expectations. The expectations I let go of are (1) that other people meet or exceed my expectations of behavior, (2) that I'll get married, and (3) that I'll be a famous actor or writer. However, that doesn't mean I've abandoned these dreams—I'm just not holding on so tightly.

In regard to expectations of others, I need to have none. That way, I avoid disappointment. I have very high expectations of how I think other people should behave, which is based on the expectations I have set for myself. I never expect anything of anyone that I don't expect of me. However, I must accept the fact that we are all different, that our world views and experiences are diverse, and that our perception of the same situation can and does differ; and because of this, it is futile for me to hold others to my standards. I probably fall far short of other people's standards too. Therefore, I need to uphold the standards I've set for myself but don't impose them on others. By expecting less of others, much of my frustration will be alleviated.

Regarding my relationship and career expectations, what I plan to do is live fully in each moment, love myself and others, and allow life to unfold as it should—with the appropriate nudges from me along the way. I will continue to work toward my goals but do it gently and consistently, without huge expectations. Expectations—especially very high ones—can lead to depression and disappointment if they're not achieved, especially those set rigidly to a timetable. If I truly live each day, appreciating it moment by moment, in mindfulness, I won't be as fixated on the future as I have been in the past. We should have goals, and we need to think about the future, but we shouldn't be consumed by these at the expense of living in the present.

I believed that I was living in the present when I moved here when in fact, I was tirelessly planning and working for the future—obsessing about it really. I'm sure it's the journey that is most important. I need to trust that if I do what I must each day and enjoy the moments in it, the future will take care of itself—perhaps even quite beautifully. As John Lennon said, "Life is what happens when you're making other plans."

Yet I have to laugh at myself because I am a bundle of contradictions—one minute, wanting to focus on the present and actually doing it, yet in the next moment, obsessing about the future. For instance, right now, my preoccupation with Neulasta and its outrageous price tag is increasingly disturbing my peace of mind. Therefore, I must find a solution. I've written down several questions for the Tel-Drug customer service rep; hopefully, now that I've received some answers, I can figure out what to do. Following are the questions and answers:

1. Q. Last time I paid $85 for the shot. The customer service rep with whom I spoke previously told me that through a pharmacy, it would be $2,500. Why through Tel-Drug is it so much more affordable?
    A. Through Tel-Drug, it is highly discounted. (That's an understatement!)
2. Q. How long does Neulasta last if stored properly?
    A. I was transferred to a pharmacist who informed me the drug has up to a year shelf life if stored properly.
3. Q. Why is the drug so expensive?
    A. It's a new formulation. Drugs developed in the past five years are more expensive in order to recoup the costs of testing and research.
4. Q. Any alternative suggestions for getting the injections without spending thousands of dollars?
    A. I was transferred back to the customer service rep who suggested calling in a ninety-day supply. (I like that answer. I requested that Phyllis call in a ninety-day supply. We'll see what transpires.)

After calling Tel-Drug, I phoned the Social Security office, and they forwarded me to an adjudicator. However, no adjudicator picked up. Instead, I was greeted with the following outgoing message: "This number is no longer part of the action unit." That was it. There was no information about whom to contact or where to forward questions. That's terrible customer service; I was appalled.

This is the stuff that makes me crazy. Not only am I trying to focus on getting well, but I also have to deal with all these financial issues. I wish I had an advocate who could take care of all this, but these are my problems. I am most familiar with the situations, and thus, I'm the best person to resolve them. And on the positive side, I feel well enough to deal with it all—at least for now.

My visitors today were Chris, a classmate from the T. Schreiber Studio, and Shelley. Shelley is five months pregnant, expecting a little boy who should arrive in June. She looks great and seems very happy. She bought the book *The Power of Now: A Guide to Spiritual Enlightenment* by Eckhart Tolle for me. She said this book put her to sleep. If it puts me to sleep, then great—I've found the cure for my insomnia! But I doubt it will because I love this type of book.

Chris brought me a box of chocolates, and he made a card for me out of black construction paper. Images he cut out of magazines are pasted in collage form on the front and inside. These images include fire, moon, clouds, a flying woman (or angel perhaps?) with a message beneath her that reads " . . . with a beautiful sadness," a masked person, and uniformed men with their fists raised (are they cheering or jeering?). The front of the card has a cutout of a woman with shoulder-length red hair and a melancholy expression, and below the picture, it reads, "Who is Deborah Ludwig?" I want to talk to him about some of the images and why he chose them.

He and I discussed at length faith, trust, change, love, and friendship. Because of his personal challenges (which I'm not at liberty to divulge), he is gaining the insight to accept life's vicissitudes and trust in God; he is learning so much about forgiveness and his own personal growth.

Chris also encouraged me to let go of my monetary worries, and I recalled what Donna said—fear and faith cannot coexist. However, because responsible money management and meeting financial obligations have been so ingrained in my head from an early age, it is understandable that these are the worries that would most preoccupy me. When something has been such a huge part of your psyche for thirty-seven years, it's impossible to let go quickly and easily, but I must keep trying for my own peace of mind. That would be real personal growth.

Chris shares his knowledge and his experiences freely. Shelley and Chris both brightened my day, and I've spent more time talking with and getting to know my roommate, Karen L.

Barbara called, and during the conversation, she put Aidan on the phone. He laughed when he heard my voice. Then Barbara asked him, "Where's Aunt Deb?" She told me that he pointed up to my room. How cute and smart—he knows where I'm supposed to be, whether I'm there or not.

February 18, Wednesday

Neulasta update: I found out from Tel-Drug that call-in orders are only for a thirty-day supply. I must submit a prescription for a ninety-day supply, so Dr. Goldberg is writing the prescription for four shots. I will have it express-mailed to Tel-Drug on Friday when I am home. The plan is to have the prescription filled before my COBRA coverage expires on February 29.

Along with some bills and insurance updates, I received a card and a letter from Ryan, a high school classmate. Here is some of Ryan's letter:

> Dear Debbie,
> I spoke to Dave this past week and he told me about your illness. I'm not sure what to say other than get well soon! Dave gave me your new address. I hope you don't mind the Valentine. I thought you might be sick and tired of get-well cards, so I went with the Valentine to try and bring a little variety and humor to your day.

Is the chemotherapy as tough as I hear it is? How are you holding up? I'm not a particularly religious person, but in your case I will make an exception and ask the Big Fella for some help.

I recently moved my family to Northern Maine. I took over as Plant Manager for a food processing facility in Houlton, Maine, this past April. Hard to believe it will be a year in just a couple of months.

At any rate, I think about you and the fun times we had back in Tell City often. I hope we can add to the memories at the twenty year reunion this August. Take care of yourself.

Sincerely,
Ryan

(I usually cringe when someone refers to me as "Debbie," but I tend to cut people who've known me my entire life some slack about it. Everyone from my hometown calls me Debbie. I started using Deborah when I moved to Atlanta in 1989.)

I really enjoyed reading Ryan's letter. I haven't spoken to him since 1999 at our last high school class reunion. It's always interesting to know what is going on in friends' lives and how they have evolved over the years—be it physical appearance, personal development, or family life. I'm glad he's doing well, and I'm sure he's a wonderful father.

Dr. Goldberg is going to schedule a consultation next week for me to meet with Dr. Rowley to discuss transplant. For standard-risk adult ALL, one form of treatment is not clearly better than another—the chemo regimen only (induction Hyper-CVAD chemotherapy and then two years of maintenance chemotherapy) versus chemo followed by stem cell or bone marrow transplantation. However, overall, in leukemia patients, clearly chemo along with stem cell or bone marrow transplantation produces higher cure rates. However, in the end, this is my decision; my doctors won't make it for me, so this is where I really need to listen for God's guidance and use the medical information available to me.

I have to supply the doctor's office with Karen's and Barbara's contact information because before any real decisions can be made, we need to see if I have a compatible sibling donor. If not, then we will have to search outside my immediate family for a donor. I have some markers for abnormal genes (not the bad genetics I was so fearful of) but abnormalities in my chromosomes that make treatment a little trickier. Unfortunately, all patients have different risk factors; because of these variations, much of the treatment is guesswork—medicine is definitely a mixture of science and art.

Trust, have faith—fear and faith cannot coexist. I just don't want to die. No, no, no—I'm going to be a cancer survivor. I will, I will, I will!

9:05 p.m.

Bobbi visited today; she just left to catch the bus. Bobbi is wise, honest, and sincere—a good soul. She gave me a hug before leaving. I think she was afraid to hug me for fear that she might contaminate me in some way. I assured her a hug would be fine. When she visits, she stays for hours, and we talk nonstop. She's not even one of my closest friends, but she's been so supportive and caring, and I have come to deeply value her friendship. I feel there is a bond between us that could sustain a friendship throughout the years—at least I hope so.

Bobbi is probably my tallest girlfriend; Natalie, a Cincinnati friend, is the second tallest. Both women have shoulder-length brown hair though Natalie's is darker. Both of them use their spirituality to guide them through adversity and help others, a quality many of my friends share.

Around 10:00 p.m., when I was supposed to have my Cytoxan drip, we had a little bit of a dilemma getting a blood draw from either line in my catheter. It concerned me because they won't administer the chemo until they get a blood return. The blood return is important because this tells them that the chemo is going into a vein and not somewhere else, which, if it went somewhere else other than a vein, would most likely kill me. Finally, a blood return was achieved.

The Cytoxan is now dripping into my veins. The last one will be administered tomorrow morning. I will also receive injections of vincristine and doxorubicin, and then I should be released. All the chemotherapy drugs being administered to me basically interfere with the growth of cancer cells, and these damaged cells are eventually destroyed by the body.

Between the thought of the impending transplant discussion and the difficulty getting a blood return, I am feeling a bit melancholy. I'm trying to stay positive, but I feel the need to cry.

February 19, Thursday

Today's thoughts turn to my creativity: I mostly express my creativity through my performing and writing (or rather, my journaling). At this point in time, my creativity is definitely challenged because I am no longer able to pursue acting. Acting, singing, dancing—all of these activities add so much joy to my life, regardless of any financial rewards. The wonderful aspect of performing is that you are sharing yourself, your craft, and your talent with others. Artists transport people into other worlds and entertain; and hopefully, if an audience member is going through a difficult time, he/she can escape his/her troubles for a little while by getting caught up in the performance or story. I think artists are incredibly brave people—true artists risk so much. The very fact that artists put their abilities and craft out there for the world to see and to judge, sometimes harshly, proves their courage. Despite the risk, there is such tremendous satisfaction in being an artist, which is why I refuse to give up my creative work.

In the long run, I definitely want my creative skills to be more in demand than they are at present and not only in the areas detailed above. Additional areas where my creativity can be put to good use include volunteer and outreach work, writing, and studying languages. These skills can be utilized to help others and make the world a better place.

I truly feel that I'm meant to give back to the world and do something amazing with my life. That is why dying within the next couple of years, even five or ten years down the road, isn't an option. Thirty-seven years isn't enough time. Faith in God, inner strength, and the love of friends and family will get me through this ordeal so that I will go on to fulfill what I believe to be my destiny—be it as an inspirational author/speaker, an actor, a philanthropist/volunteer for the Leukemia & Lymphoma Society, or all three. It's possible! Oh, and I definitely intend to experience a loving family unit of my own.

But at the moment, I am where I am. Life circumstances have brought me here to this crossroad. I have to live each day, moment by moment, enjoying who and what is present in my life and not worrying too much about the future. Now is all I have; it must not be squandered or taken for granted, and I can and will utilize this time to express and expand my creativity.

My appetite is not very good. I may ask for some antinausea medication. I usually don't need it, but it could help settle my stomach. Dan will be here around 5:00 p.m., and mac 'n' cheese is sounding pretty good for dinner tonight. I love comfort food. I will need to keep some distance from Aidan because he's not been feeling well; he may even have a small virus.

I'm feeling rather despondent today. Depression always surfaces within a few days following chemo treatments. The side effects—fatigue and nausea though minor—make me feel wimpy, and though I try to stay positive, it is a challenge. Wallowing in self-pity and crying is a good tonic and actually helps me prepare to start fighting again. It's the cycle of experiencing grief, working through it, and then facing the cancer so that I can defeat it by using all the positive energy I can muster. Some people don't like to use the word "fight," but I am a fighter. This is the toughest battle I've ever faced, and I damn well will fight it. I plan to wear the title of Cancer Survivor—I am a cancer survivor.

Marni called, and we talked for about twenty or so minutes. Then bless her heart, she decided to make a trip out to see me before my discharge tonight.

5:45 p.m.

Marni arrived around 3:30 p.m. and stayed for two hours. I helped her fill out her Screen Actors Guild (SAG) ballot (the SAG Awards are this Sunday night), and then we talked for a long while. She brought me a gift bag filled with lovely items that included a warm, fuzzy brown hat, a crossword puzzle book, a small journal, a framed photo of her and me when we worked on *Ed* (we look like sisters), *The Writer's Block* book, and two gorgeous scarves. One of them is a lime green color with big white polka dots, and the other is varying shades of pink and tan stripes.

It took us both being in New York City to develop our friendship, but better late than never. We knew of each other in Cincinnati but didn't personally know each other. Marni is one of the founding members of the Cincinnati Shakespeare Festival. Marni's visit meant so much because I was feeling quite low. She will never know how much her visit helped me because she made me laugh, and laughter is sometimes the best medicine.

February 20, Friday

Last night was tough emotionally. Every time I leave the hospital, I feel this way—a combination of relief and tremendous sorrow. I'm glad to be out of the hospital, but when I think of the amount of toxins pumped into my body over the past four days, anger and frustration bubble like hot lava beneath the surface and then explode. On the way home, in the car, Dan and I rode in silence. Thankfully, it was dark because although I fought to hold back the tears, they flowed freely down my cheeks as I struggled to remain silent.

Upon arriving home, I went straight up to my room where I could at least release the sobs quietly behind closed doors. Barbara came in to check on me a little later. I had no energy. I confided in her that I was sad, scared, and overwhelmed by the decisions to be made regarding transplant.

Today, I didn't have the energy to put away my clothes, toiletries, and gifts that I'd brought home from the hospital last night; so instead, I rested. Digestion problems are still plaguing me. Dan express-mailed the Neulasta prescription that Dr. Goldberg wrote for a ninety-day supply. We'll see if it gets filled.

February 21, Saturday

Before we left for the clinic this morning, I changed my catheter caps and the dressing around the incision area. I should've asked Barbara to help me because

I almost passed out. I had to lie down on the bathroom floor for a moment to regain my composure. After a few moments of deep breathing and relaxation, the dizziness passed, and I completed my task.

Dan drove me to Hackensack to receive my Neulasta shot. I'm still feeling weak . . .

February 22, Sunday

Today is Dad's sixty-second birthday. When I talked to him this morning, he thanked me for the card and said it made him cry. The card shows a little girl holding her dad's hand, and the sentiment it expresses is that little girls always need their dads, even when they're adults. It made me cry too, but it's so true. My dad has always been there for me—*always*—and I will continue to need him until the day I die or he does. Even if he dies before me, I'll hold on to his spirit.

I was still feeling blue yesterday, but this morning, I decided to get dressed and organize my room. "I'm not dead yet," I snapped at myself. "So get up and do something!" Filing papers, writing bills, and organizing mail were among the tasks completed. I can only feel sorry for myself for so long, which is a good thing, I think.

Katie arrived in the early evening. We had an interesting conversation that lasted until almost midnight. She made me feel really valued by letting me know that I was like a big sister to her, a mentor even. She hadn't realized how much she counted on me and depended on my support when she was coming to the New York City area from Alexandria on a regular basis to pursue acting during the summer and fall of 2003. She felt I always knew the next step (I didn't) and that I was so organized (I was). It is nice to be needed, and the fact that my going to New York to pursue an acting career gave her the courage to do so as well is very flattering. Maybe I *can* be an inspiration to people. I was very touched when she revealed that she's felt lost without having me to talk to or to lean on. I assured her that no matter where I am living, she can always count on me for anything she needs—encouragement, advice, support, friendship, and love.

I first met Katie in 1994 when we both performed in our first play in Cincinnati, which was a community theater production of *Ten Little Indians*. I played the lead, Vera Claythorne; she played the spinster, Emily Brent. What is funny about this is that I am five years older than Katie, and she was playing Emily Brent when she was twenty-two. Katie is about my height, dark hair, big brown eyes, and very pretty. She and her husband, Kevin, are expecting their first child. She is four months along, and on March 8, she will find out the sex of the child. I can't wait until that little mystery is revealed.

It's pleasantly surprising, but only three days after leaving the hospital, I feel good. I know my counts will start dropping soon, but right now, I feel fine. My priorities at the moment are staying hydrated and well fed, practicing excellent oral hygiene (don't want any nasty mouth sores), and moisturizing my skin (it's so dry, especially the skin on my cheeks).

This week, I've been reading the Lance Armstrong book, which is giving me more inspiration and hope. He had experienced pain for a very long time and delayed seeing a doctor. By the time he did see a doctor, he had stage 4 testicular cancer that had spread to his lungs and to his brain. By all accounts, he should be dead, but he's not. His survival is probably largely due to a strong, athletic body and an even stronger constitution to live; I possess both as well. Okay, in truth, my body isn't as athletic as it once was; however, I believe that my high level of physical activity in previous years has been a positive factor in how I've handled my treatments.

I've been very hesitant to research prognosis statistics related to adult ALL. I refuse to view myself as merely a number. I am a flesh and blood human being with a huge spirit and an indomitable will. I'm not going to stop fighting right now—no way; too many people depend on me and vice versa.

Today's *God Calling* message was appropriate. I needed these words very much. Here are some highlights:

> YOU must trust. You have much to learn in tuning out fear and being at peace. All your doubts arrest My work. You must not doubt. Doubt delays. I died to save you from sin and doubt and wrong. You must believe in Me absolutely. You must trust Me wholly.[20]

February 23, Monday

Karen L was at the clinic today. I met her father, and I introduced them to Katie. He told me, "I've heard so much about you."

I replied, "I've heard a lot about you too."

Dr. Goldberg said that Friday through Monday will be the critical time with regards to my chances of getting infections. Then by Tuesday or Wednesday, my white blood count should be on the upswing. I don't have to return to the clinic until Friday, at which time, I'll receive my chemo shots—cytarabine into the spine and vincristine into my catheter. I also have a consultation with Dr. Rowley to discuss transplant.

February 24, Tuesday

Today's reflection focuses on change: Change is essential. If we don't change, we cannot grow or learn or become better—we stagnate. Even unwanted change, perhaps *especially* unwanted change, is an excellent opportunity for growth because it forces us to adjust our lives, not remain in the status quo. Facing cancer has made me so ready and willing to make changes now and not wait until I'm cured. Waiting would be a waste of time. They're all worthwhile modifications though some are definitely easier than others. My current goals include developing a new mind-set—a fresh means of dealing with frustrations, annoyances, and problems—and finding innovative strategies for structuring my world so that I am living a creative, abundant, and soulful life.

9:15 p.m.

We're all tired this evening and have retired to our respective rooms to enjoy some alone time. I have experienced some pain today, mostly bone pain in my skull and forehead regions. The pain is not severe enough to take pain medication, but it is annoying. Yet I feel energized; I can't seem to unwind. I am looking at *The Writer's Block* book Marni gave me . . . hmm . . . maybe a writing exercise would be good for me right now, so here goes.
Describe your first brush with danger:

> *The Giant Bumblebee!*
> It was a sunny summer day in 1969. One of those summer days when running through the yard, barefoot and feeling carefree, was one of the most joyous experiences in the world. The warmth of the sun caressed my toddler face, and playing within the confines of the tiny yard, my whole world felt safe and secure.
> My family lived in a small trailer park on the southwestern side of town until I was four. The plastic swimming pool, tool shed, and swing set (two swings and a slide) barely fit in the diminutive front lawn that served as my playground. Despite the lack of space, I roamed freely and with wild abandon.
> Dressed in little pink shorts, a pink and white striped sleeveless top and my hair pulled up into two very high pig tails tied with pink ribbons, I pretended to be a little princess. I loved my yard, my swing set, and running around barefoot. What freedom for a three year old! I was the oldest child, so of course, I ruled. My sisters were a mere one and two years old, so they were inside (probably napping) at the moment.

I was twirling, running, and laughing in the yard, the dry grass crunching beneath my feet. It hadn't rained in a while so the grass wasn't as lush as it normally would have been, but I didn't care.

Suddenly, I stopped dead in my tracks as a terrifying sight appeared before me. Despite the searing July heat, my tiny body was frozen stiff. There, sitting menacingly on the metal stair rail, was a giant bumblebee. It was gigantic! In fact, it was almost as big as me. Terrified, a sharp scream escaped me—scream after scream after scream, pleading for help.

My mother came running out of the trailer and frantically inquired as to what was wrong. She scooped me up in her arms and tried to calm me down. Screaming and crying uncontrollably, unable to articulate what I had seen, I pointed my shaking, elfin hand to where the bee was resting on the rail. My mother turned and seeing the object of my terror, smiled. She hugged me and comfortingly rubbed my arms. She walked over to the shed, picked up a broom, and carefully swatted at the gargantuan bee. I crouched behind her and peeked out to watch her slay the dreadful creature. She swatted the rail one more time, and to my relief, the bee flew away!

Laughing and clapping, I beamed up at my mother. The bee was gone! I was saved! I was so relieved because the bee was at least twelve inches in diameter. Mom had rescued me. As always, she was there for me, and I knew I could count on her for protection. But for that one brief, chilling moment, I had been stalked by a giant bee and had found myself terrifyingly alone in the world.

As I've matured, I know there is no such thing as a bumblebee twelve inches in diameter (at least I've never seen one), yet I remain convinced of its size. When I envision this incident with the bumblebee, it is indeed and always will be as large as I imagined it—nearly as large as the three-year-old me.

February 25, Wednesday
5:25 a.m.

I'm obsessing again. I woke up at 4:48 a.m. and haven't been able to get back to sleep. This scenario is way too typical these days. What is occupying my mind? Per usual, the issues consuming me are (1) Social Security disability payments, (2) the new insurance plan, (3) the Neulasta order, and (4) W-2 forms not yet received. I know I'm going to be fine, but the fact that I have to repeatedly engage in follow-up calls is so infuriating. I wish someone else could do it all for me, but these are my responsibilities; and when I feel fine, it is easier for me to take care of them myself and not involve a third party.

Today's thoughts are on self-worth/self-love/self-improvement: I'm slowly realizing that I am a wonderful being, and I am learning to love myself. I am worthy of love—I am discovering this more every day as I work through the haunts and mistakes of my past. I have seen the loving-kindness extended to me by family, friends, and acquaintances. Self-love and believing I am worthy of love shouldn't be difficult, but it is, and I'm sure this is true for many people.

I also believe in my strength and goodness though much work is still needed on my temperament. The smallest annoyances can easily set me off. This is the aspect of my personality I like least—being quick to anger. It is counterproductive, does not make me happy, and destroys the goodness I long to put out into the world. I need to harness that spark of angry energy and convert it to positive energy. I am supposed to be more compassionate, not more cantankerous.

Today's mail call: (1) The *Perry County News* arrived. There was a very nice article about my infomercial in it and my acting career progress to date, detailing my work in Cincinnati and New York. (2) A statement from my insurance company arrived for my December hospital stay, which was billed at around $82,000—for ten days! My insurance carrier is contracted for about $15,600 of it while my responsibility is about $550. I'm so fortunate to have health insurance. What devastating financial situation would I find myself in if I didn't have it? That's a scary question.

Something seems really wrong with the health care system in this country when a provider has to write off approximately 80 percent of the bill. This demonstrates to me how inflated, or out of control, medical costs are and also how inadequate and unaffordable health care coverage is in this country. There are so many uninsured people out there, people who go bankrupt in order to get the treatment they need or go without treatment because they can't afford health insurance or a doctor's visit. Health care reform is a serious issue that needs to be addressed in this country. If I didn't have family members who were able to help financially with my medical needs (Barbara and Dan, mainly), I'd be in a lot of trouble because I am broke. Thank God for Barbara and Dan.

February 26, Thursday

Katie left around noon. I enjoyed her time here so much; she said it was good for her too. After Katie's departure, I wrote ten thank-you cards for the gifts in the friendship box, finished reading the Lance Armstrong book, and did some laundry.

And the big coup—the Neulasta arrived. Four syringes were packaged and at a bargain price. I may not even need them all if I go through transplant in late April or May. At least I have them should I go through all four complete cycles, and I will only have to purchase one additional injection. But for now, financially, I'm fine. Alleluia!

Aunt Addie called and left a message while we were out. This is the second call I've missed from her. Aunt Addie knows all too well what Mom and Dad are going through and feeling; she lived through a similar situation with her son Mike, my cousin who had esophageal cancer.

February 27, Friday

Today was a difficult one. I had an intrathecal injection of cytarabine after the transplant consult with Dr. Rowley, which was informative and eye-opening, especially to the seriousness of my disease. In people less than fifteen years of age, cure rates are very high for ALL; however, I am old for an ALL patient, and that works against me. With the Hyper-CVAD induction regimen followed by two years of maintenance chemotherapy, five-year survival rates are only 30-40 percent. Per a copy of the French study that Dr. Rowley gave to me, if you add transplant into the picture, the five-year survival rate increases to about 44 percent.[21] For some reason, I thought the cure rate was quite a bit higher, around 58 percent, though I can't recall where I got that number. To me, 44 percent seems rather dismal.

This afternoon, when I got home, I read through both studies and highlighted relevant information. I fear that Mom and Dad are going to be disappointed when they read it. I'm sobbing right now writing this. I'm scared and frustrated because I don't want my family to be upset or frightened, and I loathe the fact that this illness is causing them pain. I can't stop crying; I'm so distraught. I should be out in the world accomplishing goals, seeing my friends, and . . . oh hell, what exemption is there from God or the universe that my life should be free from suffering? I'm not any more special than anyone else. However, I always thought that if I got sick, I'd be much older, not cut down in the prime of my life.

Life isn't fair, and I've held many emotions inside over the past couple of months. Much of my frustration stems from the fact that most of the time, I feel good; therefore, I sometimes minimize the seriousness of my illness. Today, the reality of my situation was clearly put into perspective—the reality I was trying so hard to ignore. I thought if I were uninformed of survival prognosis statistics,

I could remain blissfully ignorant. I can't let the numbers discourage me. I am not a statistic; I am a human being.

My faith, positive attitude, and fighting spirit must shine through this dark place in which I am dwelling. I still haven't truly let myself grieve although today's cry was a start—loud, long, and heaving. I don't want to wallow in self-pity or be negative, but I have to keep this entire situation in perspective and face the reality of my mortality.

My mortality is a factor; it is real, and as much as my loved ones don't want to face it, they must. I feel guilty expressing my thoughts of death because people don't want to hear that I might die. I understand their fears, but by not addressing the mortality issue, they're putting a lot of pressure on me to ignore a very real possibility. I need to face it and come to terms with it so that I am less scared about making my decision to go through transplant.

Of course, I don't want to die. I want to live a beautiful, productive, wonderful long life; but that may not be my destiny. None of us is guaranteed tomorrow. The bottom line is that I have a decision to make, one that will be made sooner than I feel prepared to make. So now, more than ever before, I need to live more fully in the present.

Shelley drove me to Hackensack today. She took copious notes during the transplant consultation with Dr. Rowley. Some transplant questions I needed answers to are the following:

1. Q. What would be the time frame of going from chemo to transplant?
    A. If I have a donor available, Dr. Rowley does not see the need to complete all four cycles of Hyper-CVAD; only two should be sufficient. Transplant would most likely be scheduled a month after my last chemo treatment so that my blood counts are back up before transplant.
2. Q. If I go into remission and then relapse, is the transplant less effective after first relapse?
    A. Yes.
3. Q. Will I have total-body irradiation (TBI)?
    A. Yes.
4. Q. Will I have a bone marrow or stem cell donor?
    A. Stem cells will be collected unless Barbara is the match. In that case, bone marrow will be collected. (This is due to her pregnancy.)
5. Q. After transplant, how long will I be in the hospital?
    A. I will be in the hospital for about four weeks unless complications arise, such as infections, organ problems, or stem cell rejection (graft rejection), which occurs when the patient's immune system rejects

the donor's stem cells. After I leave the hospital, there will be a good amount of recuperation and monitoring at home—at least a month.

6. Q. Will I be getting chemo, radiation, or both to prepare for BMT (number of doses, length of time prior to transplant)?

   A. I will receive both. Chemo will consist of six intrathecal injections (posttransplant) and two days of Cytoxan before transplant. Total-body irradiation consists of radiation administered thirty minutes, two times per day for four days.

7. Q. Minitransplant, is this a possibility?

   A. Not an option for me. A minitransplant is a less intensive approach to preparing the body for bone marrow transplantation. It is a good option for older patients or more fragile patients—people who may have damaged organs such as lungs, heart, or kidneys, and/or who may not tolerate the side effects of total-body irradiation and high-dose chemotherapy, both of which are used to prepare the body for bone marrow or stem cell transplantation.

I just reviewed the notes Shelley took. I'm quite impressed with the amount of information she captured and am especially impressed with her correct spelling of several technical terms. I most likely will decide to have the bone marrow transplant, but before any absolute decision is made, I need to know if either of my siblings is an acceptable donor. That will definitely be the deciding factor as to when transplant will take place.

Eleonore and Russ visited this evening; we celebrated Russ's birthday, which was yesterday, with dinner and cake. They're both an integral part of my life right now, and I'm so glad I have them—they take very good care of all of us in this household.

10:45 p.m.

Barbara and I had a really good conversation tonight about the transplant information, my current emotional state, and the need for me to keep living my life. She mentioned that she had noticed how energized I was when I returned home from my day in the city on February 15. She's right—I felt fabulous. Now that the weather will be getting nicer and the cold and flu season is coming to a close, I will definitely get out more.

The weekend before I check into the hospital next month might be a good time to revisit the city. I could stay with Beckie and Nelson and see all my other friends. I plan to go to Tell City, Indiana, over the Easter weekend to visit Mom and Dad. Dr. Goldberg said that travel would be fine because my blood counts will be back up. He also said I could plan a vacation if I wanted. When my counts are up, I can do whatever I want, so I should go out and have fun. Keep living; I'm not dead yet.

Talking with Barbara has not only made me feel better, but it's also given me much-needed encouragement. My sister loves me, and she feels badly that she doesn't spend a lot of time talking with me. Being pregnant, I know she is really tired. Plus taking care of a fourteen-month-old and working a full-time job doesn't help either—of course she's exhausted. I understand her lack of time for me, and I'm not resentful of it, which is why I spend so much time writing in this journal. Journaling allows me to express my thoughts, sort through issues and emotions, explore dreams, and formulate plans.

February 28, Saturday

My frame of mind is much more positive today. I'm still scared, but my faith and the will to persevere have conquered some of that fear. I need to allow myself to deal with the fear by experiencing it; otherwise, it'll get locked up inside me.

I went for a leisurely walk around the neighborhood this afternoon. Afterward, I practiced breath meditation and walking meditation. I found that during walking meditation, I was much more focused, and my mind wandered less. In the *Insight Meditation* book, it suggests that if you are planning to work on both together, do walking meditation first and then breathing meditation. I will try that sequence tomorrow.

February 29, Sunday

I did both walking meditation and breathing meditation today. I did the walking meditation first. This helped me to be more centered during the sitting meditation, and my mind wandered less. I'm learning to enjoy meditation and beginning to incorporate it into my daily routine. They say it takes three weeks to form a habit; this would be a good one to develop.

I discussed bone marrow transplantation with Mom and Dad this evening to give them a realistic picture of what I'm facing. I tried to give them encouragement by stating the fact that even though the statistics seemed more dismal than I'd originally thought them to be, I am not a number, and I don't plan to give up easily.

I read some of *Seeds of Light*. The book is filled with guided healing visualizations. I am using meditation and other self-healing practices as a means to aid modern medicine's magic because I believe that integrating Eastern and Western healing techniques is a powerful antidote to illness.

March 1, Monday

I listened to the *Health Journeys: A Meditation to Help You with Chemotherapy* cassette last night. I can't believe I've waited weeks to listen to it. I had discovered it in the bottom of the bag with the wig Mom purchased for me from the Shoppe on Fifth. The shop must include this complimentary cassette with purchases.

As I listened, powerful emotions swelled up inside me, and tears of joy flowed down my cheeks. There were several images my mind conjured that particularly moved me. The cassette begins with instructions to lie or sit comfortably and breathe. Belleruth Naparstek, the creator of these guided imagery tapes for Health Journeys (the company she owns and operates with George R. Klein), guides the listener through the story. Her gentle low voice is accompanied by relaxing music. She asks the listener to imagine a place, preferably outdoors, that is safe and peaceful—it can be real or imaginary. I immediately envisioned an ocean view. For me, the ocean's vastness and the constant, steady rhythm of the waves striking the shore are incredibly soothing. I love feeling the wind blowing through my hair, the sand between my toes, and the smell of the salty sea air. I imagined myself at the place where I had spent an afternoon back in 2001 with my friend Jason, a college friend who studied theater with me at Indiana University and who had moved to Los Angeles where he still resides.

Jason and I drove to the shore although I can't recall where in Los Angeles exactly. We found this small secluded cove surrounded by large rocks and trees with the ocean in front of us, waves crashing on the beach. It was a glorious day—blue sky, sunshine, soft breeze. We sat there for hours and talked, listening to the crashing of the surf, the screeching of the seagulls, and watching the tiny sand crabs scurry about each time a wave swept in. It was perfect, so this is where I situated myself for this guided imagery journey.

The healing images I recall most vividly from the recording include "a fountain of shimmering liquid bursting from the ground," and "one special being, most likely someone who loves me or once loved me very much, stepping forward to let me know it was time to allow the healing liquid into my body." This special person I imagined to be my mom. A ribbon appeared and stretched from the fountain to me, acting as a passage to allow the healing liquid to reach me, penetrating my body's tissues, bones, and cells.

The two images that evoked the most emotion were the special being (Mom) and the healing liquid penetrating my body, which was getting rid of "old pockets of fear, pain, and resentments" that would allow me to forgive others and myself.

I quote Belleruth Naparstek, "You are healing, and you will continue to heal. It's time to be fully well, to again share your gifts with the world, to love and appreciate who you really are."[22] This quote, in particular, moved me to tears because this healing really is about healing my entire being—not just the physical cancer, but also the psychological and spiritual cancer.

I felt so relaxed and peaceful afterward; it was quite cathartic. I attempted to listen to the affirmations side of the cassette but fell asleep before it ended. In fact, I slept straight through the night until 7:30 a.m.

9:30 p.m.

My doctor's visit was fine. The white blood counts are up, but platelets are forty-eight thousand and hemoglobin is 9.1, which are low; however, Dr. Goldberg feels that since the white blood counts are fine, the platelets and hemoglobin will soon follow. I'm going to monitor my legs for bruising and petechiae (pinhead-sized red spots under the skin that usually indicate a low-platelet count), and if either appears, I will call the clinic.

Some petty annoyances plagued me today. The main one was a collection notice. Verizon sent the $42.50 I didn't pay from my final phone bill (for service in my West New York apartment) to a collection agency. I didn't pay this because UTC was supposed to delete the long-distance setup charge from my account that wasn't utilized during my hospital stay in December (this charge had been included in my final Verizon bill). In the past, I would've immediately gotten on the phone and ripped into someone. But now that my goal is to reside in a state of equanimity, I took a deep breath and decided to address this situation when I felt ready to deal with it, to not stress over it, and to remain calm. All will work out in the end, and I have much bigger issues right now to deal with anyway. So there *has* been some personal growth.

March 2, Tuesday

Today was a productive low-stress day. I wrote my blogspot.com entry, set up a blogspot.com account, posted the entry, and sent an e-mail notice about it to friends and family.

Joyce from the Social Security office called me with follow-up information about my claim. All the paperwork had been received and transferred to a caseworker. Thank goodness this is finally being reviewed because I am quickly running out of money.

I went for a long walk and incorporated walking meditation into it. My mind only wandered about ten times during the relaxing hour-plus trek. I focused on the warmth of the day, the soft breeze on my skin, the muscles rotating in my thighs and calves, the way my feet hit the ground, and the "lift, move, place" mantra on which I was concentrating. I felt so mindful and centered.

This evening, I watched the Super Tuesday results on CNN. John Kerry has essentially wrapped up the Democratic presidential nomination. John Edwards is pulling out of the race tomorrow. I have a feeling this is a going to be a brutal race for the White House, and Kerry definitely has his work cut out for him.

March 5, Friday

Today's *God Calling*:

> *Fear is Evil*
> HAVE no fear. Fear destroys hope. It cannot exist were love is or where Faith is.[23]

I'm definitely being told something important about fear's insidiousness because I keep hearing from people and reading in books about fear's danger. Fear, I believe, is the source of all evil in this world.

Trusting God and releasing fear are guiding me throughout my cancer struggle. The "no fear" and "trust" mantras are becoming so ingrained in my psyche that I almost feel brave. I want to approach life and all its obstacles with serenity and use positive thoughts to formulate effective solutions. There will be no more trembling hands, pounding heart, or shallow breathing to betray my fears. Peacefulness will reside in me.

I finished my next blog entry. It's titled "I'm Enough."

> *I'm Enough*
>
> A life-threatening illness, major loss, or any tragedy for that matter, forces us to examine our own history. Leukemia forced me to examine mine. I have spent hours replaying scenes from my life and the choices I have made in an effort to discover why leukemia chose me to be its bedfellow. I've devoured books explaining the "biology of biography"—how our past shapes and influences our tendency toward health or illness, how clinging to old hurts and grudges can cause

sickness, cancer and even death, how poor health habits contribute to disease, and how de-valuing ourselves destroys our spirit and self-esteem. In essence, I've become an excavator partaking in a personal archeological dig that I hope will provide enlightenment.

Enlightenment, though, is a long, sometimes painful process. Until my illness, I took for granted my body, mind, and abilities. I have always been athletic, of above-average intelligence, and relatively popular. I was Most Valuable Runner four straight years during high school track, consistently an honors student, and voted Basketball Homecoming Queen my senior year in high school. The following is a story of early achievement that should have assured me an abundance of confidence, yet that confidence never quite materialized.

One of my earliest victories occurred on a sunny, Sunday afternoon during my fifth grade year. Every spring the American Legion sponsored the Junior Olympics in which students from the local grade schools competed in events such as the soft ball throw, running races, high jump, and long jump. At the end of the competition, there was an awards ceremony where gold, silver, and bronze medals were presented to the winners of each event.

That day was quite exciting because I'd just won my heat in the fifty-yard dash. After all heats were completed, we were informed there had to be a run-off for first place. My opponent, from a rival grade school, was Angela who stood about a head taller than me.

My father walked with me across the grassy field to the starting line. Angela was already there with her older brother. I overheard him say, "Look how little she is," which only bolstered my resolve to win. Dad told me not to pay attention to his comment and then gently nudged me toward the starting line.

My heart was pounding and nervous energy coursed through my veins as we waited for the official's gun to go off. After what seemed an eternity, the gun exploded and we raced down the track. I soared past Angela and crossed the finish line well ahead of her. I took home the gold that day, along with a confidence I had not previously possessed. However, in the following years that self-esteem began to erode as I developed an unhealthy obsession with my appearance and self-image.

Actually, in the confidence realm, I am, and always have been, a bundle of contradictions. An example of this is that I'm a *calculated* risk taker. People tell me that I am so courageous, that they could never do the things I do—act, sing, or move to the New York City area. My response to them is, "If you really wanted to, you could and you would."

It's not that I'm so audacious, but rather I'm terrified of having regrets, so I force myself into situations with which I may be uncomfortable because I am compelled—almost neurotically so—to at least try. Fear, more than courage, is the impetus for many of my actions. I've been afraid of everything my entire life, even success. I reject being defined by one's financial status, and though that may sound admirable, unfortunately, I've substituted other definitions of "success" that have proved unhealthy. For me, success, or the perception of it, was linked to my physical appearance and my image—that the world saw me as a confident, sophisticated, attractive woman.

So, realizing my unhealthy pre-occupation with image and appearance, I decided to explore my past in order to understand why and how I created these neuroses, and more importantly, how to alleviate them. I needed to objectively assess how familial, peer, and societal influences shaped me—for better or worse, why I allowed the negative ones to diminish my self-esteem, and then formulate the necessary steps to take so that they no longer interfered with my quality of life and mental well-being.

Propriety—being a "good girl" and abiding by the rules—has dictated my life. My mother, one of the sweetest, most loving, selfless women I know, cares too much about how society views her and her family's reputation; she is also overly protective of her daughters. Mom's fears and concerns, conscious or unconscious, definitely influenced me. There was always an unspoken pressure to conduct myself appropriately, make good grades, and excel at whatever endeavor I was pursuing. Forgetting a homework assignment could send me into an emotional tailspin, especially if I could not get back into the school to retrieve my homework. Anxiety would overwhelm me because I knew that the next day I would be humiliated in front of my classmates by receiving a hole-punch in my conduct card for not having completed the assignment.

It's heartbreaking to think about that anxious, scared little girl. In life's grand scheme, missed homework assignments are pretty inconsequential, but it established a lifetime of feeling intense anxiety when deadlines were, or potentially could be, missed or when I was running a bit late for a meeting (I'm chronically on time). I've always pressured myself to be perfect, but perfection is unnecessary. My conclusion is this: Alleviate the need for perfection and you alleviate much anxiety.

As mentioned previously, throughout my childhood, appearances were a big issue with my mom, though not in the physical or monetary sense but rather in the realm of conduct. Heaven forbid should we have gotten into trouble with the law, or worse, gotten pregnant as teenagers. My greatest fear was that I would lose my parents' love and respect.

The bottom line is that I was a really good kid. I've always played by the rules and spent my life trying to please others, and in pleasing others, tried to be the best at whatever endeavor I pursued. If I wasn't the best, was it worth doing? If I hadn't been the fastest runner on the track team, would I have stayed on it? I liked being the best because it strengthened my fragile ego.

Three childhood memories particularly stand out as contributing to my fractured ego: my best friend rejected me after she became a cheerleader, which translated in my mind to my no longer being popular or pretty enough to be her friend; a boy commented that my nose was big (I had no self-consciousness about my nose prior to that moment); and a friend's grandmother gave me a backhanded compliment about how attractive I was at fifteen in spite of my "having been such a homely child" (I'd been homely?). These unkind actions and comments sparked the obsession with my appearance, which only intensified as I transitioned from grade school to high school. Reading fashion magazines and watching glamorous celebrities parading around on television made me achingly aware of my physical inadequacies. I longed to be one of the beautiful people and thus began a two-decade quest for the perfect makeover.

This quest included years of exercising, not out of the joy of moving my limbs and generating health, but rather to achieve a svelte, sculpted body. I failed at many diets because it was absurd for me to be on a diet in the first place.

In 1998, the obsession with my nose culminated in a rhinoplasty surgery that then led to a septoplasty surgery in 1999 to correct some asymmetry from the rhinoplasty. The irony is that thousands of dollars later, to this day, my nose remains crooked. At that time, I was also scrutinizing my crows-feet, under-eye bags, and cellulite. My youngest sister berated me for this behavior, saying that I was not looking at the whole package but instead picking myself apart, which proved not only destructive to my self-esteem but also to potential relationships.

In 1999, I found myself in a romantic fantasyland and completely lost all sense of myself. My first mistake was assuming that I knew the type of woman this man desired. My second mistake was trying to mold myself to fit that imagined woman. I gave him no opportunity to know the real me because I didn't believe I was good enough for him. Instead, I tried to transform into a woman I imagined he'd find desirable, and the fact is I had no clue what that was. What a complete waste of both our time.

Once the fantasy ended, I went into therapy, and it only took two counseling sessions, so I must have been relatively well adjusted, regardless of my lunatic behavior. Or perhaps, more accurately, I longed to put that embarrassing episode behind me. A new century was beginning so a fresh perspective was in order; it was time for some changes. I made plans to get on with my life, beat a bad cop in court, wrote and performed some cabaret shows, recorded a demo CD, and moved to New York City for a new adventure.

Unfortunately, after moving to New York, I still focused far too much attention on my appearance. I found myself emotionally and physically drowning even further under the pressure of being an actor in the New York City market. I worked, I struggled, I played—I took action to create the life I'd envisioned. Then leukemia annihilated the dream.

After being diagnosed with leukemia, I committed myself to uncovering some uncomfortable truths about my past. I started to understand the significance of my Body Dynamics teacher's response when I revealed to her how I always felt I needed to stand up straight or be "pulled together." She said, "Somewhere along the line, someone made you feel that you were not enough." I initially resented her comment because my childhood was wonderful. However, her words continued to haunt me, and over time, the veracity of her statement began to resonate with me.

The blame cannot be attributed to one person, including myself. However, I did allow others' comments and actions to chip away at my self-esteem for nearly thirty years. It took cancer to open my eyes to the value of my life, my body, my mind, and my talents. Now that the decoration of Deborah has been stripped away, I can see myself more clearly.

My long, auburn tresses have fallen out, my eyelashes have thinned, and I rarely wear make-up these days, but when I look in the mirror, I see clear, pretty blue eyes shining back at me. My body, which is strong in spite of the toxins pumped into it, is carrying about ten pounds more than normal in preparation for weight loss during the remaining chemotherapy treatments and then bone marrow transplant. My waist remains small, although it is thicker than normal, my legs are strong and muscled from years of running, and my breasts are full. (I must admit, I like my breasts.) Is this what the perfect woman looks like? No, and that's okay.

The years I've wasted bemoaning my perceived physical deficiencies saddens me. I always felt I had to be better and prettier, but now, I know that I am enough. Cancer made me look deep inside and for that I'm thankful.

"I'm enough" is one of my new mantras. By honestly exploring my emotional and behavioral responses to past hurts, I hope to move beyond destructive thought and behavior patterns. This healing process will take time, but no matter how long it takes, I will continue to work on self-acceptance and self-love, knowing that I am enough—actually, more than enough.

An excitement is beginning to materialize about my writing, which is making my life so fulfilling. This is another form of work that stimulates creativity and passion, like acting; however, unlike acting, writing is work I can embrace right now.

March 6, Saturday

I've been experiencing many good days recently. As usual, I began the day with my rituals of prayer, affirmations, and spiritual readings.

In the afternoon, Barbara, Dan, Aidan, and I went for a walk. It was amusing watching Aidan toddle around, picking up rocks, leaves, and dirt and then shoving them into his mouth—everything goes into his mouth. His capacity for joy amazes me—it is so pure—and his curiosity is insatiable. When he's excited about something, he raises his little arms in the air, his eyes widen, his eyebrows lift, and he beams a broad smile. He can hardly contain himself. And he's so bright; he's like a sponge soaking up everything. The other day, he placed his sippy cup on a coaster. No one told him to do it. But he'd seen Barbara, Dan, and I do it many times, so he copied our actions. It's pretty remarkable that a fourteen-month-old child is using a coaster, and he's done it a couple of times since, not just that one time.

Being involved in his life is a true gift because Aidan teaches me things—especially about living in the present. He is neither concerned about tomorrow nor about yesterday; he is always immersed in the now. Observe a child four or five years old or younger, and you'll see what I mean.

March 7, Sunday

Tonight, as I was putting Aidan to sleep, I experienced a moment of complete immersion in the present. Aidan was inconsolable after Barbara and Dan left for the hospital. Barbara had been vomiting most of the day, and her doctor feared she was getting dehydrated, so she instructed her to go to the hospital. I did everything I could think of to comfort Aidan to ensure he felt safe and loved. He sat on my lap, cradled in my arms as I gently rocked him back and forth, tears cascading down both our cheeks. I was so moved gazing upon his sweet little face. His crying broke the silence, and I could feel our two hearts beating. It was one of the most precious moments of my life.

After twice attempting to put him in his crib, the third time was a charm. I watched him sleeping, finally at peace. Gazing down at that little boy, I experienced a deep, unconditional, almost-heartbreaking love. Nothing else mattered in that moment, and it allowed me to know the extent of the love I am capable of feeling and giving.

Shortly after I'd gotten Aidan to sleep, Eleonore and Russ pulled up in the driveway. They had come to take us to their home because apparently, Dan is sick now too.

March 8, Monday

A customer service rep from my insurance company assured me that I'm set up in the system and gave me the lockbox address so that I could overnight my premium payment, which Eleonore is handling today. Tomorrow, I need to call Phyllis and the Chartwell people to give them the new contact information for my individual health plan.

The woman with whom I spoke was helpful and kind; yet I noticed that while I was on the phone with her, I was shaking, and there was an urgent quality to my voice. This concerns me because I'm trying to live with less anxiety, yet when I'm faced with a situation where there is potential conflict, I get nervous. I loathe being nervous. I want to feel serene, calm, and confident when broaching potentially contentious issues. How do I do this? I breathe and relax yet still find myself trembling. Is it the chemo? Is it caffeine? Who's to say? All I can do is keep striving to achieve peacefulness.

As of 9:35 a.m., neither Aidan nor I was sick. If we were going to be ill, we would've been by now, I would think; hopefully, that's a good sign. Illness crept up on Dan very quickly. He regurgitated as soon as he arrived at the hospital with Barbara.

Today, I am hanging out at Russ and Eleonore's home and have planned a big writing day. I'm working up in Eleonore's office, which is actually a loft with a gorgeous view of the wintry outdoors. It snowed last night. A crisp blanket of white covers the yard, but the streets are clear because the temperature has reached the forty-degree mark, and the snow is melting rapidly.

2:44 p.m.

I just got off the phone with Susan. What a lovely intrusion—I'd been working on a blog entry when she phoned. She'd called Barbara and Dan's home, and Barbara gave her the phone number here. I was quite surprised to hear her voice on the other end of the line. She was glad that I sounded so well, and we talked for a good thirty minutes. She would like to schedule a visit this spring.

Susan and I became friends when we both worked at Cigna in Cincinnati. She was in the health care division; I worked in the group department (life, accident, and disability). She moved into Ravenswood Apartments where I lived with Karen. Susan and I started hanging out, going for walks, and partying on the weekends. Just as our friendship was solidifying, she received a severance package from Cigna and eventually found employment in Miami and relocated to Florida. I never had the opportunity to visit her in Miami. A few years later, she moved to Pittsburgh, her current city of residence. I have visited her there on several occasions.

Near the end of our conversation, she said that if neither Barbara nor Karen was a match, she would be tested to see if she might be a compatible donor. (Many of my friends have offered to donate marrow.) She also spoke about possibly doing a fund-raiser of some sort to help with all my medical expenses. She is the third person to make such a suggestion—Lani and Karen B were the others. I continue to be touched and amazed by the generosity of my friends.

9:35 p.m.

Aidan and I are home. Barbara and Dan were feeling better, so they retrieved us around 7:30 this evening.

March 9, Tuesday

It has been an amazingly productive day, and it's not even half over. Of course, I've been up since 6:00 a.m. In only a couple of hours, I prayed a rosary, listened to my affirmations, played with Aidan, called Chartwell and Hackensack with updated insurance information, e-mailed my latest blog to Mom, and read *The Four Agreements* by Don Miguel Ruiz.

The Four Agreements was a gift (included in the friendship box) from Michael S, a Cincinnati theater colleague. Michael S founded New Edgecliff Theatre, which staged its first production the fall of 1998 around the same time Ovation Theatre Company staged its first show; thus, we have a common bond.

The Four Agreements reinforced everything that I've been exploring and thinking about in my own life; I could've written this book. I read it in about two hours. I think these agreements are pretty good advice.[24]

I feel like I'm enjoying my life so much more now than over the past few years—even with cancer. I know much of this enjoyment has to do with trying to live more fully in the present. I have awoken every morning over the past week with an excitement and anticipation to start the day. I hope this feeling of satisfaction remains with me when I'm in remission and cured.

March 11, Thursday

Well, I spoke way too soon about not getting sick—oh my. Tuesday night around 7:30, my stomach started to hurt; by 8:00, I was in the throes of Barbara's, Dan's, and Aidan's (yes, he ended up sick too) stomach virus. It was a vicious little bug. Fortunately, the worst of it only lasted for about eight hours. I laid down most of yesterday, not rising from my bed until 3:30 p.m. because I didn't fall asleep until 4:00 a.m. This evening, Dan informed me that his parents were home today and throwing up. So we all got sick despite the precautionary measures taken. I was so sure that if I wasn't showing signs of being ill on Monday, I was in the clear. Guess not.

Today's *God Calling*:

> *Seek Beauty*
> DRAW Beauty from every flower and Joy from the song of the birds, and the colour of the flowers. Drink in the beauty of air and colour. Think of yourselves as My expression of attributes, as a lovely flower is My expression of thought, and you will strive in all, in Spiritual beauty, in Thought—power, in Health, in clothing, to be as fit an expression for Me as you can. Absorb Beauty. Look for beauty and joy in the world around. Laugh more, laugh often. Love more. I am with you. I am your Lord.[25]

Seek beauty. What a lovely way to look at the world: to appreciate everything surrounding me. For example, a tiny flower sprouting up from a crack in the sidewalk can elicit a smile from me. Or what beauty could one find in a homeless person curled up against a building, sleeping on a piece of cardboard on the sidewalk, and trying to conceal him or herself from the stares of passersby whose life situations are more fortunate? In this instance, I see the beauty of the human spirit and its will to survive despite indigence and loneliness. I see the beauty of people's compassion as they try to assist these disadvantaged individuals. I see the beauty of and have appreciation for my own life and give thanks for this. I may have cancer, but I have a place to live, plenty of food to eat, and people who care whether I have a place to live and food to eat. I am most blessed. If you look deeply enough, you can find beauty in just about anything, even suffering.

Now to pack for my trip . . .

I arrived at Beckie and Nelson's apartment around 7:00 p.m. I just got my workout in for the week by trekking through Penn Station, then down and up the stairs in the subway. This was quite taxing on my respiratory system. The baggage I was carrying was not so much heavy as bulky and hard to manage, so it was a struggle lugging it through the subway. I was breathless by the time I reached my destination and decided at that moment to take a cab back to Penn Station on Sunday.

When I stepped off the elevator, Beckie greeted me with a huge hug right outside their door. Nelson arrived home about a half hour later. We stayed in and watched *Survivor* and *The Apprentice* while we dined on pizza. I had one glass of Cabernet.

They like me bald and said that I looked great. Well, they're being kind. How wonderful to be spending the weekend with two of my best friends in the world. They open their home and their hearts to me so freely. Nelson and Beckie just fit together. They are an attractive couple whose relationship gives me hope for my own romantic possibilities.

As stated previously, Nelson started out as an acquaintance. I met him in 1996 through his ex-girlfriend when she was my assistant director for *Talley's Folly* in which I played the role of Sally Talley. I did not become friends with him until I started hanging out with Karen B. Nelson not only became one of my dearest friends, but also a fabulous dance partner. This Latino man with a killer smile and dark brown eyes has quite the moves when it comes to salsa, merengue, cha-cha, and rumba.

In April 2002, he moved to Los Angeles; and it was there he met Beckie, a lovely British dancer. When he relocated to New York, she came with him. When they moved to the city in August 2003, I was thrilled. I had only been in the area one year; and though I had made some friends, it was so wonderful to have a good friend, whom I trusted, living nearby. The first time I met Beckie, I liked her immediately. She is a warm, sincere, funny, beautiful woman. She and Nelson have been so good to me, even before I was diagnosed with leukemia.

I'm looking so forward to seeing all my friends. I feel like a kid in a candy store; there is so much excitement brewing within me. But in this moment, I'm quite happy being here with Beckie and Nelson in a lovely apartment in the Union Square area of New York City.

March 12, Friday

I was up this morning with Beckie and Nelson. They both left early for their respective jobs, so I had much of the morning to myself before heading out to see friends. I meditated, then did some reading.

While reading *Yoga Journal*, I had a revelation about control. There is so much of life that we cannot control. I am, unfortunately, a control freak. I know this about myself. I need to learn to let go, live in the present, and deal with problems when they occur. Presently, I anticipate problems and fret about them before they even materialize. This behavior has to stop because there may never be a problem, and then I've spent time needlessly worrying about it. Control is a matter of distrust, of not trusting that I will be okay.

After reading, sipping coffee, and pulling myself together, I left the building to meet Marni and Aaron at the Coffee Pot. Lani showed up for a little while too—what a great surprise! Aaron, another Cincinnati actor friend who recently relocated to the area, finally joined Equity and is performing in his seventh show in New York City. Marni recently did a sketch on *Saturday Night Live* and is leaving for Washington DC on Sunday to work on *Comedy of Errors* at the Folger Theatre. She has upcoming auditions scheduled in Massachusetts and DC. Lani is working to get STARK's CD released, copied, and marketed. She feels focusing on her music has been the right move. It's heartening to see my friends doing well, looking happy, and, hopefully, flourishing in their careers.

After hugging them all good-bye, I headed to the Upper West Side. I arrived at the Chinese restaurant and waited for Tony. It was extremely windy outside, which made it feel even colder, and walking up and down the subway stairs was kicking my butt. My hemoglobin level must've been low. In addition to breathlessness, my left arm felt a little tingly as if there were a lack of blood flow. I tried relaxing it, taking deep breaths, shaking it, making fists. I get a little nervous about any physical oddity in my body these days.

During lunch, Tony and I talked about me, and then we talked about him and his writing. At a friend's request, he wrote a TV pilot and is also working on a screenplay about Mozart's sister. He's actually meeting with someone about optioning it.

After lunch, Tony rode with me on the subway to Fifty-ninth Street where I got off. He told me, "You look great. You sound great." I think my healthy appearance is a relief to people because until they see me, they envision me looking sickly—underweight, sunken eyes, and sallow skin.

We quickly hugged good-bye in the subway car, and I hopped off. I had to walk four long blocks east to 59 E Fifty-ninth Street. I arrived at Elysabeth's theater, 59E59, around 4:00 p.m. Elysabeth was my director and producer for *Prince Hal*. After giving me a hug and inquiring about my health, Elysabeth gave me a tour of the facility. The design is very contemporary and sleek—steel, concrete white walls. The building houses three theaters—two proscenium and a small black box. Restroom facilities for the actors are attached to the dressing rooms (which I've been told is unheard of in Off-Off-Broadway and Off-Broadway theaters in New York City), the box office is located at the entrance inside the building, and a sizable office is on the second floor. It is a state-of-the art facility. I would've loved to have had a cup of coffee with Elysabeth and chat longer, but I was running late to meet Joseph.

I headed toward Fifth Avenue and caught the R train to Twenty-eighth Street. As it turned out, I needn't have hurried because he didn't get out of *Hurlyburly* rehearsal until 5:15 p.m. While I waited, I caught up with some former classmates and Terry.

Joseph finally appeared, and to my chagrin, some of his *Landscape of the Body* crew and cast mates had organized an impromptu gathering at the Black Door for this evening. *So much for getting to really talk with him*, I thought to myself. While we were at the bar, only two women from the show joined us.

About twenty minutes after we sat down, Joseph asked, "What do you have to tell me?"

"A lot," I replied. "But this isn't really the place to do so."

I think he knew I was disappointed that we didn't have time alone, so he asked me about my schedule for Saturday and Sunday. We decided to meet for coffee at 4:00 p.m. on Saturday, someplace quiet where we could talk. There's so much I want to share with him—insights, transplant, and how much I value his friendship.

Joseph was already standing up when I got up to go to the ladies' room. He grabbed me around the waist and asked, "Where are you going?" then kissed me twice on the mouth, like the last time. And he kissed me again when we parted company. He baffles me, yet when I gaze into those gorgeous dark brown eyes, I long to lose myself in them. I wish I didn't have these feelings for him, but I do, and they're getting more difficult to fight.

After leaving the Black Door, I headed back down to Union Square. Nelson, Beckie, and I went out for Indian food. We ordered mixed seafood curry, a lamb dish, and, my favorite, chicken tikka masala. We dined family style in order to sample everything. Nelson ate way too much, and I really did too, but it was impossible to stop eating because the food was so delicious. I drank more than I should've this evening. I consumed almost two glasses of Cabernet with Joseph, and then before we left for dinner, Beckie and I had Frangelica on the rocks. I opted for iced tea with dinner and refrained from drinking any more alcoholic beverages.

On a different note, I recently found out that Katie is having a little girl, who will be named Emma Marcelline. Katie sent the sonogram photos to me via e-mail. The baby's tiny facial profile was visible: the chubby cheeks, the button nose—so precious.

March 13, Saturday

I was up early with Beckie, and we headed out to do some shopping. We called Nelson around lunchtime to meet us at Penang, a Malaysian restaurant in Soho. The food was scrumptious. The hot Malaysian tea was smooth and sweet. I need to find out how to make it. After lunch, I headed up to Chelsea to visit Dan G.

Dan G is the friend who sent me the *Sex and the City* DVDs. My friend Scott, another founding member of Ovation, connected me with Dan G over e-mail before I moved to the Northeast. Dan G and I e-mailed each other for months before we actually met. One Friday night, I met him at Food Bar in Chelsea. In no time at all, we were talking about everything. No topic was off-limits, and at times, it got a little racy. I couldn't believe how quickly we opened up to each other. The next day, I received an e-mail message from him declaring, "Oh my god, you're my new best friend!" I'll never forget it. I told him I felt the same way.

It has been so long since we've sat down together to talk. However, we picked up right where we left off, which, I believe, is the sign of a true friend. He made hot tea for me and coffee for himself. We sat in the living room and talked about me and my life at the moment and his life and challenges. He had some gifts for me that he had intended to include in the friendship box but then decided he would rather give them to me in person. He gave me a journal, a box of note cards, and the *Chicago* DVD, which he signed (he worked with producer Martin Richards on this film). The cover designs on the note cards are four different styles of dresses—Deb dresses, he called them. He said they reminded him of me and dancing. They're very colorful (yellow, pink, polka dot, and floral) and quite feminine.

Dan G told me that the next time I'm in town to give him a couple of days' notice and let him know what Broadway show I'd like to see, and he'd get tickets. I hugged him good-bye and headed to the T. Schreiber Studio to meet Joseph. This time, *he* was waiting for me.

We walked around the corner to a little coffee shop. I ordered a large hazelnut coffee, which was steamy and delicious. I talked to Joseph about transplant and all the risks involved. While explaining the total-body irradiation, tears welled up in my eyes. He gently placed his hand on my arm. I shared with him how difficult it is for me to talk about death with those closest to me because it's something they don't want to hear or think about. However, because it's a real possibility, I need to talk about it. He told me jokingly, yet with sincerity, "Since I'm such a dark, morbid person, you can talk to me about death—you can talk to me about anything." I smiled.

I told him why I loved him as a friend. I prefaced it with, "I don't know you that well," which elicited a surprise reaction from him; I continued, "Well, I don't. I don't know anything about your family or past relationships. I've definitely shared more about myself than you've shared about yourself. Regardless, I have enjoyed your friendship. You make me laugh, and I trust you completely." I also told him that when I find people I really like, they're stuck with me unless they distance themselves from me repeatedly; then at some point, I stop reaching out.

We talked about *Hurlyburly*, which opens on May 6. He has been cast in the role of Phil. I also finally found out his age, forty-one. I assured him that he didn't have to tell me, but I was curious. He told me, "I don't mind telling you, but I want you to guess first."

Well, I wanted to guess forty-one, but I went a bit younger and guessed thirty-nine. I went with thirty-nine because he revealed to me that he had only practiced law for three years; I had assumed it was longer. He asked, "Is that too old?"

"Yes," I kidded, "I prefer twenty-eight-year-olds." I laughed and then said, "No, I think yours is a perfect age."

We talked for about an hour. The coffee shop was closing, so we had to leave. We stood on the sidewalk on Seventh Avenue and continued talking. He hugged me, kissed me, and said, "If you need anything, let me know." And he reiterated, "You can talk to me about anything," then added that he loved me. I know he meant as a friend. I told him that I loved him too, and for the first time, I initiated the kiss. We hugged tightly, and as I gazed at the top of the building in front of us, I smiled.

He walked with me down to Twenty-third Street. We laughed and chatted about dancing, Beckie and Nelson, and him buying a computer. He walked with his arm around me to keep me warm. He said, "I forgot what a slip of a woman you are."

I laughed, replying, "Yes, that's why I almost always wear shoes with at least a two-inch heel." I was wearing my athletic shoes today.

We arrived at the subway entrance, and Joseph said, "Take care, sweet pea," as he gave me a hug.

After my lovely visit with Joseph, I headed back to the apartment. About 9:00 p.m., we headed uptown to Babalu for salsa dancing. Our group was small but fun. Karen C showed up as did Peter and his girlfriend. It was basically a private party because no one else was there. I've never seen the place so empty, and it remained empty until we left. We had the entire dance floor to ourselves, which was awesome because we didn't have to worry about colliding with anyone or having our feet smashed. I danced three salsas and two merengues.

When we weren't dancing, we were congregating at the table. Karen C took a cute photo of her and me with a Polaroid camera. This camera produced a tiny photo, about one-inch square. It was a darn good picture too.

We left the club around midnight. We all said our good-byes at Forty-fourth Street and Eighth Avenue. On the way to Seventh Avenue to catch a cab, Beckie and I were acting very silly. We weren't drunk, but we were laughing as if we were. I was freezing, so Beckie had placed her wrap around both of us. We were laughing, being obnoxious, and I'm sure people thought we were intoxicated. Nelson, meanwhile, was walking in the street, attempting to hail a cab and I think a bit irritated with our pseudobacchanalian joviality.

Then the right heel of my brand-new sandals got wedged in a crack in the sidewalk. We were stuck—I couldn't move! This provoked even more outrageous laughter as we doubled over. After a couple of attempts, I freed the heel by yanking my foot from the crevice. I checked the heel for damage, and thankfully, there was none. Nelson nabbed a cab, and Beckie and I tumbled in, giggling hysterically. We did calm down quickly once we were in the cab. However, it felt so good. I haven't laughed that hard in so long, and I think it was very healing for me.

What an amazing day, and dancing was the perfect end to it! I was winded after each dance, but it felt so wonderful to move my body like that again. I felt active, graceful, and beautiful; best of all, I felt like my old self.

March 14, Sunday

My mind is on Joseph. I need to nip these feelings in the bud right now. However, I checked my voice mail around 10:15 a.m., and there was a message from him. This is mostly what it said, "D. Ludwig. How are you, sweet pea? It's about 9:45 a.m. I've been up for a while and getting ready to leave for rehearsal, and I wanted to say hello. I also wanted to reiterate how great it was to see you and how great to be seen by you (a laugh). Hope you're doing all right this morning—just very wonderful things for you. See you soon. Talk to you soon, sweet pea. Bye." I was very happy to get his message. He definitely didn't have to call me, so maybe I am on his mind too.

Jen, a cast mate from *Prince Hal*, showed up right on time, and we headed out for lunch. We took Nelson's advice and went to Spice, a Thai restaurant, located a few blocks from their apartment.

Jen and her husband are looking to buy a house outside the city, mainly because they are planning to start a family. She has a couple of interviews with legit talent agents as well as a literary agent who is interested in writing a book based on her one-woman show, *Kicking and Screaming*, about her years as a Rockette.

I haven't seen Jen in at least six or seven months, maybe longer, so it was fabulous being able to spend such quality time with her. We finished dinner and walked back to the apartment. We hugged and said our good-byes; then she was off.

I went upstairs, grabbed my bags, and said good-bye to Beckie and Nelson. Beckie then hailed a cab for me, and the driver dropped me off at Penn Station. He told me that he liked my scarf (referring to the one tied gypsy style on my head). I smiled and graciously replied with a simple thank-you.

The train ride home was uneventful but pleasant. This had been the best weekend I've had since Karen and Jeff's wedding, September 20, 2003. I thanked God for giving me the time and the well-being to be able to spend a weekend with friends.

March 15, Monday

I was up early. I made some coffee, then went online to answer e-mails. I received an amazing message from Karen B. A friend of hers, Jeff B, is running in the Flying Pig Marathon in Cincinnati on May 2; he is running for the Leukemia & Lymphoma Society's Team in Training. He has already been assigned a leukemia patient for whom he is raising money, but he is also going to put my name on his jersey during the race. I'm continually amazed by people's generosity.

I packed and pulled together books, my computer, CDs, and the framed photo of Aidan. Dan drove me to the hospital and stayed there until I was mostly settled. From my bed, the Manhattan skyline and a small regional airport were visible. It's definitely better than looking at the parking garage or the side of a building.

I called Mom to let her know my room phone number. I called Joseph to let him know where to contact me and to let him know how great it was to see him this past weekend. I have basically put out a plea, via e-mail, for phone calls because Shelley may be my only visitor this time. It can get very lonely here.

Karen called and told me to log on to Amazon.com to select some meditation and guided imagery CDs that she could send to me. I'll do that next week. She also informed me that Priscilla, a coworker of hers, and Priscilla's prayer group will be praying for me Wednesday evening. Priscilla told Karen to encourage me stay open to any energy I may receive that day. How wonderful life is when two people I don't know are helping me through their actions—Priscilla by prayer, and Jeff B by running.

On a completely different note, Karen L was here last week. One of the nurses shared with me that she is in complete remission! Yeah! I need to contact her. When I tried to e-mail her last week, the message bounced back as undeliverable, so I'll try again next week. I'm very happy for her. She must be ecstatic.

March 16, Tuesday

I had just finished breakfast when the nurse started the methotrexate drip. There is a two-hour primer drip, and then the twenty-four-hour one begins. The pH level in my urine is good, 8; they want it above 7, so they'll be monitoring my urine pH level in addition to my vitals. I must be vigilant about rinsing my mouth with the sodium bicarbonate mix and drinking cold beverages (hot beverages are not allowed because they can irritate mouth sores if you have any). Hopefully, I will be as successful avoiding stomach and mouth sores this time as I was during the last B cycle.

One of the most annoying things about these hospital stays is the incessant taking of vitals. Vitals are taken every few hours. During the day, it's fine, but at night—ugh. Usually, I pretend to be asleep, but it's hard for me to ignore the aides because I feel the need to acknowledge and thank them.

My nurse just brought a copy of my blood counts in, and everything has dropped.

	March 15	March 16
Platelets	129,000	109,000
White blood count	5.4	4.9
Hemoglobin	8.7	7.9

The white blood count is still within the normal range, but because the hemoglobin has dropped, I'll be receiving red blood cells later in the week. My glucose is high, but I am told that's due to the steroids being given to me with the chemo. I will also be receiving potassium later today because that is low.

I've been talking with my roommate, Ella.* A week ago, she went to her doctor for a follow-up appointment; blood tests were taken, and she was sent to Union Memorial. She stayed there for five days before being transferred to Hackensack. She has since been diagnosed with leukemia though I don't know which type.

Ella is an eighty-four-year-old widow who has two sons, a daughter, and five grandchildren and lives alone in a four-bedroom Cape Cod-style home. Ella is scared and frustrated. A permanent catheter was inserted into her arm, and she's fretting about how she'll care for it over the next six months. I shared with her my experience taking care of my own catheter—how a nurse came to the house twice to train me and how supplies are delivered on a regular basis. These supplies include dressings and bandages for the insertion area, injections of saline to clean out the lines and heparin to prevent clogging, and a container for disposing of biohazard waste. She will need a nurse to help her with this. It is one thing having the catheter placed in the middle of your chest where two hands can do the job, but when it is placed in an arm, you only have one hand available to do the work. She's not helpless, but when you're not feeling well and you don't have much freedom of movement, catheter care can be challenging.

We talked for about an hour; then my phone rang—it was my always-dependable, loving mother checking in on me. After Mom's call, I decided to listen to some music. "She Bangs" from Ricky Martin's *Sound Loaded* CD was playing on my headset. It's a fun song with an extremely fast tempo. I can recall Nelson and I turbo salsa dancing to this song at Viva's in Cincinnati. It was the fastest salsa I've ever danced. To move this quickly, one is forced to take tiny steps so as not to lose one's balance. It was such a blast!

Barbara rang about 5:40 p.m. while on her way home from work. We spoke for about twenty minutes. I could hear Aidan fussing in the car, but he soon fell asleep. She talked to me as she maneuvered the SUV home in the snow. We discussed my chemo, her work, and her conference in Miami this weekend. Since Dan is flying down to join her, she's extending her stay so that they can enjoy some couple time. It'll do them a world of good to spend time together without Aidan or me. Russ is staying at the house on Saturday to help with Aidan, Natalie will be here Sunday, and Barbara and Dan will return Tuesday.

Mom made her final call of the day around 8:00 p.m., and Karen called shortly thereafter. At least my family is keeping me company via phone. I've only heard from Joseph, but none of my other friends have touched base with me. I'm sure they will though . . .

9:05 p.m.

Katie called. I told her that she and Joseph were the only two friends who've called, and she replied, "Well, you did say Wednesday in your e-mail."

"You're right," I replied, recalling that I had written that I would probably start getting lonely around Wednesday. Okay, so I'm a spoiled brat and a whiner.

After hanging up with Katie, I picked up my copy of *Seeds of Light* by Elizabeth K. Stratton, MS. I've been trying to commit to memory some of the meditations that are most relevant to my situation. The chapter "Healing Your Body" focuses on the seven chakras of the body.[26] I was reading the meditation "Self-Healing" and came across the following:

> On the count of three, you will receive a symbol of healing: one-two-three.
>
> Breathe. Accept this symbol of healing. Visualize it in the area of your body that is now healing, and trust that it will continue to generate healing energy and new life.[27]

As I read this, I didn't receive a symbol, but instead a jolt of energy straight to the fourth chakra, which is in the chest area where the heart is located. I began to cry. This is the area of love and compassion. There is no mention (at least not in the books I've read recently) of blood or the circulatory system being associated with any of the chakras. However, the heart pumps blood throughout the body, so it would make sense that if one were heartsick, their blood would be sick as well.

When I review much of what I've been exploring about my past, so much of the pain initiates from matters of the heart. My heart is what needs the most healing—I am sure of it, and I feel that with this awareness, healing is on the way.

* Name change

March 17, Wednesday, St. Patrick's Day

My nurse brought in a copy of my blood counts:

	March 16	March 17
White blood cells	4.9	8.0
Red blood cells	2.32	2.52
Hemoglobin	7.9	9.0
Platelets	109,000	117,000

The methotrexate drip is finished, and a blood sample was taken to determine how much of it is in my system. The first of four bags of cytarabine will begin shortly.

I spent more time with Ella. She doesn't have any activities to occupy her time, nor does she turn on her TV, so I decided to keep her company. Plus this is good experience for me. When I become a volunteer, I'll be talking to other cancer patients, so this is valuable experience to prepare for that. It makes me feel good to know that I may be helping someone who is lonely, frustrated, or scared.

I can tell I'm starting to lose my appetite. I hardly touched my veggie burger, but I did manage to eat the pasta salad and lemon ice.

Shelley arrived around 2:30 p.m. She is such a good conversationalist; I could talk with her for hours. She stayed until 4:30.

Dinner arrived at 5:15, which is way too early to eat. I wasn't even slightly hungry. I ate some of the tomato rice soup, about a third of the salmon, and half of the mashed potatoes. I lose my appetite after several days of chemotherapy—the side effects usually hit on the third day. Still, I force myself to eat a little bit, even though it's difficult.

At 6:00 tonight, there was a prayer being said for me at a Quaker prayer meeting in Cincinnati. I tried to stay open to its energy, but I was receiving phone calls, and nurses were coming into the room for one reason or another. It's very difficult to focus on meditation or prayer here due to all the interruptions by nurses and aides and the dose-rate calculator's constant beeping. It's not an atmosphere conducive to serenity. Perhaps I need to concentrate harder, but I always like to acknowledge the people who come in to help me. I want the healing power of the Quakers' prayers, so I hope I was aware enough to receive the positive energy. That was so thoughtful of Priscilla and her prayer group. God bless them.

Many phone calls came in today. I knew I could count on my friends.

March 18, Thursday

The final two cytarabine drips today will be given at 12:45 p.m. and 12:45 a.m. If all is well with the methotrexate level in my system, I should be out of here tomorrow. I will also receive red blood cells before I leave. The hemoglobin level is around 8, which is well below the normal range of 12-15; therefore, the doctor thinks it necessary to have an infusion of red blood cells to prevent my hemoglobin level from dropping too low over the weekend.

My skin is getting so dry. The first week or two after chemo, I battle dryness. It's a good thing friends have sent many different facial and body lotions. Lotions are great gifts for someone undergoing chemotherapy.

It is time to take my meds. Sometimes, it is nearly impossible to take six pills at one time because I feel as though I'm going to gag. Plus the meds upset my stomach, so I always try to make sure that I've eaten something before taking them.

Snow remains on the ground, and the New York City skyline is obstructed by clouds for the third day in a row. I thought I'd be more depressed today, but I'm doing all right despite fatigue and no appetite. I try to maintain a friendly attitude with the nursing staff, even when I'm down. They're all so helpful, and I'm very grateful for their care.

Today's inspiration is from a Believe card:

> *Expectation is everything. Every day can be your day, if you expect it to be.*

> —Bob Moawad

I like this quote because it sets *daily* expectations. Expectations we set for today, not future days, weeks, or years. I've begun to realize that my life is much richer when I live in the present. By focusing on the present, hopefully, the future will take care of itself.

6:30 p.m.

Lani arrived around 4:00 p.m. and stayed for two hours. Fortunately, a friend drove her here, so she didn't have to take public transportation. I am coming to realize more and more how much I treasure her friendship.

Today's CBC results:

	March 17	March 18
White blood cells	8.0	6.5
Red blood cells	2.52	2.45
Hemoglobin	9.0	8.4
Platelets	117,000	119,000
Glucose	166	123

I am receiving red blood cells at the moment. To date, I've had no negative reactions from platelets or red blood cells. I tolerate the blood products well, which is a good thing since I receive so many of them.

8:00 p.m.

Mom called. She's calling back in a few minutes because I had to rush off the phone to go to the bathroom. With all the fluids being pumped into me, plus all the liquids I am drinking, I'm urinating constantly. It can be quite excruciating when you have to wait to relieve yourself. Plus I have to take the time to unplug my power source, and if bags of chemo or blood products are hung on an immovable IV pole, I have to rearrange those to a moveable one—bother! In this particular instance, I was standing on my bed reaching for the bag of red blood cells and nearly lost my balance. The hospital staff would love that bit of news: CANCER PATIENT KNOCKS HERSELF UNCONSCIOUS TUMBLING OFF THE BED. But I was victorious in my objective to free the bag. All this maneuvering can be frustrating, but I deal with it; I am little Miss Self-Sufficient if there are no nurses readily available.

Then another obstacle halted my progress toward the bathroom. Drat! I forgot that I was hooked up to the blood pressure monitor (blood pressure is monitored any time a patient receives blood products). I tore off the armband and hurried to the restroom as quickly as possible with the IV pole in tow. Unfortunately, by the time I returned to the bed, the blood pressure machine was beeping, and the armband puffed up before I could get it back on my arm. *Oh well, I'll try to squeeze it down,* I thought. Ha, that's not as easy to do as one might imagine—I needed the nurse's help for that. When the nurse came in, I looked at her sheepishly, and she laughed at me. At least I provided some comic relief.

March 19, Friday

It is snowing again. I am so ready for warm weather. The cold and snow make me very melancholy. I desperately need the warmth of the sun. I've felt cold all winter, even in the security of a warm, comfortable home. The chill in my bones sometimes feels permanent, and that scares me—I long to feel warm and safe.

Today's *God Calling*:

> *Courage*
> I AM here. Fear not. Can you really trust Me? I am a God of Power, as well as a Man of Love, so human, yet so divine.
>
> Just trust. I cannot, and will not fail you. All is well. Courage.
>
> Many are praying for you . . . [28]

Courage is difficult to hold on to all the time. I try to be brave; but sometimes, it seems my world is spiraling out of control, and I am helpless to stabilize it. I will continue trying to put my trust in a higher power than myself. I have to let go of my fear and my need to control. I must accept that I cannot control what is happening in my body at this moment in time. I can use my mind to help improve my condition, particularly my state of mind, and prayers to give me support; but in the end, I need to "let go and let God."

9:40 a.m.

My blood work came back, and here are today's results:

	March 18	March 19
White blood cells	6.5	10.4
Red blood cells	2.45	2.61
Hemoglobin	8.4	8.9
Platelets	119,000	110,000

3:15 p.m.

I said good-bye to Ella. I leaned over her bed, kissed her on the cheek, and told her I'd keep her in my thoughts and prayers. She said she'd do the same for me. I hope I made her stay a little more bearable. I spent quite a bit of time with her Tuesday and Wednesday, but yesterday and today, I didn't have the energy. I hope she continues to fight the good fight.

I told the nurses I wanted to walk out, not be wheeled out, and they acquiesced. Dan and I left as everyone at the nurse's station waved good-bye.

It is always emotionally difficult for me when I leave the hospital—this is the fourth time, and every time, I cry. I feel beat-up by the end of the chemo treatment, and I'm relieved to be going home. Still, on my release days, there is an overwhelming sadness that lingers over me like a dark cloud. Fortunately, we picked up Aidan from day care; his smile cheered me up. As we were leaving, out in the hall, there was a small plastic pool filled with an assortment of colored rubber balls into which Aidan took a nosedive. It was so funny. I told Dan, "You need to get one of those for him." He flashed me a smirk.

Home at last, and I immediately crawled into bed.

March 20, Saturday

Shelley and her husband, Dan D, picked me up this morning and drove me to the clinic to get my Neulasta shot. It was good to see Dan D because I haven't seen him in a while.

Upon my return, Russ was at the house, babysitting Aidan. He's going to stay here the whole time that Barbara and Dan are gone because they felt Aidan would be better off staying in his own environment, especially sleeping in his own bed as opposed to spending four days at his grandparents' home. That's fine by me. I was looking forward to spending some time alone, but actually, it's kind of nice having someone here with me. I played with the little guy quite a bit today, prepared my own meals, cleaned up the kitchen, and organized my room. I have some bills to sort through, but I'll deal with all that later.

Extremely dry skin, terrible gas, brittle nails, a scratchy throat, and feeling flushed are the annoyances I am dealing with at the moment. I shouldn't complain, though, because I could be experiencing more unpleasant side effects such as mouth sores, nausea, infections, and vomiting.

March 22, Monday

Natalie arrived late afternoon on Sunday. We've been talking, eating, playing with Aidan, and hanging out with Russ. Natalie and I have had some really wonderful conversations about spirituality and personal growth. She shared much with me today about the weeks following her father's death and how she coped, or didn't. I shared with her insights about my life, and life in general, that

I've been discovering since my illness. We did some energy work last night and were pretty in tune with each other's energy fields. Natalie is exploring energy work as possibly a side job or simply something to do to help others, regardless of monetary remuneration.

It was a gorgeous day to drive to the clinic though it's still dreadfully cold out. At least the sun was bright, and the sky an intense blue. Natalie and I listened to music—Sheryl Crow and Madonna. We sang along to the music, and boy, it felt good to sing again.

I didn't receive any blood products today although I will most likely get platelets Wednesday because they have dropped to forty-three thousand. Hemoglobin is up to 10.1, but the white blood count is down to 4.5.

Russ and Natalie cooked another delicious meal this evening—chicken parmesan with mushrooms and pasta, parmesan/oregano bread, wine . . . it was scrumptious. While they cooked, I tried to entertain Aidan. I know that I say it repeatedly, but the wonder and intensity with which he experiences everything is so pure and beautiful. For instance, he was playing with the Styrofoam container in which Natalie transported all the Graeter's ice cream she brought with her. His system was as follows: He would drop five of his pacifiers in the container and then try to put the top on it (always the wrong way). Then he'd take the top off, retrieve the pacifiers, put them on the floor, pick them up, drop them back in the container, try to cover it up again, etc. He repeated this process many times as if trying (and he probably was) to understand the mechanics of it.

He also likes to stir things. He was watching Natalie stir the mushrooms she was sautéing. I held him up so that he could see, and naturally, he then wanted to stir what Natalie was stirring; so we let him, but only briefly because the pan was very hot, and I was afraid he'd burn himself. To distract him from the stove, I gave him a wooden spoon, pulled a clean saucepan from the cabinet, and set it on the floor. He was quite happy to stand next to it, stirring the empty pan and pounding the wooden spoon against it.

Sometimes, when I'm watching him, I can't help bursting into tears because I fear I won't see him grow up; and he won't know how much I love(d) him. Then I get mad at myself and resolve, "I'm his godmother, and before God, I made a promise to be there for him. And I damn well intend to keep that promise." He is going to need me, and I am going to be there for him. He's my little man.

March 24, Wednesday

Today's *God Calling*:

> *Know Me*
> SEEK not to know the future. Mercifully I veil it from you.

So remember that this evening time is not to learn the future, not to receive revelation of the Unseen, but to gain an intimate knowledge of Me which will teach you all things and be the very foundation of your faith.[29]

I think this one is so appropriate for the way I am trying to live more in the present and not concern myself so much with the future—focus on the now. It amazes me, reading these *God Calling* messages, how often it occurs that I read the exact message I need most on a particular day to help resolve an issue, reinforce a decision, or inspire me.

It's almost 8:00 a.m.; I have showered, prayed, and repeated my affirmations. I am sitting here, typing in bed with tissues stuck up my nose, which has been bleeding since last night. I blew some major clots out this morning—gross. I have a feeling this is a platelet issue. I have a doctor's appointment today, so I'll be sure to address it.

On a different note, it has been wonderful having Natalie here. She has been very helpful—cooking and cleaning—and she scored big points with Dan for bringing Skyline chili from Cincinnati.

Barbara and Dan returned from Miami yesterday. It was really good to see them—especially Barbara because I haven't seen her since Monday, the fifteenth.

Yesterday morning, about 5:30 a.m., I had a lovely meditation experience. A soft pink glow painted the sky as the sun crept up from the east. I was not tired. I'd been awake since 4:00 a.m., so I decided to try a different sort of meditation—incorporating all that I've learned to date and meditating without the guidance of a CD.

I rose from the bed, arranged my pillow on the floor, lit the candle, opened the blinds, and began meditating. I alternated my awareness between sounds, breath, and body sensations. I also utilized "choiceless awareness" (a state of receptiveness where we simply open up to whatever object or sound arises—in this instance, planes, birds, trees, a flickering flame). I sat for thirty-five minutes. That's a record for me. The world is so serene at that time of the morning. I am actually becoming more of a morning person. However, much of that has to do with the fact I am only getting about five hours of uninterrupted sleep at a time. Once I have made it to seven or eight hours without waking up, I'll feel better. My sleep patterns are very erratic these days.

8:50 p.m.

It was an interesting day. We arrived at the clinic around 11:30 a.m., and they put me in a chair immediately. No wonder my nose was bleeding so much—my platelets had dropped to twelve thousand, so I received a unit of platelets. My white blood cell count was 0.3, so I have no immune system. My hemoglobin level was 9.2, which is low, but not low enough to receive red blood cells. My nose is still bleeding, but not nearly like it had been last night and this morning.

It is still unknown whether Barbara and/or Karen are HLA (human leukocyte antigen) matches. (Human leukocyte antigens are proteins on the surface of most tissue cells and give an individual his or her unique tissue type.)

I really hope we know something by the end of the week. I want to get on with this process. If neither is a match, then the search for locating a nonsibling donor must begin. Of course, it wouldn't surprise me if they both came back as matches.

I was approved for Social Security disability benefits but won't receive my first payment until July 14 for June. This is because the claimant must be disabled five months before benefits are payable. I need money desperately; so I guess I remain completely financially dependent on Barbara, Dan, Mom, and Dad for a while. I have a couple $550 bills due to HUMC. I'll try to pay those next week. There are some questionable bills that I need to follow up on. However, I refuse to stress out about any of it.

Natalie stayed with me during the clinic protocol. She sat with me and read a book while I received my platelets. I reclined in the blue leather chair with my head tilted back so the bleeding in my nose would slow down.

While in this position, I overheard a conversation between two leukemia patients and decided to approach them to listen and ask questions. The woman, who was probably around my age, was a transplant patient back in 2001. She said that she did pretty well with the TBI (total-body irradiation) except that her esophagus got really dry, and she was unable to swallow food, so they had to feed her intravenously. The guy is having his transplant in May. Both of them had sibling matches. She has five siblings, and one was a match; he has six siblings, and two of them were matches. Oh, how I long for one of my two sisters to be a match! There is only a 25 percent chance that each sibling will be a match.

Later in the afternoon, after we'd returned from Hackensack, Natalie got sick. She is staying with a friend tonight. Hopefully, she's not contagious, and this is just a slight case of food poisoning or mere stomach upset. It really scares me to be around sick people when my immune system is nonexistent. I feel terrible wanting her not to be here, but if I get sick or get an infection, it could be very serious—I could even die. I'll say a prayer for her tonight.

March 25, Thursday

Lisa called tonight from the light booth at the Aronoff Center for the Performing Arts' Fifth Third Bank Theater. Ovation opens *Jeffrey* tomorrow night; tonight is "pay what you can" night. It was great to hear her voice, and she told me that I have inspired her to grow her hair down to her waist; then she is going to have it cut off and donated to make wigs for cancer patients. I think that is an incredible gesture on her part, and she has great hair, thick and curly. I spoke briefly with Joe too. He's not only directing the show, but he also had to step into a small role when one of the actors dropped out.

Natalie returned about 4:30 this afternoon, feeling much better.

March 26, Friday

Miracles do happen! Phyllis called about an hour ago to give me some good news for the weekend—Barbara is a match. Of course, we were hoping that if only one of them were a match that it would be Karen because she's not pregnant. However, I am thrilled to have one compatible sibling donor. It's definitely more complicated with Barbara, but we'll make it work. I am so thankful.

Many prayers have been answered. I've been shedding tears of joy and thanking God. I wish Barbara could be happy about being the match—her lack of enthusiasm is bittersweet for me. I know she has concerns for her unborn child, and rightly so. She knows this will greatly increase my chances for a successful outcome, but what impact will it have on her unborn baby? I do not want anything to jeopardize her pregnancy, so I was thinking about waiting until after the baby was born to have the transplant. We'll have to see what the doctors say. I hope at some point, Barbara can be glad that she's the one who will be giving me back my life. What an extraordinary gift. Karen was a bit disappointed. She really wanted to be the match, but we work with what we've got, and thank God I have Barbara.

Today's *God Calling* message was fitting:

> *Follow Your Guide*
> YOUR petty fears are groundless. So leave your foolish fears and follow
> Me, your Guide, and determinedly refuse to consider the problems of
> to-morrow. My message to you is, trust, and wait.[30]

Fear that neither of my sisters would be an HLA match lurked in the back of my mind; however, part of me kept believing that one of them would be a match. I wish I could say that I had had complete faith that this would work out as it has, but I didn't. However, I did trust that the HLA results would be as they were supposed to be, that even if neither Barbara nor Karen was a match, somehow, I would be fine—even if I had to find an unrelated donor. But I must admit that I'm so relieved to have a sibling donor.

I called my family. Then I called Natalie. She was in her car, driving back to Cincinnati, and she told me, "I didn't cry this week, but this makes me cry."

I then called Karen B, and she said, "You made my day—no, you made my month! No, you just made my year!"

I just spoke to Lynn. I was glad to be able to give her a bit of positive news. I will see her in a couple of weeks on Good Friday. Neither of her parents is doing very well, so I wanted to check in and see how she was holding up. We talked about how enduring our friendship has been, thirty-one years. I reiterated to her that no matter what I might be going through or where I am, if she is hurting and needs to talk to me, I will always be there for her.

March 27, Saturday
1:27 a.m.

I am back in the hospital. I woke up about two and a half hours ago with a fever of 101 °F. I'm supposed to call the hospital if my fever exceeds 100.5 °F. The nurse paged Dr. Siegel, the on-call physician, who called me back almost immediately. Knowing that I was neutropenic, he told me that I should be admitted. So while he made the arrangements, I packed a bag and (dreading it) woke up Barbara. She was none too happy about having to drive me to Hackensack at midnight because it's a forty- to fifty-minute drive in each direction, but it is one of those situations where it had to be done.

When we arrived at the hospital, I told her to drop me off out front. There was no need for her to come in with me. Other than the fever, I felt fine, so I didn't need anyone to hold my hand. Plus I didn't like her driving alone so late at night. When I got out of the car, she said, "Call me if you need anything. You know me, when I'm woken from sleep, I'm grumpy. But it doesn't mean anything." I smiled and waved as she pulled away.

Upstairs on 5PE, the nurses greeted me, and one of them even said, "You look better than me."

Naomi is my nurse. Once she changes my catheter dressing and hooks up the IVs, hopefully, I can drift off to sleep.

I have some chills, my head hurts, and a gland is swollen. My throat is a bit scratchy, which produces an annoying cough, and my anus hurts (I guess I should mention this to the nurse). It's hurt before, but maybe this time, I'm getting hemorrhoids. This is not the time to be embarrassed. What if it's serious? I can't be worried about my dignity when my health is on the line. I'll see how it feels tomorrow morning.

11:45 a.m.

The results of my CBC came back; today, along with the antibiotics, I will receive electrolytes, magnesium, potassium, and blood. Instead of receiving Cipro orally, I am receiving an antibiotic intravenously.

I will be here at least through the weekend. They are testing for any infections, and I will not be released until my temperature has remained normal for at least twenty-four hours. Oh, my anus no longer hurts, so I don't have to broach that embarrassing issue with the nurse—whew!

March 28, Sunday

Dr. Siegel just handed me a copy of my blood work results. I will receive blood and platelets today because my hemoglobin count is 6.8 and my platelets have dropped to eight thousand.

Ah, the cellophane window that protects my catheter incision has arrived, so I'm off to take a shower. Showering always proves to be a challenge with the lines extending out of my chest and being hooked up to the IV pole, but I manage. The cellophane window measures approximately five square inches. It is basically plastic wrap with surgical tape around all four sides. The window adheres to the skin and covers the catheter's insertion area to protect it while showering.

3:30 p.m.

I've been listening to the conversation going on next to me that is between a mother and her daughter. The daughter is the patient. Only a curtain divides us, but the mother speaks quite loudly, so you can hear everything. I can tell they have a close relationship, but the mother tends to make the daughter irritable at times. Of course, the mother means well, but it's that whole dynamic of the mother saying, "I know best" and "Here's what you should do," versus the daughter saying, "No, you don't" and "I know what to do. Don't make me feel stupid." That's pretty typical behavior between mothers and daughters, actually. As much as I love my mom, I find we sometimes butt heads in the same manner.

March 29, Monday

My lab results have arrived.

	March 28	March 29
White blood cells	0.5	2.2
Red blood cells	2.6	2.7
Hemoglobin	6.8	8.3
Platelets	8,000	27,000

All counts are on the way up. Around noon, Dr. Goldberg informed me that I was being released. And because my counts are on the rise, I can stop taking my meds.

Dan picked me up about 2:30 p.m. I checked out at the nurse's station, and we headed home. I have to say, this hospital stay truly made me realize how much I love being at Barbara and Dan's home and how much I loathe being hospitalized.

Once home, I sorted through my mail. The two CDs and cassette from Health Journeys that Karen ordered for me arrived today. CD 1 is for stress reduction, the other is for healthful sleep, and the cassette is relaxation and meditation music, which I'm listening to at the moment.

March 30, Monday

I spoke with Emily, Dr. Rowley's nurse, with whom I discussed preliminary steps for transplant. My health care company requires that I have a gynecological exam and a dental exam to clear any problems that might be lurking in these areas before they give approval for transplant. I have no dental coverage at the moment. I guess Barbara and Dan, or Mom and Dad, will need to cover that expense—or I'll charge it. I'll schedule a gynecological exam with my physician in New York City while I'm there visiting friends in May.

I confirmed with Emily that Karen came back as a 50 percent match (not acceptable) and that Barbara is *the* match. Barbara has to go in for a blood workup, and since she's over thirty-five, an EKG will be needed. They will do her HLA typing at that time, so all of the tests can be done during one appointment. Hackensack will retype both of us, which is standard procedure.

I have to have tests completed also—HLA typing, EKG, CT scan, heart MUGA (multigated acquisition) scan, and pulmonary tests. All these tests were done back in December, but I've been through four rounds of chemotherapy since then. Barbara or Dan and I need to attend an allogeneic transplant class. A timeline for all these procedures needs to be figured out before we can schedule the transplant.

I spoke with Susan tonight to give her more information about the transplant process. At the end of April, she is speaking for the Leukemia & Lymphoma Society to recruit participants for their Team in Training, and she is going to use some of my words from my blog entries to reach people. Her dedication to the cause has become more personal because I have been touched by leukemia.

She was a Team in Training participant several years ago. She rode in two one-hundred-mile bike rides, one in Lake Tahoe and the other in Santa Fe, and in the process, raised money to help fight leukemia. Since then, she's had some significant knee injuries and can no longer participate in these biking events. However, she can do fund-raising and recruiting.

March 31, Wednesday

This morning, gazing out the window as I meditated, I found my concentration stray from focusing on the breath to focusing on a small tree in a yard across the parking lot. I began contemplating the tree's nature. It probably stands all of eight feet tall, has a very narrow trunk and a few branches, and is devoid of leaves. It looked fragile and scrawny, and its vulnerability touched me as I watched it swaying in the breeze. Then I remembered it possesses strong, sinewy roots, grasping tightly to the soil deep beneath the earth's surface.

This underwhelming sapling will someday transform into a glorious, robust refuge for many life-forms. Its trunk will be wide and sturdy, and it may reach heights of forty or fifty feet; its branches, adorned with emerald leaves, will expand in every direction toward the sky. Birds, insects, squirrels, and numerous other life-forms will seek shelter in its branches from the wind, rain, and sun. These creatures will discover a playground and a home. Human beings will derive pleasure gazing upon the tree's beauty and find comfort in the shade beneath its boughs.

As the seasons change, so will the tree. Its green leaves will transform into an artist's palette of the most gorgeous hues of crimson, brown, gold, and orange. As winter approaches, it sheds its autumn cloak, revealing its gnarled, bare skeletal branches, now exposed to winter's chill. Spring arrives, attiring the tree with green buds and/or colorful blossoms; soon thereafter, it once again dons a gorgeous lush green summer frock. The cycle is complete, and then it begins again.

When one contemplates the beauty and substance of a tree as well as the fact that it is an oxygen-producing plant that enriches the planet, it is inconceivable how people can be apathetic about the destruction of the rain forests and woodlands for the sake of monetary gain. The earth's natural resources are finite, so someday, these forests may no longer be at our disposal to enjoy or destroy (as some seem wont to do). Hmmm . . . it is interesting how one small thought can evolve into larger issues relevant in today's world. Meditation really does help us connect to everyone and everything. We are not isolated beings; we are all bound to one another and to all life-forms on this planet. This interconnectedness is one more thing I am learning on my spiritual journey.

I spoke with Emily again today. She will be contacting Barbara next week. Barbara must have a separate consult with a doctor not directly associated with my case; Drs. Goldberg and Rowley pose conflicts of interest. She will need to see a high-risk obstetrician as well. These doctors will ensure that what is done is safe for both Barbara and the baby.

It is almost midnight—I haven't been up this late in a long time. I'm going to listen to the guided imagery tape now and then off to dreamland. There are decisions to make and tests to endure over the next two months before transplant, but for now, I must relax and prepare myself for the next phase of this fight.

Jeff and Karen at their wedding
rehearsal dinner.
September 19, 2003

Karen B, Nelson & Beckie at Nelson
and Beckie's apartment before a party
October 2003

Marni (right) and I working
background on the set of
Ed—November 6, 2003 (We look
like sisters!)

Aidan—11 months
This is the photo I kept next to
my bed every time I had to be
hospitalized.

Lisa and I at Barbara and Dan's home when she, Tim, and Joshua visited me in January 2004—about one month after my cancer diagnosis.

Lynn and I at my parents' home Easter weekend 2004

Lani and I in my hospital room at HUMC—June 10, 2004 (Day 9)

Kimberly (left) and Maria (right) with me in my hospital room at HUMC after BMT—June 17, 2004 (Day 18)

Andrew and I (Andrew
is about one month old)
—September 2004

Mom and Dad at Barbara and Dan's home celebrating
their 40th wedding anniversary—October 23, 2004
(actual anniversary date is October 17)

Susan & Doug on their wedding
day—November 20, 2004

Family photo—November 2004
Front row: Andrew (3 months),
Aidan (23 months)
Second row: Barbara & Dan
Third row: Alyssa (15 years old)

Dan D & Shelley
(Daniel—6 months old
—sitting on Dan's lap)
—December 2004

Natalie and I at Lori & Jeff P's wedding—
May 7, 2005 (also my 39th birthday and my hair has
grown back so curly!)

Katie & Emma—July 9, 2005 (nine
days before Emma's first birthday)

Cindy & I at Karen and Jeff's
home in Cincinnati the week before
Christmas 2007

Russ & Eleonore—May 2008 (It's
unbelievable that I didn't have a photo
of them together until this date!)

Andrew and Barbara with me one
year after BMT—June 1, 2005

PART II

TRANSPLANT AND RECOVERY

April 1, Thursday

April has arrived. My day consisted of the following: prayer, meditation, affirmations; organization of videos, books, and photos that I dug out of boxes in the basement then lugged up to my room; revisions made to two previous blog articles; and a medical update written to post on my blog. The items I retrieved from the basement were art history books, a wine text, fun girly self-improvement books, and French tapes and texts.

I received several phone calls today, one of which was from Nelson calling to check in and inquire if I'd be game to attend a party that he and Beckie want to throw the weekend I visit in May. I replied in the affirmative, especially since that's my birthday weekend. Also, a nurse from Dr. Rowley's office phoned to schedule my organ function tests for April 14 at 8:45 a.m. I'll prepare myself for a long day.

April 2, Friday

I'm becoming quite attached—okay, I must stop there. Attachment is exactly the opposite of what Buddhist philosophy teaches, which is nonattachment; so rather than use the word "attached," I'll say that I'm "committed" to my morning rituals. These rituals provide a sense of purpose and create peace. I say a rosary, listen to and repeat my affirmation tapes, meditate for twenty to forty minutes, read from *God Calling*, *365 Tao*, and *The Miracle of Mindfulness*, and then write in my journal. I'm taking advantage of this time, which seemed in short supply before, to devote to my spiritual well-being. These activities have strengthened me physically and fostered a positive attitude.

I selected a Bliss card for today's inspiration:

Be absolutely determined to enjoy what you do.

—Gerry Sikorski

Over the past six to eight weeks, I have discovered more activities that bring me bliss. I am surprised by how much I've enjoyed developing my writing abilities and practicing meditation. I would love to turn my writing into a career, perhaps in conjunction with acting and volunteering. Whatever career the future holds for me, the creative element must remain. Living an artistic life excites and inspires me. I'm presently pursuing some of these activities—my writing is one example—and not postponing them until I am well again. I don't want to wait. There is too much living to do in this moment.

My personal, career, and spiritual goals give my life meaning. I completed reading Viktor Frankl's book *Man's Search for Meaning*. The book's premise is summed up in his statement: "There is nothing in the world I venture to say that would so effectively help one to survive even the worst conditions as the knowledge that there is meaning in one's life."[31] Frankl goes on to quote Nietzsche: "He who has a *why* to live for can bear almost any *how*." I believe these statements to be true, for without purpose, one merely exists. Meaning and purpose are different for everyone. Each of us must figure out what makes life worth living and what we are supposed to achieve. I would not want to live in a world where I felt helpless or useless, so I strive to discover my purpose(s).

April 4, Palm Sunday

At the mall today, Aidan had his picture taken with the Easter Bunny. I thought he'd be scared of the giant rabbit, but no—as soon as Barbara released his hand, he waved at the bunny and ran up to where he was sitting. Once Aidan was seated on the bunny's lap, he tried to feed the Easter Bunny a Bob the Builder cracker. The child is definitely not shy. Even after the picture was taken, he wanted to go back to see the bunny again.

Today's reflection is from *365 Tao, Practice*:

Spiritual success is gained by daily cultivation.

Whatever system of spirituality you practice, do it every day. If it is prayer, then pray every day. If it is meditation, then meditate every day.

This methodical approach is assuring in several ways. First, it provides you with a process and a means to maintain progress even if that particular day is not inspiring or significant. Just to practice is already good. Secondly, it gives you a certain faith. If you practice every day, it is inevitable that you will gain from it. Thirdly, constant practice gives you a certain satisfaction.[32]

Prayer and meditation provide a sense of serenity, a feeling of well-being, and a connection to the divine as well as to the greater world. This morning, I said a rosary, listened to affirmations, and then meditated for thirty minutes. The focus of my meditation alternated between the breath and body sensations. Once I became centered, I began repeating the lines from the Prayer of St. Francis.

I've started rereading Caroline Myss's book *Anatomy of the Spirit*. I read the chapter about the fourth chakra and understood it better than I did when I read it last fall. As I contemplated the questions for self-reflection at the end of the chapter, I realized that over the past few months, I have answered them here in my journal. The essays I've written, "I'm Enough" and "Forgiveness," have quite thoroughly explored the hurts of my past and how these wounds injured this chakra. Following is the "Forgiveness" essay:

Forgiveness: Letting Go of the Past

Healing not only includes self-love and self-acceptance, but perhaps more importantly, forgiveness. Clinging to old hurts and grudges and harboring resentful feelings toward people who've wronged us are destructive behaviors. We do great harm to ourselves by not forgiving, and much illness we suffer is caused by the inability to forgive and the retention of resentments.

I thought I had forgiven many people (mostly men) from my past, but as I continued to examine my history, I realized that I had not. Too much of my identity has been invested in holding onto the memory of past relationships and scrutinizing how those relationships were beneficial, or detrimental, to my personal growth. In addition to discovering that I had not forgiven my transgressors, I discovered I had not even forgiven myself. Actions that have proved harmful to myself include: reliving past relationships, analyzing the reasons they failed, convincing myself of all the positive aspects regardless of the negative ones, and then, either repeatedly falling for the same type of guy or shunning the dating scene altogether. I finally reached the point where I didn't trust my judgment when it came to men.

As I wrote in the *I'm Enough* essay, there have been many people from my past whom I allowed to hurt me and to inject—consciously or unconsciously—their toxic actions or words into my psyche, thus eroding my self-esteem. I am encouraged, however, because I have forgiven the little girl who abandoned our friendship once she was a cheerleader, I've forgiven the old lady who made the "homely child" comment, and I've even forgiven the guy who made fun of my nose, which led to a lifetime of obsessing about that facial feature. These people and their actions were relatively easy for me to forgive. It has proved more challenging to forgive those who broke my heart.

For a woman in her late thirties, there have only been five guys with whom I've had a significant romantic involvement, though these were not necessarily relationships. (There have only been two involvements that I would consider "relationships.") I don't date much. Okay, I'll be truthful because I can hear my friends' voices in my head. I don't date at all—at least I haven't for many years. Most of my friends think I am too picky and part of it is pickiness, I suppose, but if the truth were to be told, I don't want to get hurt again. As much as I love being in a romantic relationship because it can be so joyful, I've been willing to live without that joy in order to escape the pain that inevitably seems to accompany it. Anyway, I was always focused on my acting career, so the last thing I needed were romantic distractions. At least I convinced myself for a while that this was the case.

However, as I have observed more and more people around me dating regularly, getting married, and having children, I've begun to realize there is something missing in my life. Many nights I've found myself tossing and turning in bed while reliving past relationships and feeling achingly alone. There is one relationship I have idealized over the years, and as a result, every now and then find myself wallowing in self-pity, haunted by the past, unable to move forward.

One day in January, at the Cancer Center at Hackensack University Medical Center, I was receiving red blood cells while sitting in a comfy, dark blue leather reclining chair and listening to a 70s CD my sister Karen had burned for me as a Christmas gift. I was writing in my journal when Joe Cocker's *You are so Beautiful* started playing. My breath caught and I released it slowly. *You are so Beautiful* always reminds me of Robert,* whom I consider to be the only real romantic love affair in my past.

We began dating the summer of 1987. While I stayed in Bloomington to attend summer classes, he went home to Detroit to work. One night I had gone to bed early and was nearly asleep when the phone rang. I reached for it on the nightstand next to my bed and groggily said, "Hello." It was Robert.

Soon we were talking and flirting. Then he said, "Listen to this; this song reminds me of you." I could hear *You are so Beautiful* in the background and smiled. To this day when I hear that song, conflicting emotions arise—albeit not as intense as they once were, which is progress after eleven years. I know pathetic, but I'm a very sentimental person.

When Robert and I fell in love, it was the way I had always imagined—effortless. It was so easy being around him. We laughed and flirted, there was no second-guessing of motives or game playing. It was merely two people enamored with each other and experiencing the pure joy of falling in love. Since Robert, there has been way too much drama with men. The drama factor is how I've come to recognize the wrong man. This is exactly what I tell my friends, too, when they're involved with someone who's making them crazy because he or she hasn't called, or they can't interpret his or her intentions. At the beginning of a relationship, it shouldn't be difficult; it should be magical. Emotional distress and frustration at this early stage in the game should signal this is not the right person. Of course, this rational thinking is easier when it's not your own heart entangled in the drama.

Robert and I were together for six years. The first two years were heavenly, the third was good, but by the fourth I should have said good-bye. I started to have a roving eye, and though Robert and I had discussed marriage, I was never ready to commit. Looking back, if I'm honest with myself, I ended the relationship long before he did. Sometimes I wonder how much of the leukemia was caused by my refusal to let go of the past, of certain memories—not only memories of Robert but also memories of other liaisons I've held onto.

About a year before we broke up, I was in my hometown for Schweitzer Fest, the annual festival that celebrates the town's Swiss heritage. Imagine a quaint little town, population 8,000. The city is laid out in mostly blocks separated by wide streets and well-manicured curbs. During the second weekend every August, there are four days of festive reverie around the old city hall building and grounds. A carnival company sets up rides for both adults and children and local organizations organize food and game booths. But the best—especially when I was not of age to consume alcoholic beverages—was the beer garden, or brau garten as the Swiss-Germans refer to it. A city street spanning the length of a block is fenced off to prevent minors from entering. Beer and ticket booths and numerous tables are set up inside this enclosure. Port-a-lets are stationed at each end of the block. A stage for the bands is erected outside the fence on the city hall grounds and overlooks the beer garden.

By 1992 I was of legal age and no longer required a fake ID. Robert had decided to go to Ann Arbor, Michigan, to see a friend. Once my Tell City weekend was over, I was heading to Cincinnati for a couple days then on to Ann Arbor. From there, the plan was to drive to Traverse City to visit his parents.

I went to the beer garden with a couple of girlfriends and ran into my ex-boyfriend, Scott.* Robert and Scott were complete opposites. During our two years together, Scott was emotionally unavailable, would neither hold my hand nor kiss me in public, always kept me guessing about our relationship, and never once said I love you. I never truly felt secure in that relationship. Robert, on the other hand, was attentive, unafraid of public displays of affection, held my hand all the time, and expressed to me exactly how he felt. Even before we were officially a couple he told me he loved me. I was astonished by his openness.

At this point in the story I must digress for a moment to provide some necessary background. Scott and I dated on and off during my last two years of high school, which were his first two years of college. It wasn't until I was a freshman at Indiana University that he realized he wanted our relationship to be exclusive. He arrived at this conclusion after a jealous tiff one night.

It was a Friday evening in the fall of 1984. All my girlfriends had gone out for the night. I had decided to stay in because I didn't feel like partying—I needed a bit of alone-time. So I was sitting in a chair in my dorm room, watching MTV, when there was a knock on my door. I opened it and standing there were three guys I had befriended, stopping by on their way to a party. I invited them in for a while. We were hanging out and talking when the phone rang. It was Scott. I asked him if I could call him back because Nick and a couple of other guys were visiting. He said okay. The guys stayed for only about fifteen more minutes and then I returned Scott's call.

"Who's *Nick*?" he snidely asked.

"He's a friend," I replied somewhat offended by the insinuation in his voice.

"Yeah, right," he responded accusingly.

"Hold on. Where is this attitude coming from? You're the one who insisted we see other people," I challenged.

He paused then sheepishly admitted, "Well, maybe I've changed my mind."

Woohoo, victory for me! So, at that moment we agreed that our relationship would be exclusive. After hanging up, I jubilantly leapt around the room. I had been so in love with this guy for years, and now he was finally feeling the same about me.

We dated exclusively until the end of my sophomore year, when due to his suspicion and jealousy (which was unwarranted, by the way), the relationship disintegrated. However, for several years afterward, it was always a boost to my ego when he saw me in public with Robert, or he would flatter me with compliments such as "there aren't many women like you." I felt quite smug knowing that I was in a relationship and he wasn't, and that he'd finally realized how wonderful I was. This was his loss, right?

Okay, back to the beer garden. Scott and I talked and after leaving the beer garden, a group of us proceeded to Braunie's (a little dive bar on Main Street pronounced "Brownie's"). I drove with Scott in his red jeep. He had taken the top off the jeep, so the summer breeze caressed my skin and blew through my long hair. It felt heavenly. At Braunie's we had one drink and then decided to go for a drive in the country. We ended up on the bank of the Ohio River. We sat on the top of a picnic table, talking for a long time and then he leaned over and kissed me. I kissed him back. I must tell the truth: it was very exciting. All we did was kiss, though, it went no further than that, but I had betrayed Robert with this action. The next day I left for Cincinnati.

There is one more bit of background information that needs to be provided at this point in the story. In June 1992, I began journal writing. The journal writing was inspired by my being cast as Aurelia Plath in the play *Letters Home,* adapted from the book *Letters Home.* The book was based on the letters Sylvia Plath wrote to her mother Aurelia from the time she entered Smith College in 1950 until her suicide in 1963.

One June afternoon, I carefully perused the bookstore with the goal of discovering the perfect journal in which to commence my writing adventures. The journal I selected had a hard-back cover decorated with George Seurat's pointillist masterpiece *A Sunday Afternoon on the Island of La Grande Jatte.* It was gorgeous. A red, cloth page marker was attached to facilitate the ease of locating where subsequent entries were to begin. I wrote without censoring myself about the encounter with Scott. I can't censor myself in my journal. I'm human and I want to be honest about myself, even when I exercise poor judgment. However, during my travels, the journal was discretely tucked into the bottom of my suitcase. Now back to the story . . .

Robert and I were in Traverse City for about two weeks. Two days into my stay there, I was watching the Republican convention on television. I already knew I'd be voting for Bill Clinton, but I wanted to be informed of both parties' platforms. Robert wanted to go to bed, so I told him I'd only be a little while longer. About thirty minutes later, I turned off the TV and went down to the basement bedroom. I opened the door and he was sitting up in bed with his back leaning against the wall. In that instant, before one word was uttered, I knew he knew about the Scott incident.

Initially I was furious—how dare he read my private journal?! In his defense, he explained that he'd been looking through my suitcase to see if I'd brought any lingerie with me. He saw the book, and curious because it looked interesting, he opened it up to see what it was. Due to the trusty bookmark, he opened the journal right to the Scott entry. He told me he did not read it, but when he saw the word "Scott" and "exciting" he threw it back into my suitcase. Needless to say, there was an enormous dark cloud hanging over the remainder of our vacation. Actually, this cloud hung over our relationship for the next year, even after I relented and allowed him to read the entry in its entirety in order to appease his curiosity—which seemed to help for a while. However, once trust is shattered it is usually impossible to repair. My indiscretion was small, or at least that's what I told myself, but this indiscretion hurt him deeply. The ego boost I received from my liaison with Scott was short-lived as I watched the man I cared about suffer because of my betrayal.

That last year Robert and I were together, we swiftly began heading down diverging roads and with the trust issue still smoldering, we broke up June 13, 1993. Actually, he broke up and in such a gallant fashion. I was in bed when he called from Ann Arbor at 8:30 in the morning. I spent the next four days in Indianapolis with my friend Maria, crying and trying to determine where my life was headed. I wanted to try to work things out, but Robert was deaf to my pleas.

I returned to Bloomington, where soon, with the help of a new friend, Matthew, I proceeded to get on with living. I'd wasted two months indulging in self-pity, smoking way too much, existing on diet cokes because I had no appetite for food, going for long walks to clear my head, and crying. Now I found myself interested in someone else—Matthew. Matthew saved me that summer. I believe God put him in my life because I needed him. His girlfriend was still living in Boston and had he been a free man, something deeper than friendship may have developed between us. Matthew made me feel good about myself again, reassuring me that I was a good person despite my mistakes. He encouraged me to keep acting, which I'd contemplated giving up because I had the idea that no guy would want to be involved with an actor, dealing with the demands of an acting career.

Yes, Matthew saved me from the darkness of despair, and it was despair. Suddenly, my outlook was so sunny. I decided that after summer classes ended I would move to Cincinnati, where both my sisters were residing. Karen was looking for a roommate because she was planning to return to school to pursue a PhD in Political Science, so she and I planned to search for an apartment. When Robert arrived in Bloomington at the end of August to move his furniture out of the house, he encountered a very different Deborah. I was no longer begging for us to get back together and we had a really good time. I told him about Matthew and my plans to move to Cincinnati.

Shortly after I moved to Cincinnati, Robert wanted to reconcile. I suggested we take it slowly, visit each other and see how things progressed. I didn't want to deal with a long-distance relationship. Plus I had discovered a vibrant social circle with many eligible guys in my new city. I thought my solution was reasonable given the hell I'd gone through that summer. Obviously that wasn't acceptable to Robert because before I knew it, he was dating someone else, engaged to her five months later, and married six months after the engagement. Talk about a rebound—boing! Do I sound bitter? I was.

There are many aspects of this relationship and its demise that I've clung to over the years. I didn't truly realize this until recently when I got sick. I must forgive Robert for the way he broke up with me, forgive him for marrying someone else so soon after our relationship ended, and forgive him for abandoning me. I had been financially dependent on him, even though I did work part-time while studying acting, so when we broke up, I was terrified. How would I survive? I was twenty-seven years old and I'd never been on my own. I'd gone from my parents taking care of me to Robert taking care of me.

More important than forgiving Robert, I needed to forgive myself for the role I played in the relationship's demise. Obviously, Robert and I weren't destined to be together. Although intellectually I know he and I would not have been good in the long-term, I have held up that connection with him as the ideal, all other relationships, or potential ones, paling in comparison. So, I must release the memories of the past and the idea that Robert was perfect and above reproach, while I was the villain. He is human, too. He was not perfect, and I deserve to stop punishing myself for a foolish action committed over a decade ago.

1987 was a beautiful year and at least for that brief moment in time, I'd experienced the type of love I'd dreamed of as a girl. That was a gift. I haven't experienced romantic love like it since, but I do hope to again at some point in my life. Every man that I consider significant in my romantic repertoire is married and has at least one child.

It's time for me to move on too. So, Robert, Scott, John,* and Dean,* enjoy your lives, your wives, your families. You all touched my life in some way for better or worse, and now I am absolving you of any negative influence you've had in my life and on my self-esteem. You served your purpose—to make me sick. (I'm just kidding, but that made me laugh.) I am ready to release you, so be free, I love you, and you are no longer a detriment to my mental or physical well-being. The possibilities are endless now, and I can let that special person into my life without reservation.

In truth, I'm not quite there yet, but at least this frame of mind is what I'm working to achieve. It's a process of letting go, which will take time, but by being aware of the process, the necessary first step has been taken.

Joseph recently commented that romantic relationships get in the way of your career. I half-heartedly agreed with him. Later as I remembered what he'd said, I thought to myself, "So what if my career is interfered with? It has been so long since I've been in love. While I lived in Cincinnati, I declared I didn't want to be seriously involved with anyone because I wasn't planning to stay. But romantic love is an exhilarating experience. To be intimately connected mind, body, and soul to another human being, to me, is about as close as one can get to paradise. I want to feel that exhilaration and connection again, including all its messiness. I want the messiness—I want to wallow in it!"

I feel that I am now ready to take the leap and give myself unconditionally to another person. Though it's been years, I still remember how wonderful it can be to be part of a couple, and I long for that connection. When I was first diagnosed with leukemia, I thought, "Thank God I don't have a husband or children to worry about, or them to worry about me." But as time passed, I felt differently. During my fight against cancer, there were many nights, while lying in bed alone in the dark, I would've loved to have had someone next to me, to hold and comfort me, to make me feel safe and unafraid. But I don't have a significant other, so I find comfort in God's love, in the support and care of family and friends, and in my own inner strength.

I've made a long list of activities I want to do, places I want to travel to, and goals I want to achieve. That list also includes falling in love again. True love has only happened once for me, but now I'm willing to take a chance. Part of that willingness requires letting go of and forgiving past injuries; the other part of healing is to forgive myself.

* Names have been changed to protect the guilty.

April 6, Tuesday

We leave for Tell City tomorrow, so I have to tie up some financial loose ends, do laundry, and pack. I am also going bowling with Dan and Alyssa today. I haven't been bowling in years. I think it'll be fun, even though I'm a dreadful bowler. Plus it'll be good to get out of the house and move my body a little bit.

Today's inspiration:

In *The Miracle of Mindfulness*, Thich Nhat Hanh recounts a story by Tolstoy about an emperor searching for the answer to three questions:

1. What is the best time to do each thing?
2. Who are the most important people to work with?
3. What is the most important thing to do at all times?

> The answer is this:
> Remember that there is only one important time and that is now. The present moment is the only time over which we have dominion. The most important person is always the person you are with, who is right before you, for who knows if you will have dealings with any other person in the future? The most important pursuit is making the person standing at your side happy, for that alone is the pursuit of life.
>
> Often we forget that it is the very people around us that we must live for first of all.[33]

I love this—it is beautiful, it is wise, it is the truth.

April 8, Thursday

It's so great to be here at my parents' home. Mom took one look at me yesterday when we arrived and declared with a smile, "You look great!" Then she gave me a huge loving hug. I think she was happy to see that I was carrying a little extra weight. I'm around 112 pounds, which is about seven pounds heavier than my normal weight.

Last night, after dinner, Lynn stopped by with Kara and Kyle. The kids found out last Friday that she was planning to visit me, and they wanted to see me too. Kyle, ten, and Kara, eight, loved playing with Aidan; he really enjoyed them too.

Mom, Dan, Barbara, and I took Aidan to the park this afternoon. Aidan went down the slides, crawled through the tunnels, and swung on the swings. I swung too. I haven't done that in years. One of my earliest and fondest memories is of being on a swing. I was wearing a little pale blue dress with white dotted swiss that Mom had made for me—she was quite the seamstress. The dress had a sailor collar edged with tiny white lace. I recall wearing that dress while swinging on a swing in the yard outside the trailer, killing time waiting for the rest of my family to be ready to leave for church. As I would swing forward through the air, the front flap of the collar would fly up in my face and make me giggle. I was probably around four years old. I love that memory—it's so pure, innocent, and carefree.

April 9, Friday

Lynn picked me up a little before noon, and we went to Caper's for lunch. Afterward, we visited her mother. I haven't seen Bo in probably more than fifteen years. She's been fighting her own cancer battle, colon cancer, since November 2001. She looks great though. She's still the smiling lovely woman I remember from my adolescence. We talked about our treatments, our progress, and our fears. It was comforting to have this shared bond though both of us would rather not have it. I could see tears welling up in Lynn's eyes at times when her mom was talking, and it broke my heart.

Mom picked me up at Bo's home, and we went to Good Friday Mass. It is my favorite service, yet I haven't attended it in years. It is particularly moving to me when I think about what this service asks Christians to remember, the sacrifice Jesus made for us through his crucifixion. I find myself tearing up and emotional every time I attend this service. The Gospel reading is written in play format and is read by the priest, the cantors, and the congregation—all taking on various roles. There are a few times in the reading that the congregation is supposed to respond, "Crucify him! Crucify him!" As an adult, I've never been able to bring myself to say those words; I just can't do it. The words are too brutal, and even when I attempt to say them, the words catch in my throat. Despite the inherent mournfulness of this Mass, it celebrates God's love for humanity.

When Mom and I returned home, Dad and Dan were planting potatoes in the garden. It was quite amusing to see city-boy Dan pushing a tiller, so I captured it on film. After he completed the tilling, he was so motivated that he helped Dad plant peas. Mom, of course, had to interject her expertise and started planting peas as well. She's such a control freak—that's who I get it from.

Karen and Jeff (and their dog, Dante) arrived late afternoon. We chatted, drank beers, and dined on pizza. After dinner, we all hung out; we're good at hanging out. That's the best thing about family (well, at least my family): being able to find enjoyment in the presence of one another without having to be constantly doing something—sitting around and talking is just fine.

April 11, Easter Sunday

After Easter Mass, Mom prepared our usual Easter feast of ham, potato salad, green bean casserole, and dessert—brownies and a white cake with chocolate icing. The desserts were left over from last night's party.

Mom had organized a family gathering yesterday evening. Almost all my relatives showed up. I spoke with my cousin Scott and his girlfriend, Fanny, for a long time. Fanny's brother recently had a stem cell transplant. He is a lymphoma patient and is doing very well. We talked at length about his situation and mine. I foresee her and Scott building a future together.

The evening was spent socializing and dining on pizza and chips. I was moved that my aunts, uncles, and cousins would take the time to visit with me. I really enjoyed reconnecting with them.

Karen and Jeff left shortly after lunch today. Once they had departed, I sat down with the transplant information I'd mailed to Mom and Dad to read again about some of the side effects and possible complications. It was sort of freaking me out. Barbara advised me to stop reading the booklets because I've already made the decision to have the transplant, and I'm going to make myself crazy.

However, later when I was alone, I allowed myself to cry. Why was I crying? Am I afraid? Am I afraid for Mom and Dad? Do I feel alone? Am I completely overwhelmed by my situation? Or am I sad to be leaving my parents tomorrow? Probably a little of all these things have contributed to my sorrow. I need to start sharing these moments of sadness, but I don't want to upset anyone. This is one of my flaws—a major flaw—and if my family or friends knew that I was suffering like this and not sharing, they'd kick my butt. I must start opening up and realize that I'm not going to inconvenience people. They want to help. They have told me repeatedly that they have a need for me to reach out.

It is always bittersweet leaving Mom and Dad. Sometimes, I fear that I may never see them again. I've always been like this where they're concerned, afraid of losing them. When I was in grade school, I used to cry myself to sleep at night, worrying that they were going to die. Mom would come into my room, sit on my bed, hold me, and reassure me that they were going to be around for a while. Of course, she couldn't guarantee that, but it was comforting for a ten-year-old girl to hear. I know that it is inevitable at some point that I will have to face their deaths unless, of course, I depart this world first. I feel like the luckiest child in the world, and I am their child—no matter how old I get.

April 13, Tuesday

Today's *God Calling*:

> *Gentle With All*
> LOVE and laugh. Make your world the happier for your being in it. Love
> and rejoice on the grey days.
>
> Just live in the spirit of prayer. In speaking to Me, you find soul-rest.
> Simple tasks, faithfully done and persisted in, bring their own reward,
> and are mosaics being laid in the pavement of success.[34]

Gentle with all . . . gentle thoughts and actions produce desired results. Again, here is a message of trust and faith. If there is trust and faith in the daily tasks of living and pursuing dreams, then the anxiety about accomplishing them is, or should be, diminished. By working in a gentle, relaxed fashion, obstacles may not seem as insurmountable; by remaining calm, relaxed, and faithful, solutions may appear more effortlessly and more frequently. I believe this to be true. When I find myself panicking or upset about a situation, or in a hurry to complete a task, it usually ends badly; or at least much grumbling and anxiety has been experienced prior to completion. However, those times I've remained calm and acted gently, all problems seemed to be resolved easily and without contention.

April 14, Wednesday

It was a long day. Shelley picked me up at 7:45 a.m., and we drove to Hackensack for my organ function tests and blood draws, which began the pretransplant evaluation phase. The tests scheduled over the next few weeks will help determine if my organs are strong enough to tolerate the total-body irradiation and transplant as well as reveal the status of my disease.

My heart MUGA scan was at 8:45 a.m. Before the scan, a lab technician drew blood, irradiated it, then injected it back into me. Next, I lay down under the gamma camera; this x-ray test will reveal the strength of my heart. Chemotherapy drugs like doxorubicin and cyclophosphamide (Cytoxan), both of which I've had in large doses, can damage heart muscle.

I was lying there for quite a while, so to pass the time, I meditated and did guided imagery exercises. These exercises helped create a sense of calm and well-being. It's too easy to bemoan my awful fate while undergoing these types of tests, so meditation and guided imagery refocus my mind in a positive direction.

After the MUGA scan, Shelley and I proceeded to the pulmonary department. Although I felt good today, the pulmonary tests weren't any easier to perform than they were back in December. I think my results were pretty good—at least the technician seemed pleased.

I decided we should head to the clinic for my blood draws before getting the EKG and chest x-ray, which turned out to be a good decision because Emily, at the Cancer Center, had to write a prescription for these tests. After securing the prescription, it was time for the blood draw. The nurse approached me and laughed, saying, "Hi, Deborah, I'm Annette. I'm going to suck you dry." She wasn't kidding either. There were probably fifteen vials she needed to fill for various blood tests to detect viruses including HIV, cytomegalovirus (CMV), and hepatitis. CMV is a member of the herpes virus group, which includes the viruses that cause chicken pox, mononucleosis, and herpes simplex 1 and 2. These viruses all share the ability to remain dormant in the body for a long time. I am CMV negative, so when I receive blood products, the blood must be CMV negative too; otherwise, I could get the virus. According to my doctor, half the population is positive for CMV, and the other half is negative.

We finally received my CBC results; then I was instructed to see Dr. Goldberg to get a vincristine shot. I didn't realize chemo was on today's schedule. This was for maintenance purposes since I will not receive chemo again until I'm hospitalized for the bone marrow transplant. I was relieved to receive the vincristine because I was concerned about not getting any chemo treatments until this whole transplant timeline was figured out. If I was in remission at this time, I didn't want to tempt fate and chance relapsing.

Karen L was at the clinic today. She was there with her father, whom she introduced to Shelley. She is scheduled to have her autologous stem cell transplant in a couple of weeks. (Autologous stem cell transplantation is technically not a transplant since one's own stem cells are utilized.)

Finally, we made it down to the diagnostics room where I had the chest x-ray and EKG—both took no time at all, which I was very happy about. We left the clinic around 4:15 p.m., and I arrived home about forty-five minutes later. Yes, it was a long day, and Shelley was quite the trooper.

Right now, I'm so itchy. I don't know whether it is from the irradiated blood or the vincristine. I've never had a reaction to vincristine like this, so I'm thinking it's the blood. If this is still bothering me tomorrow, I'm going to call the doctor. I want relief—this itching is driving me mad!

April 15, Thursday

My taxes are done. While I was standing in line at the post office to mail my tax returns, Sandy, a talent manger with whom I'd worked briefly prior to getting sick, called me for a print go-see. Of course, I had to turn it down. I explained my situation; naturally, he felt bad for me, but he said that I sounded like I had a good attitude. I requested that he keep me in his casting files, and he told me to call him when I was ready to start working again. I replied that I would and thanked him. It was encouraging to get the call.

April 16, Friday

Today's inspiration is from a Friendship card:

Shared joy is double joy; shared sorrow is half sorrow.

—Swedish proverb

This, to me, is the definition of "friendship." We share our joys, and those who are true friends will be happy and celebrate with us. When sorrow, grief, or fear is experienced and we allow our friends to share in this, these moments seem less traumatic. Shared experiences are such a monumental part of any friendship. True friends will be delighted, even if a bit envious, when good fortune appears and supportive when hard times arise.

April 19, Monday

I haven't written in my journal for a couple of days because I was either involved in other activities, enjoying the beautiful weather outdoors, or catching up on sleep. My sore throat has really interfered with sleep. I have been waking around midnight, 1:00 a.m. or 2:00 a.m.; then I can't get back to sleep. I toss and turn all night, attempting various ways to soothe my throat—gargling with salt water, spraying Chloraseptic down my throat, or sucking on cough drops. This is the fourth day I've dealt with this malady, and there seems to be no likelihood of relief any time soon.

Bobbi sent this e-mail message to me today. It is a good reminder of the lingering power of prayer. It cheered me up.

> Hey
>
> What's shakin'? I was just reading your journal—bits and pieces—and I had this thought . . . regarding the Quaker prayer meeting. Prayer is not a linear concept. We tend to think of prayer in terms of our life here and now. Prayer, I have learned, crosses all boundaries of time and space. That energy will get to you whenever you have the chance to receive it. In fact, it's still out there if you want to take a moment now and then to receive it.

This is the great thing about prayer. I think it's wonderful you have those in your life that tend to you spiritually. I have the same. We are blessed. Whenever you feel at all alone or afraid or weary, just stop and close your eyes and feel us. We're there in your heart. You can't get rid of us that easily.

xo
Bobbi

Later, I received an e-mail from Karen B urging people to partake in her EuroK Flying Pig Challenge.[35] During the Flying Pig Marathon in Cincinnati on May 2, she will be gathering people near her apartment on Erie Avenue, which is along the marathon route, to cheer on her friend Jeff B as he runs by. Jeff B, who is running for the Leukemia & Lymphoma Society's Team in Training, has already raised over $2,700 for his sponsored patient. He is going to run with my name on his shirt as well.

Karen B has put out a challenge to her friends, family, and acquaintances to help raise money to alleviate some of my medical expenses. How amazing is that? My friends and family are such a huge form of emotional support. I know that I am enormously blessed and give thanks for it daily.

April 20, Tuesday

A radiation consult and CT scan are scheduled for Thursday. I am really getting sick of hospitals, doctors' offices, and diagnostic exams. I know enduring all of this will make me better, but I'm fed up with it.

April 21, Wednesday

I drove myself to Hackensack today because no one was available to drive me. I was a bit hesitant at first to drive myself because the last time I had a CT scan, I was flushed and didn't feel well afterward. However, all was fine today. Sadly, as I am feeling more capable of caring for myself, I am nearing the transplant phase of my treatment. This phase will most likely find me more dependent on others than I was during the chemotherapy phase.

Lori called this morning before I left for my appointment. We spoke briefly because she was getting ready to board her flight from Chicago to St. Louis. She said she'd call back and fill me in on what's going on in her life, but she wanted to find out how everything was progressing on my end. She did let me know that she is planning a move to Seattle to be with Jeff P, whom she's been dating since I moved to the Northeast. Should they get married (which I can totally see happening), they plan to return to Cincinnati after about three years.

Lori is a friend from Cincinnati. She gave me the Bliss, Hero, Dream, and Believe cards, which were in the friendship box. I met Lori shortly after meeting Karen B. The night I met Lori, Karen B had organized a girls' night out. There were six women in our party, and we spent the evening at Havana Martini Club, located in downtown Cincinnati. When Lori arrived at Karen B's, I took one look at her and thought, *Oh great, I'm hanging out with a model.* She is tall, and at that time, her straight smooth blonde hair fell slightly below her chin. She had it pulled back in a short sleek ponytail and was wearing a light blue sleeveless sweater that accentuated her blue eyes. Of course, I grew to love her quickly because she is as beautiful on the inside as she is on the outside.

11:25 p.m.

I shouldn't have done it, but tonight, I retrieved one of my transplant books and reread it. The pretransplant section includes suggestions for "Getting Your Affairs in Order." I don't have a will, and even if I did, I don't have a thing to bequeath to anyone. But it made me think. My family would need to know the location of my life insurance policy, I want both the "Prayer of St. Francis" and "Amazing Grace" sang at my funeral, and I want to write a message to be read to family and friends after the sermon. (This is the performer in me—even my funeral will be a production!) The passwords of e-mail and various financial accounts need to be shared with family. The addresses of friends who don't have e-mail (or whose information is not stored in my cell phone) need to be noted so that in the event of my death, they can be contacted. And the most important loose end is Aidan. I am his godmother, and I long to remain a presence in his life. As a Catholic, he will celebrate many sacraments as he grows into an adult and beyond, and I want to be sure he receives cards and messages from me on those special occasions (as well as high school and college graduations) regardless of my presence in this world.

Thinking about all of this has made me incredibly sad, and I've been sobbing for almost two hours. Part of me wants to organize all of this information, and another part feels that if I do, I'm preparing to die. On the other hand, if I don't put these things in order and I do die, none of my wishes will be known. Still, I'm afraid that by doing these things, I'll be saying, "Okay, I'm ready to die." I'm not ready, and I'm so scared.

Most days, I am able to avoid this type of thinking; but every now and then, thoughts of dying creep into my mind and wreak emotional havoc. I pray so often for strength, courage, and faith. I don't want to be afraid. I don't know how to alleviate my fears, and I find it difficult to surrender these to God (it's the control freak in me, I know). Somehow, I've got to find a way, as the saying goes, "to let go and let God."

Tonight, I wanted so much to wake up Barbara or to pick up the phone and call Karen or any of my friends, but I just couldn't do it. I know every one of them would be fine with me calling late—they'd probably even appreciate being able to listen to and console me. But I'm too stubborn and don't want to impose upon or burden anyone with my problems. So I turn to God and hope that he will provide me with the courage I need. I don't know why I prefer to suffer alone. Perhaps I don't want anyone to know how frightened I truly am. Aha! Right there, I wrote, "suffer alone." If I've truly turned to God, I shouldn't feel alone, right? Maybe I don't possess the faith I thought I had, even though I talk to God daily, pray, give thanks for all the wonderful people and successes in my life, and seek guidance in difficult times. But perhaps this isn't enough.

Another source of consolation for me has been this journal. Its pages have been a nurturing place for me to sort out my feelings with complete honesty. I always feel better (and feel better now) by writing my feelings down on paper (or in this instance, typing on a computer screen). I've decided to place this on my blog site in order to share my emotions with family and friends. Maybe I don't have the courage to verbalize my feelings, but I can definitely write about them.

The bottom line is that I plan to live. There is so much to accomplish. I must see Aidan grow into a man, so I have to muster the courage and the faith to get through this next phase of my treatment. It's a very difficult time right now, but I will continue to fight.

Now that I've processed this emotional turbulence, I feel calmer. I am going to turn off the light, listen to a guided meditation tape, and then, hopefully, soon will drift off to sleep.

April 22, Thursday

I feel more emotionally stable this morning. I've been awake since 7:15 a.m. and have prayed a rosary as well as said additional prayers for healing and strength. I have listened to God and believe it would be a good idea to get my affairs in order. I've been planning to do it for a while, even before I got sick, so I need to bite the bullet and do it. Then if need be, I can revise my wishes as I get older and my desires change. That's the plan, and interestingly enough, it doesn't frighten me today.

Last night, I allowed negativity and fear to creep into my thoughts. Yet I try to say "Be gone" to negative thoughts. Negativity of any sort is counterproductive. Creative thinking, thinking outside the box, is the key to success and surmounting obstacles. This type of thinking will help me to achieve better results in both my professional and personal life. Up to this point, I've pretty much employed tried-and-true methods and played by the rules, especially in approaching my acting career. Well, perhaps it's time to toss the rule book aside and replace it with fresh, creative ideas.

I try to think for myself and not to be influenced by others but instead make my own decisions based on facts and my values. There have been times when I've allowed others to influence me, and usually, I end up feeling badly. I know what I stand for and why, and those ideals cannot be compromised.

And it's not just my values, but also my dreams that must be steadfastly held on to. In the past, I've transformed dreams into reality—forming Ovation Theatre Company, performing Lanford Wilson's one-woman play *The Moonshot Tape*, writing and performing cabaret, making a demo CD of some of my favorite songs, just to name a few. I intend to continue turning dreams into reality. The following Dream card says it all:

Never fear the space between your dreams and reality.
If you can dream it, you can make it so.

—Belva Davis

Today, I met with Dr. Ingenito, the radiation oncologist. He explained the total-body irradiation procedure to me. Over a four-day period, I will receive two doses of radiation per day. They will radiate my entire body from head to toe. The number one goal of the radiation therapy is to suppress my immune system, which will prevent my body from rejecting Barbara's stem cells. Dr. Rowley, my transplant doctor, will take care of the other end, preventing Barbara's stem cells from rejecting the host (me). Dr. Ingenito discussed the side effects with me too. He told me that nausea is the most common side effect, vomiting being a less common one, and diarrhea almost never happening. He added that if the chemo hasn't rendered me infertile, radiation most likely will; and probably two to three months after transplant, I will experience premature menopause. "It's almost inevitable," were his exact words. Other possible long-term side effects include developing cataracts or a secondary cancer, which could be another type of cancer or leukemia again.

A physicist took body measurements after I met with Dr. Ingenito; then I headed to another area of the hospital to have a CT scan of my chest. This information will be used to plan my treatment and to determine the appropriate dosage of radiation to be administered. It's all pretty scary, yet I'm amazed at the positive results doctors can achieve by utilizing the current technologies available to them.

April 23, Friday

The soreness in my throat has lessened in severity, but I am still coughing nonstop. I am also really congested, so I can't taste anything, which is extremely frustrating. Susan and Doug, the man she's been dating for a while, are taking me to dinner tonight. If the congestion does not clear up, I will not be ordering much food. What's the point of eating if you can't enjoy it? Right now, I can faintly taste the coffee I am drinking. Hopefully, as the day wears on, my taste buds will improve.

I watched the video *A Patient's Story*, which Barbara's dentist gave to her for me to watch. The woman in the video is a patient of his. She was treated at the Cancer Institute of New Jersey for ALL. She was diagnosed in 1997 and was pregnant at the time. The baby was born healthy, thankfully, despite her having endured chemotherapy. The patient went through chemotherapy induction and then two years of maintenance chemotherapy. She had neither a stem cell nor a bone marrow transplant, yet she remains in remission and has had another baby.

I might find hope in this story of being able to bear a child, but she was twenty-seven years old when diagnosed; I was thirty-seven. Ten years makes a significant difference in the fertility arena. Plus as Dr. Ingenito said yesterday, "If the chemotherapy hasn't rendered you infertile, the radiation almost definitely will." Of course, one never knows what miracles lie ahead, but I don't think I'd be willing to subject a fetus to live for nine months in my body after all it's been, and will be, going through. I can always adopt, which had been my plan before illness struck.

Today's inspiration comes from a Bliss card:

Choose to be happy. It is a way of being wise.

—Colette

Too often, people want to wallow in their misery. Wallowing in misery is okay for a while because emotions should be experienced, but at some point, you have to make the decision not to be miserable. Negativity will infect you and the people around you, which is no way to live. We have control over our actions and our emotions. We can choose to be happy or sad, and I choose to be happy. Now I'm off to see the dentist.

A total of $294 later, I received a more thorough checkup and cleaning than I had anticipated, so I'm definitely set for another six months to a year. Dr. Beckwith found a very small cavity on one of my wisdom teeth and is going to see if Dr. Rowley wants him to fill it prior to or wait until after transplant. The dentist felt I'd be okay to wait if Dr. Rowley prefers.

I received Lani's CD today in the mail. The title of STARK's CD is *The Curse*. Lani wrote all but one song on it. She's got a great voice, and she's written really gutsy lyrics. I'm too prudish to write lyrics like hers, but she's writing from her heart and her experiences, which is what an artist does.

Maria wrote a lovely e-mail message to me. She must've read my most recent blog entry regarding "putting my affairs in order." Here's what she writes,

> I know how making out a will is depressing. My Dad had me write a will when I graduated from college and started living on my own. As you know he spent a long time as a Trust Officer for the bank. He says everyone needs a will—it's not for the person making the will; it's for his or her family. Dad says (and he saw plenty of this) that if someone dies without a will it costs the family court fees to obtain guardianship of that person's affairs—no matter how big or small. And I know what you mean about not having anything; that was how I felt when I made out my first will.

> I assigned my Dad guardianship of everything. It gave him the right to handle all my affairs as he saw fit. I don't know how much it would cost your parents in court fees, but it doesn't matter because I know you trust them and why put them through any unnecessary grief if something happens. Of course, now Aaron and I have a will. The most depressing part was picking guardianship of the kids if anything should happen to both of us at the same time. But it is absolutely necessary and I feel better knowing that we are able to control what happens to the kids, and they won't be put in state custody or something awful like that while family members duke it out in court. Please have a will made up—for your parents' sake—everyone should.

> I'm sure it must be hard, thinking about writing words to Aidan. It makes you feel as if you're accepting death. How many times have I thought about Mr. Byrd in high school and what he used to say every time someone asked him if we *have* to read or do an assignment, you know he would say, "Chillens, the only thing you have to do is breathe." Of course he was right, like it or not.

> I know you're a fighter. You are one of the feistiest people I know—always have been. And you have always been a planner. We all do things for the next generation to let them know what life was

like when . . . or to show them how much we love them. I do it for my kids—you can do it for Aidan. It's ok.

I know you are sad from time to time. When Nathan is crying and I don't know why, I ask him, "Why are you sad little boy?" No one likes to see or hear about anyone they love being sad. But I know why you are sad and I'm sorry I can't make you feel better. All it takes for Nathan is turning him upside down and kissing him on the neck.

Take care of yourself Deborah Kay.

I love you,
Maria

And then Lisa wrote me,

Hi there!!

I just read your blog. You big Goof!! You don't have to be "Deborah the brave." You can call me *anytime* and *I mean anytime*! If you get in one of those moods again please don't hesitate. I love 2:00 a.m. chats, and I would especially love one with you. The thing that upset me most about the entry was that you were sad by yourself. Okay, everyone should be able to be sad by themselves occasionally, but you have had your turn and the next time you better pick up the phone and call. I'll be there with the newest cancer jokes . . . I've been broadening my repertoire.

I can't wait to hear from you again. I'm always thinking of you. Go ahead and get your affairs in order if it makes you feel good, but I'm counting on you being at the old people's home with me one day.

Love you,
Lisa

April 26, Monday

I just cannot seem to shake this cold, so I've confined myself to bed. I'm dumbfounded by the vast amounts of phlegm and mucus that can reside in one's nasal cavities—jeez! My throat feels somewhat better during the day, but at night, the soreness becomes unbearable. I have a raging headache on the right side of my head that especially hurts when I cough, which is all the time. So to put it simply, I feel lousy. The cold has been hanging on for over a week. I'm trying to will it to go away. Okay, that's enough whining for now.

Despite my ill health, I had a lovely weekend. Susan and Doug visited. This is the first time I've met Doug, and I haven't seen Susan since I was in Pittsburgh in September 2002. They seem like a great couple, and it would not surprise me if a wedding is planned soon. They arrived Friday at 7:00 p.m. We hung out at the house for a while and drank some wine. Dan, Barbara, and Aidan kept us company. Aidan loved Doug. Aidan always has so much fun when people he's never met show up. At first, he acts shy, but once he warms up to them, he wants their undivided attention.

Susan brought me an early birthday present, or rather present*s*. The gift bag was filled with two different types of lotions, a package of AA batteries, an MCI calling card with 670 available minutes, and a book titled *Meeting Faith: The Forest Journals of a Black Buddhist Nun*. I can't wait to start reading it—it looks fascinating. After opening my gifts, Susan, Doug, and I left for a late dinner at McCormick & Schmick's.

On Saturday, Barbara, Susan, Doug, and I drove into the city. Before Barbara drove all of us into the city, we took Susan's car to the Far Hills train station so that she, Doug, and I would have transportation home. (Barbara planned to return home right after Shelley's baby shower.) While Barbara and I attended Shelley's party, Susan and Doug went downtown to see Ground Zero. We left the party around 2:15 p.m. and met Doug and Susan back at the parking lot.

Barbara left the city while Susan, Doug, and I headed uptown to Central Park. We sat in a Starbuck's on Sixtieth Street for a long time, talking and relaxing. Afterward, we checked out the new mall across the street and then had dinner at an Italian restaurant on Ninth Avenue. I was beginning to feel worse by the time we got to Penn Station to catch the train to Far Hills. My throat hurt, and I was coughing more frequently. We had a long train ride back, and all I could think about was getting home to brush my teeth and gargle salt water.

I probably shouldn't have spent the day running around the city, but I felt an obligation to make sure they had fun during their visit. It was wonderful to see Susan. I've known her for over ten years now, and only two of those years did we spend together in Cincinnati. The rest of the time she has been living in Miami or Pittsburgh.

Susan and Doug left early Sunday morning, and I spent the day in bed nursing my cold. I am doing the same today. I have to get rid of this cold before next Wednesday; otherwise, I'm not going to have a very pleasant stay in the city, and I have made many plans.

It's the ideal day to stay in bed because it's rainy and cold. I have been reading, praying, silently repeating affirmations, listening to meditation music, and resting. I need another cup of coffee. The hot liquid helps loosen the phlegm trapped in my throat. My nose is sore from blowing my nose—I'm going through tissues like there's no tomorrow. Okay, again, enough whining!

Today's *God Calling*:

> *I Make the Opportunities*
> NEVER doubt. Have no fear. Watch the faintest tremor of fear, and stop all work, everything, and rest before Me until you are joyful and strong again.
>
> Deal in the same way with all tired feelings.
>
> Times of withdrawal for rest always precede fresh miracle-working.
>
> My Work in the world has been hindered by work, work, work. Many a tireless, nervous body has driven a spirit. The spirit should be the master always, and just simply and naturally use the body as need should arise. Rest in Me.
>
> Do not *seek* to work for Me. Never make opportunities. Live with Me and for Me. I do the work and I make the opportunities.[36]

This says to me that after long periods of work or a difficult struggle, one must step back and allow herself/himself a period of rest and recuperation. A break in order to refresh is necessary. I feel that during this period of my healing, I am preparing myself for the next phase of my life and all its accompanying opportunities and obstacles. I had been chugging along at one hundred miles per hour, not taking care of myself, stressing out over money, and trying to create as many opportunities for myself as possible. I was not trusting in the whole process or going at it with a relaxed attitude. I will use this time to regroup. I will try to trust that right now, if I "simply and naturally use the body as need should arise," the result will be complete healing, plenty of creative work opportunities, and a more balanced life.

April 29, Thursday

I was at the clinic yesterday for my vincristine shot. Afterward, I met with a social worker to discuss the transplant, any concerns or worries I might have, and to complete preadmission paperwork.

My cold is slowly getting better although I am still coughing and blowing my nose often. However, my throat is no longer sore, and I slept through the night for the first time in two weeks.

Today's *God Calling*:

> *Disharmony*
> SEEK and ye shall find. Shall find that inner knowledge that makes the problems of life plain.
>
> The difficulties of life are caused by disharmony in the individual.
>
> But so often My servants lack power, conquest, success, supply, harmony, and I think I fail in My promises because these are not manifested in their lives.
>
> These are but the outward manifestations that result from the obedience, honesty, order, love—and they come, not in answer to urgent prayer, but naturally as light results from a lighted candle.[37]

I interpret the above passage to mean that when we hold on too tightly to our wishes and desires, we hinder progress; by naturally and simply letting these desires and wishes manifest in a state of relaxation and faith, we will find prosperity, success, and love. However, by grasping tightly, we choke and destroy our dreams and goals. So "lighten up and trust" is what I believe this message means.

April 30, Friday

It's Susan's birthday. I received an e-mail message from her letting me know that she'd received my card and writing to tell me about her recruitment meeting for the Leukemia & Lymphoma Society's Team in Training:

> Hey Deb,
>
> Thanks for the beautiful card. On Wednesday, I spoke to possible recruits at the Leukemia Society Team in Training informational session. There were only four people there, but that is good.
>
> The two Society reps started the meeting out by welcoming everyone and then they played a video. I am in the national video when I did my ride in 2000. (I will show you sometime, an actor, I am not . . .) I kept getting teary-eyed during the video because I remembered the

great experiences I had and wish I could do it again for you. However, knowing the treatment you had, and will have, was the result of research that I helped fund, made me happy.

One of the athletes in the video was a survivor from the early 90s. He said when he had his transplant, he was in the hospital four months, but the survivor he just talked to that day said he was only in a week![38] That is progress! I feel very confident in your recovery.

On behalf of you, I am going to continue to volunteer to help recruit Team members. I may try to do a forty-mile bike ride, but we will see . . .

Have a great weekend.
Susan

May 2, Sunday

Barbara presented me with birthday gifts this evening since I will be in New York City on that day. The gifts included (1) a pair of black crop pants, (2) a coral off-the-shoulder, short-sleeved top, (3) a lavender off-the-shoulder, cap-sleeved top, (4) a Lycra halter top, (5) matching earrings and necklace with beads of varying shades of pink, and (6) a paint-by-numbers kit. The picture to be painted is John Constable's *The Hay Wain*. We'll see how closely I can imitate Constable's artistry; a painter I am not. The card she included is so beautiful. The verse is about what it means to have a sister—the special bond, the friendship and unconditional love.[39] I'm so blessed to have her as a sister.

May 3, Monday

My throat feels better today. I can smell and taste, which is progress, but my nose keeps running . . .

I meditated for the first time in at least two weeks and did not cough once during the session. Afterward, Katie called to touch base about meeting later this week when we're both in Manhattan. She's made me feel better about the whole "putting my affairs in order" situation, especially with regard to Aidan.

Today, in the mail, I received a birthday card from Lynn with a check for $300 in it. Her generosity made me cry. I will call and thank her tomorrow evening. Hopefully, my voice will be in better shape so that I can talk; I'm very hoarse at the moment.

Today's thoughts/reflections focus on change: I'm working with change as a positive force to let life evolve, to be present in the moment, to remain open to whatever opportunities may arise, and to deal positively and easily with obstacles that result from change. I have been working toward these goals for months now, and though I still have a long way to go in realizing them, I have made some progress.

One example of this progress is how I have been approaching insurance and billing issues. In the past, I would immediately get upset and anxious about a bill that shouldn't have been charged or a collection notice that was received in error. But now, because I'm aware of that agitation, I instruct myself to remain calm and breathe, thus enabling me to approach the situation with some equanimity. I try not to judge my unacceptable behaviors and attitudes when they occur but instead make note of them. This awareness and presence allows me to deal more effectively with life's aggravations.

May 4, Tuesday

Dan and I attended the allogeneic transplant class today at HUMC. I picked up an advance directive form and will complete it before transplant. I'm appointing Barbara to be the person responsible for making medical decisions for me should there come a time I am incapable of doing so. Mom will be listed as the first alternate, and Karen will be listed as the second.

I called Lynn this evening to thank her for the card and the money. She told me that she had wanted to give me some money to help me out when I initially moved to the New York area, but she was unable to do so at that time. However, now she was financially able to give and added that she would rather help me than a stranger. That makes sense.

May 5, Wednesday

I saw Karen L today at the clinic. As I was sitting in the outer waiting room, I saw this gentleman walk through. We looked at each other as if we knew the other, and then almost simultaneously, recognition occurred—it was Karen L's husband, Larry. I rose out of my seat and walked toward him, and we hugged. He informed me that Karen L was having her autologous stem cell transplant this afternoon and that she was in the chemo room getting her final treatment. I told him to please tell her that I said hello and that I'm thinking about her. He assured me that he would relay my message.

He left to run some errands as I returned to my chair. Then it hit me—I wanted to see her. So I got up and marched back to the chemo room. I stuck my head in, and there she was sitting in the chair straight in front of the door. Our eyes met, and we both smiled. I walked over to her and gave her a warm hug. I sat down, and we talked for only a few minutes—I didn't want to tire her, and I had my own appointment to keep. It was great to be able to see her on this very important day. I had felt compelled to see her and am so glad I followed my instincts. I know she appreciated my telling her in person that I would be thinking of her and praying for her and that I loved her. I hope and pray she does well and that soon, we both will be back to fully living our lives. When I left, she said, "We're both going to make it." We hugged again.

I returned to the waiting area. It was taking forever to see Dr. Goldberg because they were running so far behind schedule. Emily found me and informed me that due to my small stature, Barbara may not have to bank any blood, which would be good news for her.

I finally received my vincristine shot. I had noticed on my CBC results that my white blood cell count was 3.8, so I asked Dr. Goldberg if it was okay to go into the city (I told him my plans). He said I would be fine, then added, "Go have fun."

I arrived at Beckie and Nelson's place around 7:00 p.m. No one was home, so I waited outside the building. Fortunately, Nelson came home early. He greeted me with his signature hug—engulfing, safe, warm, and loving.

He told me, "You look great! I was walking toward the apartment and thought, 'What a pretty girl standing there.'"

Of course, that comment made me feel wonderful. Beckie arrived about twenty minutes later and presented me with a stunning spring floral arrangement of lilies, roses, carnations, and several other varieties I couldn't identify (I have such limited flower knowledge). The colors—yellow, orange, purple, white, lime green, peach—were gorgeous.

I was on my own for several hours this evening because my hosts had a dinner engagement that had been previously scheduled. I assured them I would be fine. I cooked a frozen tomato-spinach pizza and watched *Dateline*. Tonight was the two-hour interview with the cast of *Friends*. The sitcom's final episode will air tomorrow night, concluding a successful ten-season run.

Beckie and Nelson walked in the door around 11:30 p.m. We talked for a while; and then the topics of the advanced directive, my will, and Aidan's mementoes came up. At first, Nelson didn't want to talk about it. My dying is not an option in his view; I know the thought disturbs him. Finally, he realized that I needed to discuss this and that I was getting these items in order because should death be my fate in the near future, this planning gives me peace of mind now. I asked them to be the witnesses for my advanced directive, and after the discussion ended, they both agreed and signed it.

May 6, Thursday

I'm hoping this trip sustains me for the next couple of months. I plan to enjoy every minute I am here, live in the present, and focus solely on the people I am with at any given moment.

It's fantastic to be sitting here at the kitchen table, writing in my journal, drinking coffee, and basking in the warmth of the sunlight streaming through the skylight. I so treasure the sun; its warmth and brightness always improve my mood. Unfortunately (and I found this out in my allogeneic transplant class), once I have the transplant, the sun is not my friend. It is imperative that I both apply an SPF of 25 or higher to my body and face every time I go outside and stay covered up with long sleeves and a wide-brimmed hat. Any sunburn could produce a serious reaction in my body, which could cause severe complications during the transplant recovery period. I am preparing myself for the long, arduous recuperation process; and just as I did during chemotherapy, I will maneuver through it with aplomb and grace. The Hyper-CVAD regimen was no walk in the park. It was an intense, aggressive treatment, yet I did well. I will use these experiences to become stronger and more resilient.

Katie arrived around noon, bearing birthday gifts that included ten dark pink tulips that I immediately placed in the vase with Beckie's bouquet, a paint-by-numbers oil painting set (Vincent van Gogh's *Sunflowers*—obviously, I had mentioned painting to both her and Barbara), and the book *The War of Art*.

After opening my gifts, we walked to Second Avenue and found a café that piqued our interest. We took advantage of the agreeable weather and dined outdoors. I sat in the shade while Katie sat in the sun—she was a bit cool.

Katie told me that as far as she was concerned, I'd already won my battle with leukemia and that transplant was just the icing on the cake that would kick this cancer out of my body for good. She added, "You've come so far since last November when we had dinner at Café Freda." At that time, I was not doing well emotionally, and she had been quite worried about me. She feels that even though I am fighting leukemia, I look healthier now than I did then. That's probably a fair assessment. I definitely feel better than I did six months ago despite the chemotherapy treatments. On my way back to the apartment, Joseph called, and we made plans to meet tomorrow.

Later that evening, I met Dan G at Joe Allen's. He looked great. His hair is very short—actually, like mine right now. We had a lovely dinner though unfortunately, I couldn't taste much of my pasta. (I was unable to taste lunch as well, which sucked.) After dinner, we walked to the Gershwin Theater to see *Wicked*. An understudy for Kristin Chenoweth performed this show, but I did have the privilege of seeing Idina Menzel play Elphaba, and she was superb. When she finished singing her first solo, I applauded fiercely and nearly jumped out of my seat. What a voice! The entire show—the story, the music, the acting, the costumes, the staging—was so entertaining and moving that I almost cried at the end. Afterward, down in the lobby, Dan G bought a souvenir program for me as well as the cast recording and Idina Menzel's CD. He bought these CDs so that I'd have more music to listen to during my upcoming hospital stay.

We proceeded to Food Bar in Chelsea for a nightcap; then he put me in a cab. I arrived at the apartment by 12:30 a.m., and Nelson and Beckie were already in bed. My left eye was irritated. I rinsed it well with water, placed eyedrops in both eyes, then went to sleep.

May 7, Friday, Thirty-eighth birthday

Horrors—I woke up with conjunctivitis! Thirty-eight sucks. I was so upset that I started crying. Beckie and Nelson did their best to console me. I phoned Dr. Goldberg's office, and someone called back to tell me that Phyllis would have to return my call later in the day because she was currently attending a conference.

Karen B called first thing this morning to wish me a happy birthday. It's just like her to be the first one to call. Lisa, Jen, and Natalie all phoned before noon to extend their birthday wishes. I lamented my pinkeye fate to Lisa who instructed me to hold a hot washcloth over my eye because that would help release the oozing matter.

After Beckie and Nelson left for work, I watched some of Donald Rumsfeld's testimony to the Armed Services Committee regarding the torture photos and the abuse scandal at Abu Ghraib prison in Iraq—what a travesty. During the testimony, Joseph called. He had been out very late last night celebrating with his *Hurlyburly* cast mates and had woken up only a short time ago. He needed to run some errands but said he'd touch base with me later. I really didn't want to see him with my grotesque-looking eye. However, I still longed to spend some time with him.

Karen and Mom phoned in the afternoon as did Lori. At 5:00 p.m., I left to pick up my prescription eyedrops. Michael D, a friend and dance partner from Cincinnati, called my cell phone to say happy birthday. Our conversation was brief because I had difficulty hearing him due to the rush-hour traffic. I found the CVS/pharmacy, paid for the drops, and returned to the apartment. The drops eased my discomfort immediately. The left eye was worse than the right one, which only had a minimal amount of infection in it.

Finally, at 7:25 p.m., Joseph called. He had decided to take a nap and ended up sleeping for hours. He apologized. I accepted his apology. I didn't feel well anyway and looked even worse. He told me, "I'll kick some ass for you tonight (meaning in his performance), and I'll call you tomorrow."

I still cannot taste anything. My throat aches from constantly coughing, and there is this odd smell and burning sensation inside my nasal passages. I feel like I'm falling apart.

Beckie, Nelson, and I headed uptown about 9:00. They had a surprise arranged for me, and although I felt lousy, I was a good sport and went along because I knew they had put much effort into this surprise. We took the subway. The R train was experiencing mechanical difficulties, so it took us much longer to reach our destination than it should have.

Finally, we exited the Fiftieth Street subway station and walked two blocks south on Broadway to Noches, a trendy Latin restaurant/club. The interior of the facility was gorgeous. There were several floors. The first floor was a bar, the second was a bar and a dance floor, and the remaining floors were the dining areas that surrounded and overlooked the dance floor. We were escorted to the fourth floor and shown to our table. The dim interior was illuminated by square colored panels of red, yellow, orange, green, and blue.

Miles, our waiter, was superb. He made numerous suggestions of spicier entrees that might allow me to taste a hint of flavor after I had bemoaned the fact I couldn't taste anything. What a shame to dine in a restaurant with mouthwatering menu choices and not be able to savor the cuisine. Nelson and Beckie wanted to order dessert after dinner, so I decided to order a cup of coffee, thinking it might soothe my throat. Dessert did not sound appealing to me. Plus if I couldn't taste it, I wasn't going to consume the calories.

During dessert, I was feeling quite sorry for myself and broke down sobbing. I was whining about the fact that this wretched pinkeye hurt and made me look dreadful, and this cough was incessant and stifling (I hadn't stopped coughing since we entered the restaurant—I'm not exaggerating either). On top of all this, I had leukemia! (Waa, waa, waa!) I know they felt sorry for me and wanted to get me out of there, but there was a surprise yet to come of which I was entirely oblivious.

Around 11:00 p.m., as we were finishing dessert, this woman comes shimmying up to our table, waving her arms in the air. I looked at this odd creature, then at the guy in front of her, then back at her. It wasn't until she plopped down in the seat next to me that I realized it was Karen B. I threw my arms around her, and the tears flowed generously. That was the big surprise—her flying in for the weekend. During dinner, Nelson and Beckie had been debating whether to have Karen B meet us at the restaurant or their apartment. I had noticed that both Beckie and Nelson excused themselves from the table several times throughout the course of the evening. I later found out that this was to make phone calls to Karen B to discuss the meeting-up strategy.

We left the restaurant and caught a cab back to the apartment. Karen B had brought some gifts with her, so we sat on the couch, and I opened them. One gift was a ceramic martini glass she'd painted pale pink with decorative figures and three words ("diva," "star," and "princess") around it. (The title Princess was bestowed on me by Dan. He called me Princess while I was living with him and Barbara when I first moved here and wasn't working.) Another present was a beautiful huge sturdy pink-and-white umbrella with UVA/UVB protection. She had purchased this to support breast cancer research, so the familiar pink ribbon logo is on it. Lastly, she presented to me a card filled with checks that totaled $1,250. This generosity brought tears to my eyes, especially knowing that many of the monetary gifts were from complete strangers. These donations were collected during her EuroK Challenge.

Thanks to my friends, what began as a really crummy birthday ended up to be quite a wonderful one. Thirty-eight is not so bad after all.

May 8, Saturday

Today was spent mostly relaxing before the party. We all slept in. After getting out of bed, sipping coffee, and chatting, we finally pulled ourselves together enough to walk to Zen Palate for lunch. Once again, this proved to be a maddening dining experience because I was unable to taste the food.

I rested most of the afternoon so that I'd have energy for the upcoming party. Karen B went to a spa for a massage; I stayed at the apartment to rest. The pinkeye had much improved, but the cough persisted.

The party began at 8:00 p.m., but no one arrived for at least thirty minutes, which is normal—everyone wants to be fashionably late. Adele and her friend Lucy were the first to show up. I met Adele through Lani when I was apartment hunting in the fall of 2002. Adele's sister had been living in the apartment in West New York that I would come to inhabit. Her sister was moving and needed someone to take over her lease. I didn't particularly like the fact that the apartment was so small and virtually no sunlight penetrated it; but because it was only $550 per month and a month-to-month lease, I was willing to make the compromise of small and dark, which is why I named it the Cave.

When Lani showed up, I discovered that she had had an emergency appendectomy the previous Saturday. She shouldn't even have been at the party. Of course, I was delighted to see her, but she looked tired and weak. STARK has their CD release party Friday, the fourteenth. I told her I'd be with her in spirit since I would be unable to attend. I'm so proud of her. She's worked so hard.

Cristina arrived. She was the only person from my acting class to attend the party, but that's okay because I don't expect the world to revolve around me (well, maybe sometimes . . .). She and I really connected in class. We discussed possibly finding a show to do together. She is so talented, and I love working with talented people because they make my performance better. I hope our friendship grows.

Jen and her husband, Phil, also were in attendance. This was the first time I've actually spoken more than a brief hello to Phil. He possesses a quirky British sense of humor. It meant a great deal to me that these friends made the effort to attend the party.

After my friends left, I snuck off to the bedroom to lie down. As much as I would've enjoyed meeting some new people, I didn't have the energy. It was a great party, and I truly appreciated Beckie and Nelson organizing and hosting it.

May 9, Sunday

I called Mom and Barbara to wish them a happy Mother's Day. Barbara informed me that Dan has a bad cold. I fear we are all spreading germs back and forth to one another in that household.

Around 1:00 p.m., I said good-bye to Karen B. I wouldn't be seeing her again before she left that evening because she, Beckie, and Nelson were going shopping while I was heading to the T. Schreiber Studio to see the matinee performance of *Hurlyburly*. I spoke with Joseph briefly afterward. His short haircut looks great; I knew it would. (I love it when I'm right.) He couldn't go out with me because he had to help strike the set due to class being in session the next day. I was a bit upset and made a hasty departure.

In his defense, he had called earlier in the day to see if we could meet before the show. I retrieved his messages around 11:00 a.m., by which time, he'd left two of them. I didn't return his call until 1:40 p.m. because I was hoping to spend more time together than merely an hour before the show.

May 10, Monday

I've decided to stay one more day since Dan has a cold. I think my sense of taste is returning because I can taste my coffee.

I'm debating whether to call Joseph. Maybe I hurt his feelings yesterday with my abrupt departure from the theater. But then again, I'm not sure I can take hearing once more "I don't have time to see you." Do I expect too much from my friends? Perhaps I do. There it is—my high expectations of others causing me grief; I must rein in my expectations. Or am I struggling with my emotions because I have a crush on him? I think I might.

If that is the case, I must quash any romantic feelings I may have for him and focus on keeping our relationship platonic. I'm sure he's only interested in me as a friend, or else he would've made a move by now. I enjoy his friendship, so I don't want to do anything to jeopardize that. I'm so ready to fall in love, but now is a really inopportune time for me to do that. Who wants to be with a sick girl? Maybe when I am restored to full health . . .

9:22 a.m.

Okay, I'm an ass. Joseph just phoned, and he'll be stopping by around 3:30 p.m. I should have known he wouldn't blow me off, but I get my feelings hurt so easily, especially regarding matters of the heart. However, I'm not going to make this into a romantic visit. It is merely two good friends hanging out.

5:20 p.m.

Joseph stayed for about two and a half hours. He has three clients to train this evening, so he had to get to the gym. He informed me that he booked the *Law & Order* job he'd auditioned for earlier this week, and his scenes are scheduled to shoot Thursday and Friday. He will play a cop. This episode is the season finale, so I will most likely be in the hospital when it airs.

May 13, Thursday

I returned to Basking Ridge yesterday. It's good to be home and lying in my own bed, but I find myself missing my friends and city life . . .

I woke up this morning feeling no better than yesterday, so Dr. Goldberg wrote prescriptions for antibiotics (a Z-pak) and cough medicine for me. During my checkup, the doctor was concerned because my white blood count had dropped to 2.2 from 3.8 last week. He checked my blood smear and didn't detect any leukemia cells, but that doesn't mean there aren't any cancer cells lingering about. My thinking is that this is all viral, so it will clear up eventually. My body has been fighting off congestion, a cough, a sore throat, fever blisters, and an eye infection. Whatever is happening in my body, it needs to change. It is not only worrisome and annoying to me, but it may also interfere with the transplant timeline. However, the transplant team at HUMC doesn't seem overly concerned, so perhaps I should just chill out.

Dr. Goldberg informed me that Barbara's marrow can be stored for up to two years. However, they want to start her part of the process as soon as possible so that when I'm ready for transplant, we can proceed without delay. I've been told by medical personnel and former transplant survivors that I will take two steps forward and then one step back many times throughout treatment and recovery. Of course, I'd prefer no steps back, but I accept that inevitability.

May 15, Saturday

I decided to sit out on the deck in the shade and enjoy the morning while I catch up on some writing. It's so peaceful out here except for the drone of air conditioners, which is only mildly irritating. Every now and then, a yellow finch finds the courage to join me on the deck to steal some food from the bird feeder.

I began working on the next article for my blog. Dan G has inspired me to write what I consider to be the best blog entry to date. This article details how others have inspired me during this trying period of my life. This is the e-mail message from Dan G after we'd seen *Wicked*, which inspired me to write the article and gave me a theme song, "Defying Gravity":

> I just wanted to tell you how happy it made me to share the magic of this musical with you. And it's interesting to me how differently I looked at it after being reminded of the experience you are going through and how certain songs have taken on new meaning. I truly believe that you are "defying gravity" right now.[40] And I pray that you continue to fly as high and as far as your dreams will take you. I know that you will get past this and continue to do amazing things with your new found courage, heart and state of mind. And I'm comforted to know that through it all you have a wonderful group of friends to support you. I mean, let's face it girl . . . you're "POP-uUUU-larrr."[41]
>
> I love you.
> Dan

("Popular" is a song on the *Wicked* soundtrack as well; it's sung by Galinda, eventually known as Glinda, the Good Witch.) Here are some of the lyrics to "Defying Gravity":

> Something has changed within me
> Something is not the same
> I'm through with playing by the rules
> Of someone else's game

Too late for second-guessing
Too late to go back to sleep
It's time to trust my instincts
Close my eyes and leap

It's time to try
Defying gravity
I think I'll try
Defying gravity
And you can't pull me down . . .

I'm through accepting limits
'Cuz someone says they're so
Some things I cannot change
But till I try, I'll never know
Too long I've been afraid of
Losing love I guess I've lost
Well, if that's love
It comes at much too high a cost
I'd sooner buy
Defying gravity
Kiss me good-bye
I'm defying gravity
And you can't pull me down . . .

So if you care to find me
Look to the western sky
As someone told me lately:
"Everyone deserves the chance to fly"
And if I'm flying solo
At least I'm flying free
To those who'd ground me
Take a message back from me
Tell them how I
Am defying gravity
I'm flying high
Defying gravity

And soon I'll match them in renown
And nobody in all of Oz
No wizard that there is or was
Is ever gonna bring me down![42]

When I listen to this song, I shed tears of joy, and chills run up my spine; it energizes me. "Defying Gravity" is about overcoming fear in order to fulfill one's potential. I'm not going to be afraid of doing the things I want to do in life. The song rejects playing by the rules because some rules are meant to be broken. When this segment of my life is over, I will remind myself that life is brief, so there is no time to be afraid. Stephen Schwartz, thank you for writing such inspiring lyrics.

May 16, Sunday

It's another beautiful day in New Jersey. I'm outside on the deck (again). I want to enjoy some nice weather before being hospital-bound for a month. I hope I don't sink into depression. I can handle being cooped up inside during the winter, but it's a whole different matter to be cooped up in the spring and summer. The plan is to thoroughly enjoy the time I have now, and part of that enjoyment includes spending as much time as possible with my dear little Aidan.

May 17, Monday

I found out today I will be admitted to the hospital Monday, May 24. On May 25, I will commence four days of radiation, followed by two days of chemotherapy. Memorial Day will be a day of rest (no chemo), and the bone marrow transplant is scheduled for June 1.

My cough has gotten better, and I am no longer blowing as much green and yellow goop out of my nose—the mucus is mostly clear. (I know . . . too much information.)

Aidan and I spent the afternoon together while Barbara and Dan met with Dr. Rowley, who instilled them with much more confidence than the other physicians had during previous consults. This process has been extremely frustrating for them because there is so little information available about pregnancy and bone marrow donation, and weighing the decision to do what's best for your sister versus what's best for your baby only further compounds the frustration.

Dr. Rowley provided them with facts and charts (which Dan covets) and no guarantees about the baby's safety (the other doctors Barbara had met with were telling her, "Oh, no problem," or at least that's how she perceived it). Of course, there *is* a risk to the fetus, especially since bone marrow aspirations are very rarely performed on pregnant women. Barbara will be only the second pregnant bone marrow donor in HUMC's history. However, Dr. Rowley will be performing the procedure on Friday, so she will be in highly capable hands.

May 19, Wednesday

Today, at the clinic, I wore neither hat nor scarf. My hair has grown out some though it is *very* short, sort of Sinead O'Connor-like. However, I was determined to be audacious and venture out sporting my new do.

My blood counts look good. The white blood count is up this week to 5.1, platelets are well over three hundred thousand, and hemoglobin is 11.6—almost normal. Dr. Goldberg performed a bone marrow aspiration, and this time, the marrow oozed out just as it should. In December, the marrow was so dried up that only a tiny amount could be retrieved. I am a little sore from the bone marrow aspiration, and Dr. Goldberg also took a sample of bone for a bone biopsy. We'll know the results Monday.

Karen L was at the clinic, and she looks fabulous. Her autologous stem cell transplant was two weeks ago, on May 5, and she is already back home. We talked for quite a while. I pray she continues to do well. I really love her despite not knowing her very well, but we are connected by our blood cancers and our having been hospital roommates.

Oh, I must include here that I had many compliments on my new look. I received comments such as "You look 'great,' 'chic,' and 'cute.'" Who knows, maybe I'll discover that I prefer my hair short—well, not this short. It felt empowering to sport my new hairdo today.

Before leaving the clinic, I signed all the pretransplant paperwork but forgot to get a copy. I'll get a copy Monday. It's detailed information about my treatment plan that I want readily available to me in case I need to reference it while I'm hospitalized.

Karen called to inform me that she has worked it out with her employer so that she can be here for two weeks after I'm released from the hospital; her boss is allowing her to utilize accumulated sick days. She will be here the week of transplant too. I feel more at ease knowing she will be with me through this experience.

Some other good news: Lori is engaged. I knew it would happen sooner or later. Lori visited Jeff P in Seattle this past weekend to help him settle into his new place. He proposed Saturday night while they were dining at SkyCity, the revolving restaurant located atop the Space Needle. They're considering tying the knot next May.

I spent another wonderful evening with Aidan. It makes my heart ache knowing I won't see him for a month or longer; I'll miss him terribly.

May 20, Thursday

Metta meditation and a long walk were part of my morning routine. The mail had been delivered by the time I returned home, and there it was—the invitation to my twenty-year high school class reunion. Before December 18, 2003, I had been looking so forward to this event. Realistically, I doubt I'll be strong enough to make the trip to Tell City in August. Cindy told me not to discount anything yet. I know that she, Maria, and Lynn are hoping I'll be able to attend. We'll see . . .

May 21, Friday

Barbara's bone marrow aspiration was scheduled for today, so she and Dan left for the hospital at 8:00 a.m. In the end, Barbara chose the side of the known benefit (sibling donor) versus the unknown risk (donation during pregnancy). Dan and she made the decision together and believed that they had done everything possible to minimize the risks to their baby. I said a prayer for them this morning.

It was a busy day for me; I ran many errands. At Macy's, I bought a couple of cute loungewear outfits (cotton pants and tank tops) to take with me to the hospital. During my first hospital stay in December, I had quickly ditched the oversized hospital garb in lieu of my own stylish comfortable clothes. My wardrobe was one thing that I could still maintain control over. After Macy's, I stopped by Godiva to purchase a box of chocolates for Barbara and Dan as a thank-you for the whole bone marrow aspiration ordeal.

Before heading home, I stopped at the UPS store to make copies of my advanced directive, the Leukemia & Lymphoma Society expense reimbursement form (for some meds), and some *Yoga Journal* articles. As I was getting ready to leave, the woman who had been making copies at the copier next to me approached me and asked, "May I ask you a question?"

"Sure," I replied.

"I noticed your hair, and it looks really stylish on you, but I was wondering if you cut it that way or if you recently went through chemotherapy?"

I told her that I had gone through four months of chemotherapy. She then confided that her sister had been diagnosed with breast cancer and that she had had a mastectomy yesterday. She also added that their mother had died of breast cancer. She confessed that she was scared. I gave her a warm hug.

Then she asked, "How do you get through it?"

I spent a few minutes with her sharing coping strategies that I had found useful over the past several months—prayer, meditation, guided imagery, accepting love and support from family and friends, and allowing myself to experience *all* my emotions. I wrote down the titles of guided imagery and affirmation CDs she might want to purchase. (I forgot to include journaling, which has been an effective tool for channeling emotions, expressing thoughts, and developing ideas.)

I gave her my e-mail address and the hospital's phone number because I had told her about my upcoming transplant. I then offered, "Anytime you need or want to talk, please feel free to call me." I gave her a final hug, and we wished each other well. I'll definitely keep her and her family in my prayers, and if she reaches out to me for help, I'll be there.

I felt so good after this extraordinary encounter and realized that God put me in that store at that particular moment because she needed help. (I had originally planned to go to the UPS store before going to the mall.)

Barbara and Dan arrived home around 6:00 p.m. She was sore and tired, so she went straight upstairs to lie down. I took some pizza and the box of Godiva chocolates up to her room, and we spoke briefly. She said that the procedure went well and added that Dr. Rowley was very pleased—he had declared that she had good stem cell concentration, which definitely bodes well for me.

May 22, Saturday

Barbara and Dan were having breakfast out on the deck when I finally ventured downstairs. I was relieved to see Barbara up and about though she was sitting in a chair with a pillow propped against her lower back because she was in a great deal of pain and would be for a few more days. I joined them, and Barbara recounted her ordeal.

Because she was six months pregnant, a bone marrow aspiration rather than a peripheral blood stem cell draw had to be done. A peripheral blood stem cell draw was out of the question because, prior to collecting stem cells peripherally, the donor is given growth factor medicine to increase the amount of stem cells in the blood stream. However, it is unknown how growth factor medicine affects a fetus or women who are breast-feeding, so the only alternative to collecting the stem cells from Barbara was a bone marrow aspiration.

I had three bone marrow extractions over the course of several months. Barbara, on the other hand, endured about seventy-five insertions in less than two hours and with a spinal only. This procedure is usually performed while the donor is under general anesthesia and sleeping. But being pregnant, Barbara decided not to put the baby at additional risk and remained awake during the procedure.

She told me that going in, she was surprisingly calm, maybe too calm because her blood pressure was 85/50. When she finally got into the operating room, nothing seemed to go quite as planned. The typical bone marrow harvest is done while the donor lies flat on their stomach, with an oncologist on each side so that simultaneous extractions can be made from both sides of the pelvis, thus moving the procedure along more quickly. At twenty-eight weeks pregnant, lying on her stomach was not an option.

The original plan was to have some type of prop on each side of her so that there would be minimal pressure on her stomach. As soon as she rolled into position, she could tell that wasn't going to work. The props were not strong enough to counterbalance the force required to push a needle into the pelvic bone, and her stomach was being pressed very hard against the table. Thankfully, the decision had been made to use a spinal as opposed to the usual general anesthesia for the procedure; otherwise, she would not have been able to communicate this discomfort to the doctors. So she ended up on her side, with only one oncologist working at a time.

She was not in pain but soon realized why the doctors want the donor to be completely out: She could certainly feel the pressure of that large needle during each of the seventy-five insertions. Just knowing what they were doing made her feel ill, so she tried to think of other things. Every few minutes, someone would inquire as to how she was doing. About forty-five minutes into the procedure, they stopped to get a quick analysis of the bone marrow sample in order to check the stem cell concentration and to make sure they were collecting enough. After another twenty minutes, she was done. She was moved to recovery, and the fetal heartbeat was checked. Everything looked good; Baby McCabe didn't even know what an amazing procedure he'd just endured.

May 23, Sunday

Barbara and Dan went to his parents' home to attend a birthday celebration for Eleonore. They're still gone, and it's almost 7:00 p.m. I stayed home because I needed to do some laundry and wasn't feeling particularly social. I have organized almost everything I plan to take with me to HUMC. Clothes, framed pictures, photos, drawings (received from Aidan, Kara, Olivia, and Eliza), CDs, my laptop computer, and books are all ready to be packed tomorrow morning. I will be moving into HUMC for four to five weeks, so I want my surroundings to feel somewhat like home, however remote that possibility may be.

I'd be lying if I said I was not feeling any trepidation about the whole situation. Many people think I'm brave and an inspiration, but I think I'm merely someone doing what needs to be done and all the while *trying* to be brave. I'm an actor—I can be quite convincing.

Mom will be phoning soon, and I'm looking forward to speaking with her and Dad tonight. I'm feeling a bit fragile . . .

May 24, Monday

I spent the morning tying up loose ends: paying bills, writing letters, checking e-mails, and updating my blog. Barbara and I then sat outside on the deck, sipping iced tea and chatting. Dan came home at lunch and grilled hamburgers. We ate outside. It was rather hot, but we were in the shade. I thought the heat felt great though since these days, I always seem to be cold. Plus this was a beautiful way for me to spend the morning before the commencement of my monthlong confinement.

Dan drove me to the hospital and stayed while I unpacked. I organized my room, placing framed pictures strategically where I could best see them. Of course, Aidan's photo went on the table right next to my bed; his smiling face will lift my spirits.

Most of the organization of my room was done by the time the nurses started coming in to take vitals, complete the admission questionnaire, and give information to me regarding an antifungal medication research study. Dan left as the nurses began filtering in and out of my room. And . . . drumroll . . . I am in remission! Dr. Goldberg gave a copy of the report to me, and I particularly like the part that reads "No evidence of residual leukemia."

May 25, Tuesday

At 9:00 a.m., I was wheeled on a gurney down to the radiation unit. The total-body irradiation was painless, but the setup was quite extensive. I was placed on another stretcher in a sitting position, legs extended in front of me and my back leaning against a wood panel. Foam triangle pieces were placed beneath my knees so that my legs were bent, positioning my knees pointing up toward the ceiling and my feet pressing flat on the stretcher. My feet were separated to a specified width, based on the measurements previously taken by the physicists. There can be no space between areas of the body, which ensures the even distribution of radiation. To eliminate the spaces, rice bags of various sizes were positioned between my legs and feet and then secured by tape. Supports were then placed behind each arm, and both my head and torso were taped to the wood panel. My head was secured to the vertical wooden panel by tape that reached from one side of it to the other across my forehead and under my chin, thus completely restricting any movement. I felt like I was about to become a torture victim.

The lights were extinguished, and an infrared laser beam was positioned down the center of my body—alignment is critical. Once alignment was achieved, a large glass panel with a wooden frame was placed in front of me, more accurately on my right side; and then the radiologists left the room. The radiation machine was turned on, and fifteen minutes of zapping the right side of my body commenced.

Once the right side was radiated, the gurney was turned around so that the left side of my body was facing the glass panel. The laser beam was again aligned;

then that side was zapped for fifteen minutes. This was a painless procedure, but I'm sure at some point, I will begin experiencing side effects. I requested to be wheeled down in a wheelchair for the afternoon session. I don't need a stretcher at the moment. It makes me feel self-conscious lying there in the lobby or hall like a total invalid as staff, nurses, and other patients walk by and gawk at me.

I was back in my room by 10:45 a.m., and Mom called shortly thereafter. Shelley also phoned. She will be visiting me tomorrow.

Kathleen, one of the chaplains, visited with me. At first, she didn't recognize me, and then she said, "Ah, the actor." We talked for about thirty minutes, and she is going to see that someone comes in to do some energy work on me.

Room service (can you believe it?) called, and I ordered lunch—tofu vegetable stir-fry and a Diet Pepsi. Unfortunately, by the time it was delivered, I was no longer hungry and hardly touched any of it. Something about being here quickly diminishes my appetite.

Cindy, Jen, and Karen B all called. Cindy is sending a package, and Jen is planning to visit Thursday evening. Karen B will be here for the transplant and then again the week of June 6.

Transport retrieved me an hour earlier than my scheduled radiation session this afternoon. Then to my chagrin, the radiation unit was running behind schedule, so I spent two hours waiting in the wheelchair. It was really annoying, and I was very unhappy, especially since I had nothing to do to pass the time.

Once I was in the radiation room, two physicists attached electrode-type devices to my body, which were to monitor the amount of radiation I was receiving. This would only have to be done once, I was told, unless an adjustment of the radiation dosage needed to be made.

I spoke with Karen, Jeff, and Mom this evening. Barbara called my cell phone while I was talking to Karen on the hospital phone, so Barbara's going to call back tomorrow.

May 26, Wednesday

I woke up, took a shower, and listened to the affirmations on the bone marrow transplant cassette. I had difficulty eating before I went for radiation. I drank some orange juice and a little coffee but couldn't stomach the pastry.

When I returned to the room, my nurse gave me a Compazine tablet to prevent nausea. I've learned these past months that it's good to get the nausea under control before it worsens. I've had three bowel movements this morning—yuck.

I find myself tearing up every once in a while. I try to be brave—not just for others, but also for myself. This is going to be a long, arduous journey. I must take one day at a time and appreciate my body's healing process. Right now, the radiation is destroying my immune system, stem cells, and bone marrow. However, I must remember that this destruction will clear the way for the infusion of new healthy, resilient stem cells. I feel reassured knowing these stem cells are being supplied by Barbara, who is a strong, resilient woman.

Yesterday, Kathleen suggested I write a letter to my body about it betraying me. I want to do this, but then again, I'm kind of hesitant to do so. I feel like my body needs as much love and nurturing as I can give it, not a berating for being bad. Still, my body did let me down. All my life, I've been so healthy, strong, and athletic. What happened? The answer to that question will probably never be answered. It's more acceptable for an older body to become ill, but not a thirty-seven-year-old one. How could this happen to me?

And I am angry that my life has been interrupted and essentially put on hold. However, despite my anger during this time, I've discovered new talents and interests, so this experience has produced some positive results. I will never know why I developed leukemia, and perhaps the answer isn't important. Rather, the journey I'm traveling and the lessons I'm learning are what is important.

On a different note, I decided to partake in the voriconazole study sponsored by the National Institutes of Health. Some information from the consent form is as follows:

> One of the most common side effects of BMT is a decrease in the number of infection fighting cells (white blood cells) in the body. Infections are caused by bacteria, viruses or fungi. When white blood cell numbers are low or the cells are weak, the body can't fight infections. For this reason, all BMT patients take drugs to prevent infection by these germs.
>
> Fungal infections are one of the worst forms of infection. One of the drugs used to both *prevent and treat* fungal infections is called fluconazole. Fluconazole prevents some, but not all, types of fungal infections. Voriconazole is a newer antifungal drug that can *treat* more types of fungal infections than fluconazole. But, voriconazole has more side-effects than fluconazole. Although voriconazole is used to *treat* severe fungal infections, it has not yet been tested for the *prevention* of fungal infections.
>
> The purpose of this study is to compare fluconazole and voriconazole in the *prevention* of fungal infections in blood or marrow transplant patients where another person is the donor.[43]

Both drugs have been approved by the FDA. I will be randomly assigned either voriconazole or fluconazole. This is a double-blind study, so neither me nor my study doctor will know which medication I'm taking. Since voriconazole is given twice a day and fluconazole is given once a day, a placebo will be given if I'm assigned fluconazole; either way, I'm taking two pills a day. I will continue the study drug until one hundred days posttransplant. During this time, I will be monitored very closely. Should an infection occur, all means of treatment will be utilized to remedy it. Perhaps this study will yield useful information for future patients, so a guinea pig I will be.

Shelley visited this afternoon, staying for nearly two hours. We walked around the transplant ward so that I could get some exercise. After Shelley left, it was radiation time again.

Barbara called shortly after I returned to my room. She put Aidan on the phone, and he giggled when he heard my voice. He said "I" for "hi." Dan slept in my bed last night, and he told Barbara to tell me that he doesn't miss me because he slept with my scent. It was a typical Dan comment that made me laugh.

I have not eaten much today due to the nausea, but I still weighed in at 117 pounds. They gave me an injection of some sort to induce urination because I am retaining water. Great, I'll be frequenting the restroom again.

May 27, Thursday

I've returned from my fifth round of radiation. I spoke with Dr. Ingenito this morning. He thinks I am doing very well and tolerating the radiation better than most patients. I'm experiencing nausea, appetite loss, diarrhea (this morning), and dry mouth—all of which he said were normal side effects. Though didn't he tell me during my consultation that diarrhea was a side effect rarely experienced? Hmm . . .

Patricia from the pastoral care office came in to see me. We spoke for a while, and I told her about the journaling I've been doing and the plans I'm making, such as writing a book and volunteering for the Leukemia & Lymphoma Society, which she thought was wonderful. After our conversation, we prayed together.

Barbara visited this afternoon. She brought with her a six-pack of Tab and a bag of Doritos. We talked for a long time, and she stayed until they wheeled me down to Radiation. I regurgitated prior to heading downstairs. Vomiting is so disgusting, but I felt better afterward.

Jen arrived shortly after I was returned to my room, which was around 7:00 p.m. She brought with her many audiobooks. She was very sweet and motherly (although she's my age) as she encouraged me to eat. I consumed half of a chocolate shake. Then she lightly scratched my back for a while to distract me from the nausea. It helped too; I almost fell asleep. She left around 9:30 p.m. and said that she'd return next week. After Jen left, both Mom and

Karen phoned, but I only spoke with them briefly because I was exhausted and didn't feel well.

May 28, Friday

This was my last day of radiation therapy. When I left, Debbie, one of the morning-crew radiologists, gave me a hug and wished me luck. They're all so wonderful. I will miss them, but I will *not* miss the radiation.

As I waited for transport to return me to my room, I conversed briefly with the mother of a little girl who was also receiving TBI. Apparently, the child had gone through transplant six months ago, and everything was fine; then she relapsed. Before the first transplant, the doctors had treated her with chemotherapy only, no TBI; this time, they're using radiation as well. The little girl looked so fragile and listless lying there in her mother's lap, and I struggled to hold back tears.

I ate a small cup of raspberry sorbet for lunch. It was the only thing that sounded appealing. The thought of most food makes me want to hurl. I've felt pretty good up until today, but now nausea is overwhelming me. My nurse has given me another dose of Ativan.

The 4:00 p.m. radiation time was pushed back, so I was able to talk to Nelson when he called; he always cheers me up. I finished radiation around 8:30 p.m., and once I got back to my room, I threw up. Since I've hardly eaten any food, I experienced dry heaves mixed with bile and phlegm, which was extremely unpleasant.

I utilized two strategies to get through radiation without feeling anxious or claustrophobic. During the morning sessions, I would do metta meditation ("metta" is the Pali word for "loving-kindness"). Meditation helped me focus my attention on something other than the radiation penetrating my body. Plus metta meditation is a way of extending loving-kindness to ourselves, to other people—those we care about as well as those we don't particularly like—and to the greater world; so I feel I was doing something beneficial. During the afternoon sessions, I would listen to music that I selected from my CD collection.

May 29, Saturday

I am exhausted and nauseous, and I have terrible diarrhea. A stool sample was taken this morning to rule out an infection. I attempted to eat some of my Frosted Flakes but was only able to swallow six or seven spoonfuls. I finally managed to take all the meds, which proved to be challenging because twice, I felt the urge to retch. Many fluids are being pumped into me in preparation for the Cytoxan I will begin receiving this afternoon continuing into tomorrow.

I've been lying here in bed listening to music and crying. Natalie called to check in on me, so I cried to her. She feels so helpless, but her listening to me was comforting.

After I hung up with Natalie, Kathleen from pastoral care came into my room to visit. She presented me with an iridescent green glass heart. The object is about one inch in diameter. She told me that she usually gives the patient a choice of colors, but I wasn't going to get that choice. She handed it to me and said, "This is for your heart. Green is the color of the heart chakra." (I knew this.) I automatically placed the object against my chest. I told her that I thought it was extraordinary that she had given this to me because during my self-healing work over the past few months, I had discovered that it was my heart chakra that needed the most mending. How synchronistic is that?

Surprise! Dan walked into my room and said, "Get your mask on. The family is here." I was so thrilled. Since the family room is located outside of the sterile environment of the transplant unit, I put on my mask. I unplugged the IV pole from the wall and followed Dan.

There he was . . . my sweet smiling little boy! Aidan was definitely amused by my IV pole and the mask covering my face. He hugged me several times while patting my back, gave my head gentle touches, and tried to kiss me through the mask. I loved this so much and struggled to fight back tears of joy. We played for a few minutes with some of his toys from Chuck E. Cheese's (they'd just come from a party there). Then Barbara and I went back to my room where we talked as she gathered my dirty laundry. I walked out with her to say good-bye to Dan and Aidan. This visit completely turned my day around. I still can't eat and am feeling nauseous, but my mental state is greatly improved.

May 31, Monday, Memorial Day

I began taking Prograf (antirejection medication) today. This will be administered twice daily. I will also be taking folic acid twice a day and B-12 once a week, which will aid in the growth of my new stem cells.

One of the clamps on the IV lines became disconnected, and I discovered blood all over my sheets and on the back of my tank top. I was a bit panic-stricken at the sight of all the blood, but a nurse quickly closed the clamp, and an aide changed the bed linen. Fortunately, peroxide removed the blood stain on my top, which is now being laundered.

I'm still experiencing diarrhea and nausea. I have no appetite, and my mouth is so parched. I need to drink more water, but I can't stomach it right now.

Barbara, Dan, Beckie, Nelson, Karen B, Shelley, and her husband, Dan D, all visited this afternoon—at the same time. It was quite the party. It made me happy to have all these wonderful people surrounding me. My brother-in-law even set up my laptop for wireless access. Everyone left by 6:30 p.m., but then I received a call from Karen B. She told me that she didn't feel right leaving me all alone as she could sense I was scared and asked if I'd like her to stay the night in my room with me. I told her that I would, so she returned to the hospital.

I fell asleep listening to the bone marrow/stem cell transplant guided imagery tape, which encouraged me to release emotions of fear and sadness and replace them with images of hope and healing.

June 1, Tuesday, Transplant Day (Rebirth Day)
Day 0

As the day wore on and the time approached for Barbara's stem cells to be transfused into me, sorrow replaced anxiety. I am losing a part of me as her stem cells replace mine and begin producing her blood in my body. My blood type will change from O- to O+, which is Barbara's blood type. This changing of blood type is somewhat unsettling to me. However, I also view this day as one of rebirth—another birthday to celebrate. It is extraordinary how this whole bone marrow transplant process works. It is truly miraculous. And not only is this a physical rebirth, but because of all the self-reflection and positive changes I'm attempting to make in my life, it is a spiritual and emotional rebirth as well. So despite feeling melancholy over what I'm losing, there is excitement and anticipation about what I'm gaining. I thank God for the new stem cells that will generate new and healthy blood in my body and grant me a second chance at life.

Around 3:30 p.m., Dr. Hsu, another physician in Dr. Goldberg's oncology group, administered the blood transfusion. The transplant was a slow intravenous infusion through my catheter of the bone marrow collected from Barbara. Karen B was already stationed at my bedside, and Karen waltzed into the room just minutes before the doctor began the procedure. The transplant, which took all of twenty minutes, was uneventful except for an intense scratchiness in my throat caused by the preservative in the blood. I was given Benadryl prior to the transfusion, which quickly sent me off to la-la land. Meanwhile, my sister and friend sat vigil, watching my blood pressure rise and fall, sometimes significantly, on the monitor. The nurses assured them that this was normal.

June 2, Wednesday

I walked three laps around the transplant unit and did the armband exercises the physical therapist had demonstrated to me. I attempted to eat some chicken broth and rice, applesauce, and cream of wheat but hardly touched any of it. I have no appetite. I am diligent about my mouth care though. Frequent oral care—toothbrushing (with the sponge brushes, which do a lousy job of cleaning teeth and gums but prevent bleeding) and rinsing—is adhered to many times throughout the day to prevent mouth sores.

I continue to struggle with nausea and diarrhea. I'm so tired, but I must remain active to some degree because being active is supposed to hasten my improvement, at least that's what the health care professionals keep preaching.

I'm not getting enough sleep. Two contributors to my sleep deprivation are the vitals checks (blood pressure, temperature, heart rate, and oxygen) during the night and the 4:00 a.m. blood draw to obtain the daily CBC results. I am almost always awakened when the aides or nurses come into my room. Of course, the taking of vitals is necessary, but it's definitely not conducive to a good night's rest. The vitals checks don't bother me during the day, even though an aide comes in every couple of hours to take them. I am very good at recording the results in the notebook on the table next to my bed. However, I'm rarely as diligent at documenting these statistics at night as I am during the day.

Many calls came in today . . .

June 3, Thursday

Karen and I walked four laps around the unit, and then I did the armband exercises. I am still feeling wiped out but working to stay strong.

Jen and Karen C visited for about an hour and a half this evening. I haven't seen Karen C since February when we had lunch at the Tomato Restaurant.

June 4, Friday

I showered, listened to affirmation tapes, and received communion. I received a lovely card from Lynn in which she declares June 1 as my second birthday. I like that.

My exercises today consisted of five laps around the ward and arm exercises.

June 6, Sunday

Today, my physical and mental states are unchanged, and the usual suspects are creating discomfort. For instance, I have had violent dry heaves—so violent, in fact, that my entire torso aches. Mucus and skin (from the shedding of the lining inside my mouth) are all that is produced when I vomit. Some blood samples were drawn. They are not worried about my kidneys but believe I could have a strep infection.

Karen B was here Friday, Saturday, and Sunday. Barbara visited after Karen B left; then Nelson and Beckie arrived. I'm definitely not alone during this ordeal, and for that, I'm eternally grateful.

June 7-19

[The entries from June 12 through June 19 chronicle, or at least attempt to chronicle, the remainder of my hospital stay. Some entries were completely indecipherable due to all the drugs and chemicals in my body, especially the morphine. Not only were my hands shaky, but also my mind was racing with thoughts quicker than I could write them down. Everything—thoughts, movements—seemed to alternate between a heightened, frenzied state of action and a slow-motion dreamlike state.

I have done my best to interpret my handwriting. Here is a sample of it:

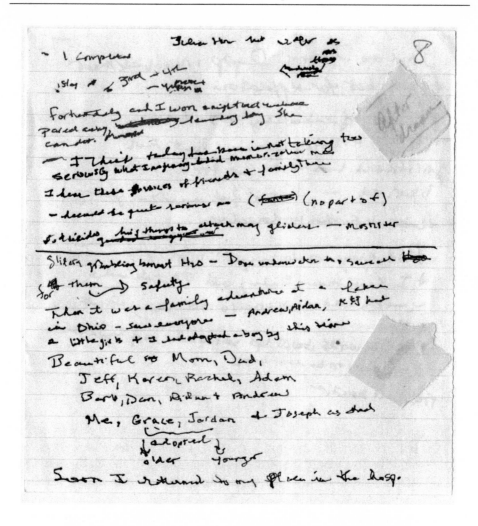

This demonstrates how incoherent and delusional I was during this time because my handwriting was so illegible. I was attempting to record the 3-day dream I had. (Written around June 12, 2004)

These entries are quite revealing as to my mental and physical states during the second week after transplant. The first several entries describe a continuous dream I had over a two-day period while under the influence of morphine. I am unsure of the actual dates, so I have ventured a guess as to the time frame. I made no journal entries from June 7-11.]

June 12, Saturday

I'm in bed. The guided imagery work has been effective in alleviating some of my discomfort, or more likely, it's the morphine working.

I've been feeling rather bizarre—in a very dreamlike, hazy, confused state—fading in and out of consciousness. It all started last night when a Reiki practitioner came into the room to do some guided imagery work with me. Karen B remained in the room with me, but I don't recall who else was present. Maybe Barbara was there? Anyway, I was already well on my way to morphine-induced delirium when the guided imagery session began.

The Reiki practitioner instructed me to "breathe in peace and breathe out negativity." I did this for several breaths. Then I was told to breathe in joy and breathe out anxiety and depression. This was repeated a few times. Then she told me to imagine that above my head was a golden ball filled with love from all the people I know . . . and thus, my journey began.

As I drifted out of consciousness, I felt myself, while in the bed, floating out of the room and begin to slide rapidly down a bright white porcelain tunnel. Normally, the speed at which I was moving would terrify me; but a great calm enveloped me, and I was unafraid. Eventually, I found myself, still lying in my bed, flying above the city and taking in all the sights below me. Throughout the days of this recurring dream, I found that upon waking, my bed would float gently back into the hospital room; however, when I fell asleep, the bed would glide out of the room and venture to different places and dimensions.

So lying in my bed, I glided out of the room and the hospital and flew over buildings, trees, hills, and mountains in both sunshine and rain. An invisible shield surrounded me to prevent me from falling and to protect me from the elements. As my flight continued, I found myself in the Midwest—Cincinnati, actually. Many people were waving to me, welcoming me back. Then I proceeded on my journey and stopped to pick up Barbara, Dan, Aidan, and Andrew (my unborn nephew, and this was before the name Andrew was decided upon).

After picking up my family, my bed ended up in a field adorned with gorgeous flowers in varying shades of pinks, reds, yellows, and purples. In this place, many friends were greeting me—Karen B, Natalie, Susan, Lynn, Cindy, some of my acting classmates, and many children of all ages. However, my happiness faded as I sensed death approaching. I could see brutish men, dressed in black clothing with hoods covering their heads and concealing their faces, shaking the railings on other patients' beds to arouse them, then carrying the patients to the death chamber. I had to escape!

Upon being captured, I demanded to be set free. However, these creatures were very strong. As they were leading me to the death chamber, I saw a little girl with bald spots on her head and brown marks on her face. My heart ached for her because I knew she was sick and probably dying.

I said to her, "You look so pretty." She gave me a big smile.

Finally, the death brutes shoved my bed into a cage. I was desperate to be free, so I used all my willpower to break the clamps that secured the gate and made my escape. Then I found myself sliding back into my hospital room.

The dream continued . . . After fleeing from my captors, I once again found that I was being pursued by those wanting to harm me. As my bed maneuvered to escape, I punched at these men and pushed them away from my bed. Barbara joined in fighting them off, and they finally gave up.

Barbara disappeared from the dream, and I found myself in a festive carnival setting where I was joined on my journey by Johnny Depp. Johnny was quite helpful during my second battle with the bad guys. Of course, his significant other was quite jealous, but I told him her jealousy was unwarranted because I wasn't interested in him. (Yeah right.)

During my second captivity, I felt as if I were sinking deeper and deeper underwater, yet I could still breathe. Somehow, I was being protected, which made me peaceful and calm. Eventually, I was able to subdue the bad guys who had sabotaged my protectors, and I conquered them single-handedly—without Johnny's assistance. I had been trapped in a tunnel filling up with water, and my bed maneuvered its way to safety as it glided out of the watery death pit. My bed was like a magic carpet, safely transporting me away from danger.

Next up on my excursion was a family adventure at a lake in Ohio. This was a very beautiful moment because Mom and Dad were there along with Barbara, Dan, Aidan, Andrew, Karen, and Jeff. Karen and Jeff had two little girls, but their children's names were Rachel and Adam. (Adam is a very strange name for a girl.) Even stranger was that I had children: Grace, a little girl, and Jordan, a little boy—both adopted. After this reunion, consciousness returned, and I found myself back in the hospital room.

The third and final segment of the dream was pretty short, but in my mind, this segment was confirmation that my life would not end any time soon. Once again, I floated out of the building and into the hospital courtyard (I don't even know if HUMC has a courtyard, but in my dream, there was one). This courtyard was filled with trees, flowers, and white pillars with ivy snaking up and around them. Taking place here was a ceremony honoring people about to die. They were queued up in their beds around the perimeter of the courtyard where I somehow ended up in the center of this configuration. Suddenly, all the beds and their occupants began floating toward an open door into a tunnel leading underground. I was part of this floating procession. When we passed through the door, darkness enveloped us. As we neared the bottom gate where we would leave this world for the next one, I could hear the guards yelling, "Hurry up, the gates are closing! The gates are closing!" Just as I was about to proceed through the gate, it shut abruptly, ejecting my bed back up the tunnel and out into the light.

Upon waking, I exclaimed, "This is a sign—I'm not supposed to die yet!" I told Karen B about this dream and that I needed to write it all down. I was frantic to record it so as not to forget it. [Later I would discover that she made several attempts to write this all down for me, but I kept drifting off to sleep.]

I was mentally out of it the day after the dream too. As I drifted in and out of sleep, I kept hearing the voices of family and friends. Joseph and I were supposed to perform in an acting contest. However, we existed in different dimensions, so we couldn't connect with each other. From my room, I could see his frustration, which frustrated me because he couldn't see me and where I was located.

I was so convinced that my family was here yesterday that I disconnected my IV pole from the electrical socket in the wall and walked, with the IV pole beside me, out of the sterile environment of the transplant unit and into the hall toward the family lounge. Of course, when I arrived at my destination, no one was there. Disappointed, I turned around and went back to my room. Surprisingly, none of the nursing staff saw me leave or return. I had been giving the poor nurses grief about my family being there to visit because I was so sure of it, but they kept assuring me that my family wasn't there. The nurses kindly and patiently reiterated this to me, but I'm sure my insistence was wearing on their nerves.

Barbara visited today. She wanted to talk to the doctor because she felt the nurses weren't addressing the fact that "I was talking out of my head," as she put it. I was still in that somewhat delusional state of seeing and hearing people that weren't there, so her concern was justified. The following exchange is what sparked that concern.

When she first arrived and after we'd been talking for a few minutes, she asked me what I'd been doing today.

I responded cheerfully, "I played with Aidan this morning—"

She interrupted me, "Deb, you did not play with Aidan."

"Oh, I know," I responded, giggling.

After reminding me that I couldn't possibly have played with Aidan this morning, she presented me with some new clothes, which Mom had sent her money to buy. Barbara and I have very similar taste, so what she selected was adorable. The items were light blue terry cloth cropped yoga pants, matching hooded jacket, a matching short-sleeved polo-type top, and a blue-and-white-striped cotton racerback tank. She also bought food items including popsicles and small frozen pizzas.

She walked two laps around the transplant unit with me before she headed home. She stayed for about four hours. The combination of medications and morphine contributed to my continued vacillation throughout the evening between lucidity and delirium. This will be great sense memory stuff for acting—if I can remember it.

June 13, Sunday
Day 12

"You are much more lucid today," proclaimed one of the nurses. I definitely feel more grounded.

My mouth and throat are sore, I have minimal diarrhea, my eyes are yellow and puffy, so eyedrops have been prescribed. Despite not feeling well, I walked three laps around the unit, did two sets of arm exercises, and while lying on my bed, executed some ballet leg exercises.

I had no visitors today, so I was lonely. I entertained myself by watching TV and listening to music. Although I had no visitors, I did receive several phone calls from Mom, Lori, Jeff, Barbara, Carol, and Beckie.

June 14, Monday
Day 13

I remain quite tired, yet I managed to get out of bed to wash my face and underarms. As I peered into the mirror, I was struck by how quickly what little hair had started growing back was suddenly falling out again. To hasten the falling-out process, I scrubbed the remaining hair off my scalp with a wet cloth.

The physical therapist came in to walk with me and to motivate me to complete a couple sets of arm exercises. After she left, I struggled to swallow the antifungal pills. These capsules are so fat that swallowing is very difficult. My appetite remains nonexistent. My eyes still bother me, and my mouth is in pain. There are no mouth sores, but the lining of my mouth has gotten very thin due to the shedding of the skin inside my mouth. The physician treating my strep infection checked in on me and decided to continue the medication protocol currently being administered.

Dr. Rowley came into my room later in the day. He says I am doing well physically, but he is concerned about my spirit. He senses that I am depressed, which I am, but I'm sure much of my mental state has to do with being so heavily medicated. The nutritionist visited me as well because she is worried that I'm not eating. I told her that I try to swallow a few bites of food, but it's challenging because food and pills make me gag.

As of today, I've been here for three weeks. It seems like forever. Mom, Karen B, and Lani called today.

June 15, Tuesday
Day 14

I showered and did my exercises, and later in the morning, a package from Geralynn arrived. In it were five LIVESTRONG yellow wristbands from the Lance Armstrong Foundation, two crossword puzzle books, a journal, and Marlo Thomas's book *The Right Words at the Right Time*. Lynn sent a card with a miracle prayer written in it.

Lani visited for about four hours. She's so wonderful to make the trip out here so often. Nelson and Karen B telephoned.

A nurse organized the medication order for when I leave the hospital. There are thirteen different drugs and a transplant kit that includes all my medications, a large weekly pill organizer, a thermometer, and a blood pressure monitor. I was given a printout of the medications and the corresponding cost of each one. Yikes! For one month, the total cost—and this is my coinsurance amount—is $458; of that $458, the Prograf is the big-ticket item at $302 (for 180 pills). The transplant kit and meds will be in my possession by the time I leave the hospital.

Overall, I am tired, my mouth hurts, and my appetite hasn't returned.

June 16, Wednesday

What a surprise—Maria and Kimberly are here! Before she departed for Cincinnati today, Karen B kept telling me to expect some visitors but didn't reveal whom to expect. It was about 4:00 p.m. when I saw Kimberly peek through the window on the door, and then I saw Maria too. I was so excited. I had no clue they were making the trip here to visit me—Kimberly flew in from Louisville, and Maria flew in from Chicago.

We talked all evening, and it was reminiscent of the times we spent together in college. We haven't seen each other in a very long time, especially Kimberly and me. It's been years. Kimberly apologized for not calling me, and I told her there was no need for an apology. I added, "The important thing is that you are here now." We talked, took photos, and hung out. It was as if no time had passed since we'd seen one another last—we picked up right where we left off. Our friendship is as intact and as strong as ever. The only difference, almost fifteen years later, two of the three of us are married with children. At 10:00 p.m., the ladies left to catch a shuttle back to the hotel.

June 17, Thursday

Most of the day, Maria, Kimberly, and I enjoyed one another's company, laughing and giggling like schoolgirls. It was so wonderful to see them, and I'm so touched that they would travel this distance to be with me. At 4:00 p.m., we hugged and kissed good-bye; then the ladies headed to the airport.

Shortly after their departure, Lani arrived. This time, she had prepared macaroni and cheese for me, and I ate almost every bit of it. This was the first substantial amount of food I'd eaten in weeks, so it's a good thing I packed on some extra pounds prior to transplant.

Beckie and Nelson showed up as Lani was leaving. Nelson brought the itinerary for my mother's flight to New Jersey in July. Beckie knew I hadn't exercised yet today, so per Karen B's instruction, she was trying to persuade me to get my butt out of bed. I was resisting her efforts and getting annoyed at her insistence because I did not feel like walking. She was annoyingly, yet pleasantly, persistent. In the end, I begrudgingly acquiesced but only made three trips around the ward.

Some good news: my white blood cell count is at 0.5. Dr. Rowley expects to send me home this weekend. Once the white blood cell count hits 1.0, they kick you out of the hospital.

June 18, Friday
Day 17

My platelet count fell to eleven thousand, so I had to have a transfusion of platelets. The white blood cell count is now 0.7. I am still experiencing nausea and didn't eat much today.

June 19, Saturday
Day 18

I'm home! I received a transfusion of blood before I left because my hemoglobin was pretty low.

Before I left, I was given a medications list outlining each drug, what it is for, dosage, and frequency. This list includes Prograf (antirejection medication and protection against graft-versus-host disease [GVHD]), acyclovir (antiviral), Flagyl, penicillin, and Bactrim (all three antibacterials), Compazine and Ativan (both for nausea), Pepcid (protects the stomach), folic acid (promotes new red cell growth), magnesium oxide (replaces lost magnesium), atenolol (controls high blood pressure), Ovral (protects against uterine bleeding), and Synthroid (thyroid medication), which I've been taking for years. All in all, I am supposed to ingest eighteen to twenty pills a day. The Bactrim is only taken Monday, Wednesday, and Friday, twice a day.

In addition to the medications list, I was also given fifteen pages of discharge instructions. These instructions covered house cleaning, care of pets and plants (gardening and repotting of plants should be avoided for up to three months posttransplant), sun exposure, hygiene, physical activity, nutrition, sexuality, complications, follow-up care, immunizations, and information about GVHD. Graft-versus-host disease is a common complication following an allogeneic stem cell or bone marrow transplant. If the donor's white blood cells are not a good genetic match, they will perceive the patient's organs and tissues as foreign material that should be destroyed.[44] Approximately 20 to 50 percent of patients undergoing a stem cell transplant with a related HLA-matched donor develop GVHD.[45]

My immune system will not function normally for one year or longer, so there are many precautions I must take. It is suggested that for the first one hundred days posttransplant, when I am away from home, I wear a mask. I hate those things; I could hardly stand wearing one for a few hours at the clinic during follow-up visits after chemotherapy. The guidelines suggest that you should always wear a mask in the doctor's office or hospital. I am to avoid large crowds, over twenty-five people, during the first one hundred days.

There are also commonsense guidelines such as hand washing and changing infant diapers (that's a no-no). I should take my temperature if I'm not feeling well because if it reaches 100.5 °F or higher, I must call the doctor, and I may be asked to check into the hospital because a temperature this high could be indicative of a serious infection. In addition to the above precautions, I must be mindful of what I eat and how food is prepared; I must strictly adhere to the low-microbial diet.

Sufficient intake of fluids is especially important, and it is suggested that I drink four to six glasses a day; however, since I am taking Prograf, I should drink more than the suggested amount. Gatorade is actually said to be a better option because of its nutrients. No alcoholic beverages are permitted either.

Then there is the information regarding immunizations. All of my childhood immunizations have been wiped out of my system, so after the first year posttransplant, I will require new vaccinations. These shots are essentially the same ones that babies and toddlers get—influenza B, meningococcal, pneumococcal, polio, and tetanus/diphtheria. I will receive all these at one-year and two-years posttransplant; plus on the second year, I will receive the measles-mumps-rubella (MMR) vaccine. My body is not strong enough to handle these immunizations now, so I must wait. I hope I don't catch anything until then. It's a little scary knowing that I am no longer protected against these viruses.

Dan picked me up around 3:00 p.m. When I walked into the house, Aidan came running to me and threw his little arms around me. "It's Aunt Deborah!" he exclaimed. It was the best greeting, and I held on to him for as long as he would let me.

After depositing the bags in my bedroom, I took a long hot bath. It's so great to be home. I spent twenty-eight days in the hospital, and I *never* want to do that again.

June 22, Tuesday

I've been home since Saturday. I have never been as sick of one place in my life as I was of that hospital. I am feeling drained of energy, so staying hydrated is essential. Also, the hydration will help my kidneys. My creatinine level went up one point since Saturday, so I've been instructed to drink plenty of fluids. Creatinine is a waste product made by the muscles, and a high creatinine level indicates that the kidneys may not be working properly. I definitely don't need the aggravation of kidney problems right now, so I am consuming large quantities of water.

Finally, my room is somewhat organized; almost everything I took to the hospital with me has been unpacked. I have to rest between organizing different bags of belongings because I'm so fatigued.

Mom arrives tonight for a two-week stay.

June 30, Wednesday

I haven't felt like writing lately—I'm so tired and unmotivated. I finally mustered the energy to answer some e-mail messages today, and afterward, Mom and I went for a walk. I've been trying to get a little exercise every day, but I'm so exhausted. I can only manage to venture short distances from the house.

My clinic visit went relatively well yesterday. My platelets are at 140,000, hemoglobin is 8.1, but my white blood count is down to 2.1 (from 2.9 last Friday).

My skin is very itchy, and there is a slight rash, so I may have a slight case of GVHD. However, if this is GVHD, I don't want it to get out of control. I want my body to be able to fight it off without having to ingest prednisone (a steroid used for combating GVHD). Dr. Rowley will check my skin again on Friday.

I've had many restless nights, so Dr. Rowley prescribed Ambien for me. Last night, I'm happy to report, I slept for seven hours straight. I am still tired today, but I refuse to sleep until nighttime.

July 2, Friday
Thirty-one days posttransplant

Today's *God Calling*:

> *The Child-Spirit*
> Courage. Face the future, but *face* it only with a brave and happy heart.
> Do not seek to *see* it. You are robbing Faith of her sublime sweetness
> if you do this.
>
> Just know that all is well and that Faith, not seeing, but believing, is the
> barque that will bear you to safety, over the stormy waters.
>
> Seek in every way to become child-like. Not only for its simple trust
> must you copy the child-spirit, but for its joy in life, its ready laughter,
> its lack of criticism, its desire to share all with all men. Ask much that
> you may become as little children, friendly and loving towards all—not
> critical, not fearful.[46]

This was the perfect meditation for me today. I've been rather depressed
lately, yet I should be ecstatic because my recovery is going quite well. There is
a sadness engulfing me, and I'm not sure why. Am I afraid to face the future?
Am I tired of feeling like such a plain Jane? Am I fed up with feeling exhausted
all the time? I would venture to say that all these factors are contributing to
this pervasive gloom. I feel that mentally I've taken three steps backward since
transplant. Prior to the procedure, I was so optimistic about the future.

The bottom line is that I must rid myself of this melancholy. Right now, I
sleep a lot or am at least lying around watching TV. I need to make myself get up
and move. As the above passage encourages me, "Face the future with a brave
and happy heart." Also, remaining in a childlike spirit, being friendly and loving
to all, and avoiding criticism and fear will help me overcome depression and face
the future with courage and trust—at least that is my hope.

July 3, Saturday

Mark phoned. He and his partner, Derek, are in New York City; he wants to
visit tomorrow. It's been at least three years since we last saw each other. Mark
was another founding member of Ovation Theatre Company (there were five of
us). About a year after the company was formed, he and his partner at that time,
Scott (also a cofounder of Ovation), moved to Chicago. I was very disappointed

when I found out they intended to leave Cincinnati. Ovation survived, but I missed them terribly.

This morning, I sat out on the deck and read the *New York Times*. Mom and I went for a late-afternoon walk. I am still very shaky, my skin is itchy, and I am constantly cold and fatigued. It is important that I make myself exercise, meditate, and write regardless of how I feel. These are all important activities for achieving well-being of body, mind, and spirit. I so desire to be healthy and strong again.

July 4, Sunday

Mom, Dan, Barbara, and Aidan went to the Bronx Zoo today. I stayed home because I knew there was no possibility of my enduring two to three hours of strolling around the zoo. However, Mark and Derek came to visit. They arrived around 2:40 p.m. We sat out on the deck, drinking Diet Cokes and talking for several hours. During that time, we caught up on life and talked politics. I haven't seen Mark since he and Scott made a trip to Cincinnati in 2001. It's weird to think of him and Scott not being a couple anymore, but they are both in new relationships and remain good friends, which I think is awesome.

I took the guys back to the train station shortly after everyone returned from the zoo. I was glad Mark and Derek were able to meet my family before departing.

I have a rash high up on my forehead that extends down behind my right ear and onto my neck. There is a bit of rash around my nose too. It is very itchy, but then, my whole body is itchy. I'm assuming this is some form of GVHD. I'll talk to the doctor about it Tuesday.

July 5, Monday

My body is still not processing food properly; I passed two loose stools before 10:00 a.m. The rash on my face doesn't appear to have spread but remains red and itchy. My nose feels a bit swollen due to the rash on and around it. I spent most of the day scratching my head and behind my right ear (sounds like I'm a dog)—miserable!

July 6, Tuesday

Dr. Rowley thinks my facial rash is due to an allergy and not GVHD. He wrote a prescription for a high-strength hydrocortisone cream. Unfortunately, the pharmacist had to order it because it was not in stock. I'm supposed to pick it up tomorrow afternoon. So the itching persists . . .

Dr. Rowley also informed me that my loose stools are due to my daily intake of magnesium oxide. Knowing that bit of information lessens my concern.

I drove Mom to the airport this afternoon. I was sad to see her leave. She has been such a big help these past couple of weeks. Now I have to fend for myself for five days, but Karen will be here Monday for a two-week stay.

I must start meditating regularly again because today, going to and from the airport, I found myself easily irritated by the other drivers on the highway. I had absolutely no patience. I don't want to be bad tempered and intolerant; but boy, it's nearly impossible to be calm and loving when other drivers cut you off, pull out in front of you, tailgate, or drive too slowly. Grrrrr . . .

July 7, Wednesday

Again, I find myself fretting about the future. I must stop it. Somehow, things will fall into place when I am ready—I must believe that. I'm making myself out to be the poor relative and the little girl who can't take care of herself, and that is not true—well, okay, right now, I *am* the poor relative. And yes, I am a dreamer; but there are many dreamers in the world, and they make good and prosperous lives for themselves, which is what I plan to do.

The activities I enjoy are ones that are not easy to make a living from, but does that mean I should relinquish them? No, instead I have to be more creative in how I go about achieving my goals. I believe that I'm meant to help and inspire people—that much I have learned from this whole experience. Another question is how to integrate all this to include a family of my own. I want it all, and I don't want to compromise one for the other.

I continue to listen for God's direction and feel that I've been given some answers. However, I'm still uncertain about several issues, one being survival jobs. Should I stick with temping, or try to get certified in yoga or Pilates where I can help people incorporate mind, body, and spirit health? Lynn thinks I should consider something in the nursing field, but I don't think I possess the constitution for that since I can't handle blood and gore. I'd probably be great as a social worker or counselor though. There is so much to consider, and I am only thirty-six days posttransplant; so right now, my focus should be on getting well and recovering my strength. And I am gaining strength—I walked about a half a mile today to and from the pharmacy to pick up a prescription.

On a different note, John Kerry announced yesterday that John Edwards will be his running mate. I'm very excited about that though the Republicans are harping on Edwards's lack of experience and his having been a trial lawyer prior to being a senator. Well, their arguments don't hold up for two reasons:

1. George W. Bush was the governor of Texas—he had no national or foreign policy-making experience prior to being elected president in 2000. At least Edwards, a senator, has served on the Senate Intelligence Committee; so he has at least gained national intelligence oversight experience.
2. Trial lawyers help the little people. For example, John Edwards won a $25 million award for a small girl, Valerie Lakey. She had part of her intestines sucked out when a swimming pool drain cover came loose, and she was trapped by the escaping water.[47] This is just one of many cases in which John Edwards has helped others, and I don't believe anyone could consider this a frivolous lawsuit.

July 9, Friday

I drove myself to the clinic this morning. My counts looked okay—the white blood cell count is up to 2.9 from 2.8, hemoglobin fell from 8.6 to 8.5, and platelets are up from 190,000 to 223,000. I feel stronger but still possess quivering hands.

Yesterday, I meditated, read, walked over a mile, and called Joseph. I left a message for him, and he called back about a minute later. He's in Montauk rehearsing a workshop production of a William Saroyan play to be performed this weekend. He returns to Manhattan Sunday. He's going to try to visit me next week.

July 14, Wednesday

Karen arrived last night. We spent the morning drinking coffee and chatting about her new house, my health, and politics.

I have developed a terrible cold as of yesterday. I am sneezing and blowing my nose nonstop. I've gone through one entire box of tissues since about 4:30 a.m. I called the doctor's office about taking cold medication. They thought it would be fine, but being so recently out of transplant, I'm going to hold off taking it unless I really must.

I thought Joseph was going to visit, but I have yet to hear from him. Oh well, I know he's busy; obviously, he has a difficult time fitting me into his schedule.

July 19, Monday

I was rudely awoken at 3:00 a.m. by a creature of some sort scratching and gnawing away at the wood above the ceiling by the bathroom door in my bedroom. It had to have been a squirrel because the noise it produced was quite loud; I can't imagine a mouse making that much of a racket. I kept fearing it would chew through the drywall and poke its head through the ceiling. The noise went on for about forty minutes, which thoroughly annoyed me; I was nearly driven downstairs to sleep on the couch.

Karen has been here almost a week now, and she's been a great help. She's up in the loft, working on the computer, making corrections to her dissertation; so I thought I'd catch up on some journaling. I'm still fatigued but overall, recovering nicely. My cold is almost gone. I have made a list of activities and goals I want to achieve by the end of August. It is always helpful for me to have an outline of some sort to guide me. The outline includes walking several times a week, daily meditation and prayer, daily journal writing, working on roles I would like to perform someday, and practicing vocal exercises to get my singing voice back in shape. Now my body needs to listen to my mind. I'm still having difficulty with that one . . .

Some inspiration from a Believe card:

> *There is always one unexpected little moment in life when a door opens to let the future in.*

> —Graham Greene

I can't say it was a little moment, but I do feel that my experience with cancer over the past seven months has opened the door to my future and forced me to reevaluate my life and my priorities. I am cancer free at the moment. I am healing from the transplant, and though it is a slow process, I feel I've been given a second chance that mustn't be squandered. Life is too precious, and taking it for granted leads to recklessness in behaviors and attitudes. I want to project light and love into the world, not chaos.

July 21, Wednesday

It is now fifty days posttransplant; I'm halfway through the first one hundred days. I still feel very lethargic, and my blood counts continue to rise and fall, but I'm doing well. Karen and I went for a mile-long walk this morning. I must make myself exercise and meditate more often (I've really slacked off on meditating). Both exercise and meditation make me feel physically energized and spiritually renewed.

There is good news to report. On Sunday, July 18, at 4:58 p.m., Emma Marcelline was born. She weighed six pounds fifteen ounces and measured eighteen inches. Kevin called Monday to let me know. He said that Katie's so in love. I can imagine. Congrats to them.

July 26, Monday

Karen left on Friday after my clinic appointment. I told her that she spoiled me. She said that she felt like she didn't do all that much. (She did.) I'm definitely more self-sufficient when no one is here helping me out. It was a good visit, and if I don't see her again before November, I'll see her then when I'm in Cincinnati for Susan and Doug's wedding. Yes, they're getting married, and Susan has asked me to sing during the ceremony.

July 27, Tuesday

Mike phoned this evening. I feel that our cancer battles have brought us closer. This bond has been forged because no one else in our families can understand what we've been through emotionally and physically. He is dealing with chronic pain, a result from all his surgeries, and is in the process of trying to find a solution to manage it. He, Cheryl, and the kids just returned from vacationing in San Francisco and Lake Tahoe. We talked for about twenty minutes, and I told him I'd call when I'm in Cincinnati in November. It'll be nice to spend some time with him and his family.

My clinic appointment today was positive. The white blood count is at 4.2, but my platelets have dropped to 170,000. Dr. Rowley does not seem overly concerned about it though. I had my second lumbar puncture, which was oh so very much fun. Dan was my driver today.

July 31, Saturday

Beginning next week, I only need to go to the clinic once a week. However, I still cannot conquer the fatigue that has been plaguing me. I know recovery takes time, but it's so hard for me to be patient. Practice, practice . . .

Lisa phoned tonight. I had been thinking about calling her today—funny how that happens. She called me from the light booth in the Fifth Third Bank Theater at the Aronoff Center for the Performing Arts (this is the place where she seems to have a free moment). Ovation opened Noël Coward's *Fallen Angels* last night, and Rick at *City Beat* gave it a wonderful review. And even bigger news, Lisa is pregnant! Joshua will be a big brother around February 8, 2005. I know that she's wanted to have another child. So many of my friends are getting married and having children. I'm very happy for them but can't help thinking, "When will it be my turn?" Still, I cannot dwell on what's missing in my life but rather be thankful for what I do have because I have so much more than many people in this world.

Aidan spent the night with his grandparents last night and was gone all day today. I really miss him when he's gone; I miss our playtime. He loves to take off my hats and put them on his head—he looks so cute in them. Then he'll pat my bald head and sometimes even tries biting it, but I put a stop to that. He's insatiably curious, knows exactly what he wants, likes everything to be in its proper place, and is a loving, high-spirited child. He's adding more words to his vocabulary: bye, hi, dog, duck, bottle, bubbles, horse, mama, dada, and hot, to mention a few. He may not be able to speak very well, but he definitely understands what you say to him. When you ask him to, he'll wipe up spills, throw away garbage, and fetch objects. Aidan has brought so much joy into my life at this difficult juncture, and I know his presence in my life has helped raise my spirits and made me fight harder to conquer this illness—I don't want him to grow up without me.

Tomorrow is August, and seven months of 2004 are gone. Sometimes, it seems I've been dealing with this illness forever; other times, it seems as though I was diagnosed yesterday. It has been quite a journey, and it's not over yet, and perhaps it never should be. I want to be healthy, strong, and living life fully again, but I don't want to forget the lessons.

August 1, Sunday

Fatigue and lack of motivation have been my constant companions for two months now. I suppose some degree of indolence is to be expected after a bone marrow transplant. My mind says "write" or "exercise," but my body refuses. At this moment, my body is winning that tug-of-war.

I've also been mulling over my acting goals. Do I still want to pursue an acting career? Do I want to stay in New York or return to Cincinnati? Am I ready to give up the dream? When I consider relinquishing my dreams of an acting career, I cringe. I love creating characters and performing. Right now, the biggest hindrance to my being a really wonderful actor is my self-consciousness, which inhibits any actor's full potential. I'm good, but I could be so much better if I could get past this obstacle. This self-consciousness stems from my desire to please, to be applauded and praised, and it prevents me from taking risks and making bolder choices in my acting. The concern with how others are responding to my performance blocks my freedom to create and sometimes interferes with my concentration in the moment. Worrying about how my work is being received is a colossal waste of time. I find that this self-consciousness is more prevalent in auditions or classes than in actual performances.

This need for approval must be eliminated. First and foremost, I should pursue my acting, or any creative endeavor, because I am compelled to do it and enjoy it. I do the work because I find a compelling story or a fascinating character to which I'm drawn. My focus should be on being the best performer I can for me, not for critics or auditors.

Acting opportunities, particularly good ones that pay, have been difficult for me to find here in New York; however, I must continue to seek them or create them if I continue on this path. I've created opportunities before; I can do it again. I've allowed New York to intimidate me a little, and I can't allow that to continue. I may not possess an MFA in acting from Harvard, Yale, or Julliard, nor do I have Broadway, Off-Broadway, or major film and TV credits, but I am talented. I've performed some very challenging roles quite successfully. I even gave a private performance for Pulitzer Prize-winning playwright Lanford Wilson of his one-woman play *The Moonshot Tape*, which he thoroughly enjoyed and for which he gave highly positive feedback. I need someone to give me a break and take a chance on me. I worked on *Ed*, *Sex and the City*, and an Oxygen network movie the month before I got sick. I know it was only background work, but I secured those jobs myself, without an agent, through perseverance—repeatedly sending out mailings to casting directors.

The bottom line is that I intend to live a creative life and earn a living doing it. Acting, singing, and writing seem so easy for some people; but I've always found these very challenging fields to break into. I have to conclude that I'm not very skilled at networking. It is imperative that my work be seen and that I meet the right industry people, so savvier marketing skills must be developed.

On a different note, my biggest fear for the future is not having financial security. I have no money right now. I want my own apartment, preferably in or close to the city, but sufficient money must be available to rent in those areas.

Perhaps at some point, I'll tire of the rat race here and move to a more serene locale. But until that day comes, I feel the need to give 110 percent to my goals. Yes, my plans were interrupted when I got cancer, but I was fortunate to be living here where I was placed in the hands of an excellent oncologist. My doctors and Barbara have given me back my life, and that life comes with responsibilities. There are dreams and goals to be fulfilled, and I plan to do just that.

August 2, Monday

I started working with *The Artist's Way* by Julia Cameron again yesterday. The book is filled with inspirational quotes, exercises to spark creativity, and suggestions for putting your goals into action. My artistic enthusiasm must be rekindled. I believe God granted me these talents to utilize, and not to do so would be akin to rejecting the Creator's wishes.

I have felt very achy today—mostly in my lower back, my left side, and my hands. I'll be sure to tell Dr. Rowley about this tomorrow. It's probably nothing, but then again, it could be something. I didn't think leukemia was a realistic diagnosis last December, but it turned out to be. One never knows . . .

August 5, Thursday

I hardly slept at all last night. I was awake from 10:00 p.m. until almost 4:00 a.m. This inability to sleep is frustrating. Sleep is when the body's cells repair themselves. I'm so tired of tossing and turning night after night after night. Sleeping pills don't even help. I'm sleep deprived and sluggish in the morning. Consequently, I find myself lying around all day watching TV. I feel like I'm wasting my days, and that frustrates me. Or perhaps, more accurately, I am allowing my body the rest it needs. There is still much healing to be done, so I must be patient.

Because of my laziness, I'm not doing anything productive, and my productive nature berates this idleness. This sluggishness and loss of energy is, in part, due to lack of sleep; but if sleeping aids don't help, I don't know what else to do. Exercise? Yeah, if I can get my behind off the sofa. It really is exasperating when the mind tells you to do something but the body refuses.

So it was another melancholy day for me. What is my problem? Where is my fighting spirit? I feel as if I'm treading water in the middle of the ocean without any rescue in sight. The transplant has been successful so far, which should make me feel elated; instead, I feel disheartened.

To add to my depression, Karen called this morning and told me that she is pregnant—about thirteen weeks along. I am thrilled for her and Jeff, but once again, I can't help feeling sorry for myself. I'm going to write this down, and then I'm going to try to forget it: Friends are getting married; friends and sisters are having babies. And what do I get? I get cancer. It infuriates me! My life is on hold for a freaking year due to developing leukemia. I feel like such a whiner, but at the same time, I've had a hellish experience. However, it is time to get back on track without resenting the good fortune of others. I am happy for my sisters and friends; I'm just incredibly sad for myself.

Another downer is that I will miss my twenty-year high school class reunion next weekend. Last summer, I was so looking forward to it, and it was still a year away. At thirty-eight, I still look pretty good though I'd look a lot better with hair and smooth skin; but even bald and scaly, I don't look terrible—though I do have bags under my eyes. Ah well, the ravages of life.

Hopefully, by writing all these negative thoughts out on paper, I can put them into perspective. I need to start meditating again on a regular basis because I'm forgetting to live in the moment.

August 6, Friday

Many thoughts have been running through my mind today. One of them is where I'm eventually going to live and how this could affect my health insurance coverage. If I live in New York and change to a New York individual plan, will I be able to retain my current physicians? Does my insurance carrier have individual health plans in New York? What would those premiums be? I have at least three more years of follow-up visits to my oncologist, so health care must be taken into consideration when contemplating a move. It's dreadful to be consumed by these concerns, but they are a part of my reality, and they deserve serious consideration because I refuse to put my health in jeopardy.

On the other hand, I don't want my health issues to prevent me from pursuing or accomplishing my goals. The health issues can guide my decisions but not dictate them.

The bottom line is that I need money. Money is the key, and I hate that because my life has never been about the pursuit of money. However, to live and survive in this area of the country, one needs a significant amount of it. This is why I find myself thinking about leaving for a place where I don't need as much in my financial coffers. But this is defeatist thinking, and I'm selling myself short. If others can make enough money to live here, then surely, I can too. I'm not an idiot, but I do need more confidence in my ability to provide for myself. I need to trust that all will be well. Life is unpredictable—I know that all too well. But that can't stop me from living each day to the fullest, loving people, taking chances, and fulfilling my potential. As my favorite saying goes, "Leap and the net will appear!"

August 7, Saturday

My handwriting remains indecipherable. This shakiness is so annoying. I am dealing with several physical aggravations at the moment. My skin is still dry and flaky. I have small bumps on my forehead around the hairline, on my neck by the right ear, and on my nose. Exfoliating does not help smooth the skin; in fact, I think exfoliating is making it worse. I feel helpless to correct these epidermal problems. Perhaps I need to see a dermatologist, but the last thing I want to do is see another doctor.

In addition to my skin issues, I am cold. I loathe being cold. I alleviate the chill by soaking in a steamy tub, but the minute I get out to dry off, I'm cold again. Even when it's eighty degrees outside, if I'm in the shade, I'm wrapped in a shawl or a blanket. The chill can't be assuaged.

On a positive note, my hair is beginning to grow back. I still look bald; however, if I look closely in the mirror, I can see new follicles coming in, and I can feel them—they're very soft. I thought my scalp would feel prickly.

Barbara is officially on maternity leave. Right now, she is making breakfast. I can tell she is tired. The baby could come at any time; then Dan and I will have to help out more around here. I hope Aidan deals well with having a little brother. It'll be a big change. Aidan is the center of our world, and he's used to receiving all the attention. It will be interesting to see how receptive he is to the baby.

August 8, Sunday

It was another sleepless night of tossing and turning. It's so irritating. Am I not tired, or do I have too many thoughts circling around in my brain? Despite my lack of sleep, I found the energy to do a bit of work today.

I pulled some plays from boxes in the basement because I want to work on some roles even though I won't be performing them. I feel this will help keep my acting chops sharp. I selected *The Homecoming* and *The Lover*, both by Harold Pinter, *The Blue Room* by David Hare, *War* by Bill Bozzone, and *A Streetcar Named Desire* by Tennessee Williams. I had been working on Williams's character Blanche DuBois in class last December before I got sick. These are plays and characters I am attracted to for various reasons, mainly because the roles are complex, some even a bit unsavory and far removed from my puritanical sensibilities. And what actor doesn't thrive on playing roles completely different from their own personality, pretending to be someone else?

August 9, Monday

The critter is back. Egad, at 4:45 a.m.! I heard it scratching and gnawing on the ceiling by the bathroom door in my bedroom (same location as before).

I fear this annoying nighttime intruder is going to chew or scratch through the wood and drywall and topple into my bedroom. Should this happen, I'm sure the animal would be as terrified of me as I would be of it. The thought of me coming face-to-face in my room in the middle of the night with a squirrel or, God forbid, a possum or other rodent kind of makes me laugh; that scenario would likely occur in an absurd comedy.

I'll tell Barbara and Dan about it again. I've told them several times about these occurrences, but they seem to think it's not a big deal. I can't help thinking that this animal is, or could be, doing some major structural damage to the house. Oh well, all I can do is report these occurrences; any action taken, or not, is up to the homeowners.

August 11, Wednesday

I feel so lethargic. I haven't been eating much lately either. I ingest only a few bites of food, then feel the urge to regurgitate, so I am consuming about half of what is put on my plate. This morning, while I was standing by the counter, spreading butter on a piece of toast, I broke out in a cold sweat and had to sit down. It was as if the act of standing was draining me of strength. I was starting to feel better a few days ago, but now I sense the onset of stomach problems.

Yesterday, I nearly passed out after my lumbar puncture. It was so painful. Oh, when will all the discomfort cease?

August 12, Thursday

I have felt really lousy the past couple of days. Nausea, accompanied by increasing fatigue, started Monday night—I threw up after dinner. I am so frustrated. I feel like at this point, after seventy days, that I should be doing better than I am, that my counts should be higher than they are, and that I should have more energy. I know the healing process takes time, but I long to feel like my old self again.

I may have caught a virus of some sort that my body is fighting off. I have had very little appetite, but because of all the medications I'm ingesting, I feel the need to eat—even if only small portions because I fear my stomach will experience even more turmoil if I take the pills without food. I must stop complaining and focus on the positive.

August 13, Friday

Tonight is my high school class reunion. It saddens me to miss it. I really would've liked to have seen my classmates.

My hair is just beginning to grow back—all over too, not just on my head. This means that I'll be shaving, plucking, and waxing again soon. I have to admit it was kind of nice not having to worry about performing these grooming rituals on a regular basis.

I'm not sure why I was feeling sickly the past few days. I never broached this with the doctor. If I start feeling worse, I'll call him; for now, I'll ride it out because I do feel better.

August 15, Sunday

So much has happened since the last entry. The most important event: Andrew Daniel came into the world at 2:27 a.m., August 14. He weighed six pounds fifteen ounces and measured nineteen inches long. He looks like Aidan did when he was born—the same eyes, nose, mouth, and coloring. Andrew is a little shorter and a tiny bit heavier than Aidan was at birth, but he's just as adorable. He was all of twelve hours old when I met him. I'm so blessed to be here for his birth.

Barbara and Andrew are doing well and will be home later today. Eleonore picked up Aidan yesterday morning to stay with her and Russ and will return him later today so that he can meet his little brother.

I stayed with Aidan Friday night when Barbara and Dan left for the hospital. Dan had attempted to put Aidan to sleep, but he continued to cry after they left. About fifteen minutes later, I went upstairs to comfort him. He had pooped, so first, a diaper change was in order. I'm not really supposed to change diapers due to my compromised immune system, but I wasn't going to let the child sleep in a poop-filled diaper. He was so good for me while I changed him. I made a game out of it, so it went smoothly. Then he started crying again.

It was quite upsetting to him when he realized Mommy and Daddy were not home. He loves me, but I'm not his parents. It breaks my heart when he cries "Mommy, Mommy" over and over, and when that doesn't produce results, he cries "Dada." All I could do was hold him, comfort him, and ultimately distract him, which I accomplished with milk and books. We sat downstairs on the couch and looked through some of his picture books. Finally, he was tired, and he pointed upstairs.

"Are you ready for sleepy?" I asked.

He nodded, so I carried him upstairs. Then he pointed to his parents' room. "Do you want to sleep in Mommy and Daddy's bed?" I asked.

Again, he nodded, so I put him in their bed and climbed in next to him. He was asleep almost immediately. I, on the other hand, was awake until Dan returned home at 4:00 a.m. Every sound or movement Aidan made caught my attention. I watched him sleeping—he looked so beautiful and peaceful. Once Dan was home, I went to my room and let him be with his son.

Thank God I felt so much better yesterday and today. I have my energy and motivation back, and it feels good. I finished the laundry this morning and also emptied the dishwasher. The house is in good shape for Barbara's return. Also, I have been working with *The Artist's Way*.

I tend to return to that book often. It really is my inspiration for living a creative life. I would love to someday meet Julia Cameron and let her know how much of an influence her writing has been on me.

And . . . I slept last night. I think I actually slept eight hours straight, which I haven't done in months. That's why I feel so rejuvenated.

10:00 p.m.

Well, Aidan loves his little brother; he always wants to hug and touch Andrew. I snapped some adorable photos of Aidan holding Andrew as they sat on the couch. Little Andrew didn't know what to make of all the attention. I hope Aidan continues to feel good about having a baby brother.

August 16, Monday

It's another rainy day. Aidan is at day care, and Barbara and Dan are both sleeping—it's almost 11:00 a.m. Barbara told me that she slept maybe one hour last night. Poor thing . . .

Today's reflections/thoughts focus on appreciating my body (I haven't done this in a while): I feel stronger and more energetic than I have in a while. I have gained a new respect and appreciation for my body—how it works, its strengths, its weaknesses. We need to lovingly care for our bodies and not abuse them. I will continue to respect my body by not smoking, cutting down on alcohol consumption, exercising more, meditating, and eating healthfully. One can only abuse the body for so long before it starts failing. Once you've dealt with cancer, you realize that no body is invincible and that illness can happen. We cannot always prevent illness, but we can take measures to ensure we stay as healthy as possible. *Never* take the body for granted. I won't ever again.

August 17, Tuesday

What is on today's agenda? There is an ongoing medical charge that must be resolved. I've been told by my insurance carrier that it is being paid; however, yesterday, I received a collection notice regarding it, and receiving collection notices makes my blood boil. If I'm supposed to pay the damn thing, I will, but I've been informed I am not responsible for it—several times. I'm trying to keep this in perspective because in the scheme of life, this is a minor irritation. I will try to resolve it in a calm, cool manner. All will be well.

8:30 p.m.

I had the opportunity to help someone again today. Carol called and asked me if I'd talk to a friend of hers who is contemplating a bone marrow transplant. None of her siblings are a match, so they have to find a nonrelated donor. I told Carol that I'd be glad to speak with her.

Debra called almost immediately after I'd left a message for her, and we spoke for about twenty minutes. I shared my experience, why I decided to undergo transplant, explained how my recovery period was progressing, and how I have dealt with any complications. By the end of our conversation, she said that I had given her much hope. I told her that I would definitely recommend transplant. She was told that her blood cancer is one that would not be cured unless she had a transplant (I was told the same thing), so of course, I think transplant is a no-brainer. I told her if she needed or wanted to talk to me again to call anytime. Helping people is so gratifying.

August 19, Thursday

I was sickly again yesterday. I returned home from the clinic with the urge to throw up. I hadn't eaten anything all day, so all I did was dry heave. I despise that feeling. Once again, I found myself lying around the remainder of the day, doing nothing productive.

I was disheartened by my blood count results. The white blood cell count was 3.3, hemoglobin was 9.0, and platelets were 150,000. Everything has decreased. I want to see the counts rise and stay up. I know that I should be encouraged because I've had no blood products since leaving the hospital in late June. I am thankful for that, but at the same time, I want the healing process to move along more quickly. My impatience is surfacing. I know six to twelve months is the normal healing period for a bone marrow transplant patient, and I am not even three months out of transplant.

I just want my life back. I want to work and earn money, go out and play with my friends, dance, dine in restaurants, eat sushi, and drink wine. Be patient, Deb, it'll all happen again.

August 20, Friday

It's unbelievable to me how many young people get cancer. Diane, a childhood neighborhood friend who is Barbara's age, has been tentatively diagnosed with multiple myeloma. Multiple myeloma is another type of blood cancer, cancer of the plasma cell.

My heart goes out to her because I know the fear and sadness she is experiencing right now. However, unlike me, she has a little girl to care for and protect, which must compound her stress. A hospital in Arkansas is supposed to be the best facility to deal with her type of cancer, yet her insurance company will not approve her to be treated there. Mom said that the employees at Branchville Training Center, where Diane and Dad both work, are trying to raise money for her by organizing car washes and a dance. I wish I had money to send. I mailed a card to her today to let her know that if she needed to talk, I was available.

August 22, Sunday

I continue to experience bodily discomfort and annoyances. For instance, the skin on my nose is so rough. I have been exfoliating it and putting lotion on it, but neither seems to help. I hope I can alleviate this coarseness because makeup looks terrible on skin that is not smooth.

There has been some pretty intense tingling in my toes, and last night, it was extremely painful. I was lying in bed, and my feet felt like they were on fire. I rubbed them for a while, and that seemed to help, but this tingling sensation has been persistent for several weeks now. It doesn't appear to be GVHD because there is no redness, rash, or itching, just a tingling sensation. I have a doctor's appointment Tuesday, so I'll be sure to mention it.

August 25, Wednesday

I'm sleep deprived again, which greatly affects my energy level. This is disheartening because Monday, I felt wonderful.

Marni visited this evening. She gave me some information about low-cost housing in New York City, and she insisted on taking photos of me with my current look so that I can get back into acting now. (Actors need to look like their headshots; otherwise, casting directors get upset.) Listening to her acting stories and adventures sparked my desire to audition again. I can't help but be moved to action by her—what an inspiration.

August 27, Friday

Yesterday, I received a large envelope from Lynn containing messages from some of my high school classmates. At the class reunion, she had set up a box in which people could place written notes to me, and some people even gave money (although no names were attached to the cash, so I don't know whom to thank). Plus she enclosed a program from the reunion, so I have everyone's home and e-mail addresses. I'll send e-mail thank-you notes to everyone who wrote to me. I was particularly blown away by a nice message I received from John, my grade school nemesis who used to call me Swig. I detested that name and at the time, him too. I guess this demonstrates how much we mature as we age. Anyway, it was very sweet of him to think of me.

Five more days until the catheter comes out. Now I need to figure what to do with the remaining supplies, mostly syringes and caps from Chartwell and Corum, as well as how to dispose of the biohazard waste I've collected. There are three Neulasta shots in the refrigerator, and because I no longer need them, I want to donate them to the hospital if possible. Because these injections are so expensive, it seems unthinkable to toss them in the garbage without seeing if they could be of use to uninsured or underinsured cancer patients.

The antifungal research drug protocol ends September 9. However, the researchers will continue to monitor me over the next year. Also, the doctors will start weaning me off Prograf over the next six months.

Inspiration for the day:

> Dream card:
> *Dream lofty dreams, and as you dream, so shall you become.*
>
> —James Allen

> Bliss card:
> *If it's not fun, why do it?*
>
> —Jerry Greenfield

Life should not be lived in drudgery. We should make the most of every day. Find those activities we enjoy and that enrich our lives and pursue them. Life should be a daring adventure, whether we are embracing dreams and goals, spending time with loved ones, or serving others and God. Even though I've been living more in the present moment and trying to fill my time productively, I feel some stagnation. Unfortunately, when a person's life starts revolving around doctor's visits and hospital stays, interacting with the outside world kind of comes to a halt. It's definitely been a challenge, but now I am daring to dream again and plan for my future.

Yet while I am planning and dreaming, I am attempting to live in and enjoy the present. It's so important to live in the now because it is all we have. The past and the future are merely illusions, and remaining attached to the past or future will cause nothing but suffering. Dream dreams, but remember to live in the moment. I must remember all this because I am a bundle of contradictions these days—one minute, immersed in the present; the next minute, dreaming of the future. I was going to say that I needed to find a balance between the two, but I think it will prove more beneficial to grant more weight to living in the moment.

August 28, Saturday

I know that Barbara and Dan are worn-out. The kids are a lot of work and need much attention, especially Andrew. But I really get offended when I try to help or offer to help, and snappish or halfhearted replies are what I receive in return. I am trying to do as much as I can to help out around here by unloading and loading the dishwasher, emptying the garbage, entertaining Aidan, watching Andrew, or cleaning up after meals when I feel well; but I still get the impression they think I don't do anything. I shouldn't take this personally, but at times, I feel underappreciated for my efforts. The last thing I intend to do is be a lazy moocher while I am living here. I want to help out because they have done so much for me. Right now, my feelings are a bit hurt.

At least it's a sunny, warm Saturday afternoon. I am sitting on the deck, doing some reading and writing. It's a bit warm for the rest of the family, but because I am always cold, the warmth feels heavenly. Aidan, Andrew, and Barbara are napping; Dan is reading on the couch in the living room. I don't always know how to react to Barbara's or Dan's moods, so I am staying out of their way and giving them some space.

On a happier note, yesterday, I received a video from Maria. She had made it during the class reunion. Not only were there several messages from classmates, but she also filmed general shots of people meandering about, mingling and talking. A message that particularly touched my heart was from Dave, my senior prom date, with whom at one time, I had a very close friendship; unfortunately, we've drifted apart over the years. Dave was also my escort when I was crowned Basketball Homecoming Queen. His lovely message made me cry. He said,

> Hey, Deb, I don't know if you can hear me. [There was much noise in the background.] We're having a great time, just started. But we really, really are thinking about you and wishing you were here.
>
> And just on a personal note, I haven't written or sent a card. It's been really hard. I don't know what to say. I'm just going to say it this way. I love you—we all do. You're strong, and you can get through this. And we *will* see you at our next reunion. We're counting on that. And I hope to see you in town soon. See ya.

At the end of the video, Maria had taped her children. Olivia sang a song for me; then Eliza danced in a circle with a doll. Nathan sat on the couch next to Olivia, who pointed out that his shoes were on the wrong feet. It was very cute, and the kids are just gorgeous—all that white blond hair. To finish the video, Maria recorded the following message:

> Hey, Deb, I hope you enjoyed the tape. I had a lot of fun making it for you. I hope you're feeling better, and we hope to see you soon. I love you. Bye-bye.

This video is special to me, and it is a reminder of how very fortunate I was to grow up in a small town in southern Indiana surrounded by true friends. I intend to attend my twenty-five-year class reunion.

The last gift I received relating to the reunion was a class photo. This was taken and sent to me from a photographer who used to work with Mom at the *Perry County News*. The notes Lynn collected, Maria's video, and this photo all made me feel as if I had been there celebrating with my classmates.

September 2, Thursday

On Tuesday, the catheter was removed. I'm still sore in the area of my upper chest where Dr. Klein had to pry the tube loose because tissue inside my body had grown around the line. This is not unusual when a catheter has been in place for an extended period of time, and mine was in for about seven months, from January 20 until August 31. I was very lucky that I experienced no complications or infections with the catheter. Many people do experience problems. When this happens, the catheter has to be removed, the infection treated, and the line reinserted.

Yesterday, I had terrible diarrhea, which hasn't improved any today. Between my digestive problems and continued lack of sleep, I'm quite frustrated.

Karen and Jeff will be visiting Saturday. They are driving from Pennsylvania where they are spending Labor Day weekend with Jeff's sister Cindy and her family. Karen has been suffering from nausea lately. Hopefully, once she's past her first trimester, the nausea will subside.

September 3, Friday

I spoke with Diane. It's confirmed: she has multiple myeloma. She will be treated at Vanderbilt Medical Center in Nashville. She goes there for a consultation next Wednesday. I will keep her in my thoughts and prayers.

September 6, Monday

Karen and Jeff's visit was quite enjoyable. They were only here for the afternoon, but in that time, Andrew provided Karen with ample baby-handling practice. She and Jeff have accepted the role of his godparents. Andrew's christening is going to be scheduled for a Sunday in October. We spent the afternoon hanging out by the pool at Russ and Eleonore's residence. Jeff also presented a get-well card to me from his niece Devon. What a sweet and caring little girl.

This is my fifth day experiencing diarrhea. I'll definitely have to inform Dr. Rowley of this tomorrow, which is the last time I see him. Going forward, I return to Dr. Goldberg's office for all subsequent visits.

I've been confining myself to my room in the hopes that my absence will make life a bit easier for Barbara and Dan. I try to be as helpful as possible, but when it comes to the children, I only want to help when I'm asked. Otherwise, I feel as though I'm infringing on or, rather, interfering with their parental obligations and desires.

I think my presence here is beginning to wear on Dan's nerves. I'm trying to figure out how to exist within this household without intruding on their family time. I think, realistically, I might be able to move out in March. Meanwhile, I am planning to be gone from September 28 to October 6, November 11-29, and then three weeks in December. The time away will give them a reprieve from my presence.

I'm trying not to take their foul moods personally. When both children are crying or fussy, there is a good deal of tension. At those times, I tend to escape to my room so as not to be in the way. That's cowardly, I know; but escaping the unpleasantness is my way of avoiding conflict, which, in Buddhist philosophy, one should not do. Aversion causes suffering. Sharon Salzberg writes in *Insight Meditation* that we can free ourselves from suffering "by recognizing and acknowledging the unhappiness and dissatisfaction in our own lives and those of the people and other beings around us." She continues, "The appropriate response to suffering is awareness and compassion, always."[48] I am aware and trying to be compassionate, but for some reason, I am resisting reaching out . . .

September 9, Thursday,
Day 100 posttransplant

To celebrate my one hundred days posttransplant, Barbara, Andrew, and I had lunch at Johnny Carino's, a country Italian restaurant. It was enjoyable dining out once again.

Tomorrow, I'm going to download the low-cost housing applications that Marni told me about and research other housing options as well. I'd like to get those applications out by the end of this month. Who knows, maybe I will be eligible.

All in all, it was a good day though I'm still experiencing gastrointestinal problems . . .

September 10, Friday

The scars on my chest where the catheter had been placed are looking good. I may or may not buy Mederma patches. It's rather odd, but I don't want to erase these scars—they're my battle wounds, and I want to remember what I went through and how I grew emotionally and spiritually. Some people want to forget the experience, but I've never been one to forget *any* experience, no matter how good or bad. Our experiences, both positive and negative, are the sum of who we are. I can no more forget about leukemia than I can forget about Robert* or Scott* or being a track star or homecoming queen or performing for Lanford Wilson. These are all aspects of who I am, and I won't expunge them from my existence. I may forgive past hurts and refuse to dwell on them, but they're never forgotten. And why should I? They've made me stronger.

* See "Forgiveness: Letting go of the Past" (April 4 entry)

September 11, Saturday

On this day, every year since 2001, a deep sadness consumes me. It has been three years now since that fateful day, and those horrific events remain vividly etched in my mind. I was glued to my television for days, watching in disbelief as rescue-and-recovery attempts were made and as volunteers poured into New York City, Washington DC, and Shanksville, Pennsylvania. At any given moment, enormous grief and overwhelming emotion would swell up inside of me and have to be released, usually by shedding tears.

I also watched in horror as some in the Muslim world celebrated the attacks on the World Trade Center and the Pentagon. (I would never cheer the murder of other human beings, not even Osama bin Laden himself; though I do understand a little bit—being aware of damaging past and present U.S. foreign policy decisions—as to why they were cheering, still, this behavior reeks of callous disregard for human life and is destructive to human relationships across cultures, nationalities, and religions.)

How can those of us all over the world who truly value human rights and human dignity and who respect others' differences create sane societies out of this madhouse the world has become? Sometimes, all of this is very disheartening, and the Western world is not guiltless in atrocities committed against mankind. None of us is innocent. Okay, my preaching is finished for now.

September 14, Tuesday

Marni was here yesterday to take my headshots. I dropped off the film last night. It was very kind of her to make the trip out to see me when she is so busy getting moved out of her apartment and ready for her job in Atlanta (she leaves Thursday). She even took some photos of me holding Andrew, which will be very maternal looking I'm sure. The funny thing is that I can be quite maternal, and I seem to be more so as I age.

Today's thoughts turn to the people I've chosen to be in my life: When I look at the people I've chosen to be in my life, they are reflections of me. They reflect my values, hopes, spirituality, and compassion. These are people who enhance my life, they make me a better person, they keep me on track with my goals and life choices, and they set me straight when I get out of line or need a good kick in the pants. I have eliminated those from my life that don't enrich it somehow. Negative people bring me down. I don't like gossip, insecurity, and discouragement because I live in possibilities. If I feel something can be achieved, I'm going to try it. I have my fears and imperfections, as do my friends. We help fight those fears and imperfections by supporting and encouraging one another to reach our full potential.

September 16, Thursday

My CBC results yesterday were as follows: white blood count is 5.8 (2.8 last week), hemoglobin is 10.7 (10.4 last week), and platelets are 223,000 (181,000 last week). I am also now 100 percent donor bone marrow, which means Barbara's stem cells have completely replaced mine—amazing!

I broached the subject of the tingling in my toes and was informed that this is referred to as neuropathy, which is a common side effect of chemotherapy—most likely from the vincristine. Neuropathy is nerve damage that can cause tingling in the extremities; I've experienced a bit of this in my fingertips too. This sensation may eventually subside or persist indefinitely.

I don't have to return to HUMC until October 7, so I'm free for three weeks. I'm also going to track my bowel movements and diet over the next several weeks. If my system is still out of whack, the doctors can see the pattern and decide what we need to do—for example, get a stool sample to test for infection and/or have a colonoscopy to check for GVHD. I'll do what I have to do although the last thing I want is someone sticking a probe up my rear. However, I will not bury my head in the sand and ignore this situation because it could be GVHD; if not treated, GVHD can be fatal. I refuse to ignore this the way I ignored the bruising on my legs last December.

September 19, Sunday

It is such a gorgeous day out. I definitely must go for a walk, maybe even do walking meditation. I haven't done that in a while.

I attempted to meditate three days ago and failed miserably. My back was aching, and I couldn't ignore the pain; my mind was racing with plans for the future, and then my cell phone rang, so I gave up. It was a futile exercise. I've really been quite consumed with planning for my future and not living in the now.

I'm considering going into the city sooner than I'd planned, maybe Thursday. Beckie and Nelson will be out of town, but they've offered their apartment to me on several different occasions in the past when they've been gone, so I may take them up on it. I feel the need to get out of Dodge. Dan needs a break from me, I think, and twelve days apart will do our relationship some good though I hope my absence is not too much of a hardship on Barbara because she can use the additional help.

September 21, Tuesday

I have decided not to flee to Manhattan this weekend. Dan and I had a really good conversation Sunday afternoon and came to an understanding. There has been tension between us lately because I felt he was nitpicking at me over my assigned chores while he felt I was failing to achieve a goal he had set to help Barbara. I've always tried to get as much done in the house as I can before Barbara and Dan arrive home each evening, but I still don't feel well much of the time, so I may not get everything accomplished. In fact, there are many days that I am still extremely tired. The tension between Dan and me was due to miscommunication.

The following is what transpired over the weekend. Friday evening, Dan came home from work and saw Barbara sitting on the living room floor folding clothes while I was on the couch watching TV. Andrew was sleeping. I had not had a chance to empty the trash yet, and Dan made a snide comment about it. I snapped a sarcastic comment back to him though I don't recall what it was. After that exchange, he gave me the cold shoulder all weekend. Finally, Sunday, he decided to talk to me. I was glad he did because it clarified his situation and brought many things of which I was unaware to light.

Dan prefaced our discussion by expressing his frustration with hearing Barbara complain all the time about being tired. Crying, she has called him at work to come home to help her because she was so exhausted. I had no idea any of this was happening. I'll admit I can be a bit oblivious, but I really thought I was helping out as much as I could. Anyway, Friday, when he came home and saw me on the couch while Barbara was working, that was the last straw; he was furious, and rightly so from his perspective. I had actually done some work earlier in the day, but of course, he wasn't there at the time to see it. Also, I was not feeling well later in the afternoon, so I was resting.

He shared with me that his goal, by assigning me chores, had been to force Barbara to get some sleep. She is going through a tough time because she is not getting sufficient rest. Night and day, she is trying to fulfill the needs of her children as well as tend to all the household tasks and in the meantime, wearing herself out. I knew she was tired, but I didn't know the extent to which she was feeling depleted of energy. She never complained to me or asked me for additional help. But that's Barbara. (Hmmm . . . sounds a lot like Mom, Karen, and me.)

Dan said that he was not intentionally trying to be a jerk to me by his insinuations regarding the quality of the household tasks that I was doing or not doing. However, he admitted to not being specific as to what his goals were in asking me to do these chores. Because of this miscommunication, I thought he was sick of my presence in his home and was being mean to drive me out. This tension between us had built up over the past few weeks, and I think my anxiety about the situation exacerbated my gastrointestinal problems.

I don't deal well with unconstructive criticism or faultfinding on a daily basis ("nagging" is what Dan called it, which made me laugh). I'm not equipped to deal with it. I either get my feelings hurt, or I get resentful and spiteful—neither of which are acceptable reactions. I'm glad we had this discussion, and taking Dan's perspective into consideration, he had every right to be upset. I will try harder to be more aware of what needs to be done and take more initiative helping out. It's the least I can do considering all they've done for me. We ended our conversation with hugs and an "I love you."

Now the air is clear, and interactions are good. We had a productive day yesterday, and I believe everyone was relatively happy. I need to remember to do little things without having to be asked. Many people turned their lives upside down for me when I was diagnosed. Although I know they don't expect anything in return, I must remember that when I am needed, I have to pull my weight. My family and friends need me as much as I need them.

Autumn begins tomorrow. I've weathered three full seasons since December 18, 2003, and my recuperation has gone quite well in a relatively short amount of time.

September 23, Thursday

It's been a good week except for those lingering gastrointestinal problems. I pray that this is nothing serious. I have had bowel movements anywhere from two to four times a day. It is really disturbing.

Monday, Lani surprised me by driving out here to New Jersey. She had the day off, so she borrowed her band's van. She called me on her way out. I wish more people would be spontaneous with their visits. She arrived around 2:00 p.m., and we sat outside on the deck and talked most of the afternoon. I made lasagna for dinner, and Lani joined us.

I picked up the photos that Marni took. Most of them are actually quite good. The main problem is that there is a shadow over my face in many of them. However, there was one picture in which my eyes really pop on the page. It's very pretty, and my nose looks relatively straight. There are a few little specks on the photo, but I believe those can be retouched. So next week, I will get the headshot made, have about fifty of them reproduced, mail them to casting directors at the network programs here in New York, and see what transpires.

September 29, Wednesday

I've been in the city since yesterday afternoon. It's exhilarating to be here ensconced in the urban hustle and bustle.

Last night, I had a lovely dinner with Jen. It was a birthday celebration. Her husband, Phil, joined us, as well as Karen C. It ended up being a baby celebration too—Jen is pregnant. March 20 is her due date.

We dined at Col Legno, which serves northern Italian cuisine. The food, service, and ambience were all good. The restaurant had a cozy rustic atmosphere. Two of the great joys in life, in my opinion, are having a delicious meal and stimulating conversation with friends. This was the perfect beginning to my city adventure.

Today, I ran a couple of errands. I dropped off the negative at Reproductions to have my headshot copied, then walked to the Actors Federal Credit Union to deposit money into my checking account. After that, I relaxed.

September 30, Thursday

I met Donna D, a cast mate from *Prince Hal*, for lunch. I haven't seen her in a very long time. She looked wonderful. Donna D possesses a serene nature, so she has a very calming effect on people—at least she does on me. We discussed the state of the world, politics, theater, and spirituality. She has been studying various spiritual practices, and I enjoyed listening to her talk about them.

Nelson, Beckie, and I watched the presidential debate this evening. Well, actually, it was more of a presentation than a debate due to all the rules and lack of spontaneity from both camps. Bush performed better than I thought he would, but Kerry consistently looked more confident and even tempered. Bush failed to disguise his disdain and annoyance with certain questions and statements. Kerry received a small bounce in the polls, but the race remains neck and neck. I don't put much faith in the polls anyway because there are numerous ways to manipulate a question to get the desired answer. And who are these pollsters calling anyway? I've never once been contacted by pollsters in the twenty years I've been a registered voter.

October 1, Friday

I had the dreaded yearly gynecological exam this morning—I loathe Pap smears. I not only experience discomfort, but also a great deal of pain. My doctor uses the thin prep pap, which, for my body, is agonizing; for about sixty seconds, I endured excruciating pain.

I really like my gynecologist. She is a kind older woman who's very thorough in exams. Dr. Goldberg instructed me to discuss hormone replacement therapy (HRT) with her due to the possibility that I may experience early menopause (another side effect of chemo and radiation). She didn't want to put me on any type of HRT because of my age, but she said to continue utilizing my birth control pills, which would supply the estrogen my body needs.

After my appointment, I went to a diner located near my doctor's office for breakfast. I called Bobbi, and she met me there. Our waitress gave great service and was so friendly. She helped to turn my day around. Earlier that morning, on the subway, two men were yelling obscenities at each other from opposite ends of the car. Everyone appeared to be ignoring them, but I could sense that everyone was hyperaware of their belligerent exchange. The negative, hostile energy permeating the subway car was so intense that I felt sick upon exiting the train. I wanted so badly to ask these guys if they knew how immature and tacky they sounded. But I knew that if I said anything, they'd probably start attacking me too. So I am grateful to the waitress at the diner because she definitely set a positive tone for the remainder of my day.

Carlos, a friend of Nelson's from Cincinnati, arrived around 5:00 p.m. Later that evening, we went to listen to STARK play at Continental. Lani is such the rocker—she was awesome. She even dedicated a song to me, saying that I inspired it; it's called "This Day." Lani gave me permission to print the lyrics.

This Day

VERSE I
Good deal
As my father would say
In the
Street where we used to play
Big deal
As my mamma would say
We'd starve
While in his arms she would lay
So what
If my hair's dirty today
What if
My dang panties can't stay
Straight up
That was yesterday
So close
Yet so far away

CHORUS
And this day is my ever-y-thing
The day I finally learned how to sing
To-day is my ever-y-thing
Otherwise
I'm nothing

VERSE 2
Hell yeah
Is the expression
BFZ
Has made quite an impression
Oh well
I'll use my sense of humor
Life's short
At least that's the rumor
Sorry
Won't be on my lips
Why me
Just won't factor in
Bite me
Will be one of my quips
Eat me
And my dust you damn wimps 'cuz

CHORUS
And this day is my ever-y-thing
The day I finally learned how to sing
To-day is my ever-y-thing
Otherwise
I'm nothing

BRIDGE
So
Good-bye to tomorrow
Fuck off to yesterday
No time to drown in sorrow
I got bills to pay
Ridin' under the radar
Just lookin' for some love
Stayin' out of the quagmire

So much shit to rise above
But

CHORUS
And this day is my ever-y-thing
The day I finally learned how to sing
To-day is my ever-y-thing
Otherwise
I'm nothing[49]

I love it! These are definitely gritty Lani lyrics. The song says to me: the past is the past, so it doesn't matter, and the future may never come, so make the most of today.

I was standing in the bar, dancing and singing along to the songs that I knew. I watched Lani performing on the stage, then looked at the friends accompanying me, and felt a wave of love and happiness wash over me. I turned to Nelson and said, "This is so amazing being here with you guys and watching a friend perform. Life, at this moment, is perfect." Nelson smiled and hugged me.

After Lani's performance, we headed downtown to a Mexican restaurant. The food was delicious, but since I'd had two Coronas at the bar, I couldn't drink the margarita Nelson had ordered for me. We took a cab back to the apartment because the high-heeled sandals I was wearing were killing my feet. I offered to pay the cab fare; but of course, being gentlemen, neither Nelson nor Carlos would allow it.

October 2, Saturday

We spent the day prepping for the party. When Karen B arrived around 6:00 p.m., she looked great but was emotionally reeling from a frustrating romantic situation, which I don't feel at liberty to reveal. Actually, I thought she seemed to have come to terms with the situation quite well by the time she arrived in New York City.

The party was a blast. My friends that showed up included Jen, who brought her friend Lori (also her publicist), Cristina, and Dan G (Dan G was quite the hit with Nelson, Beckie, and Karen B).

When the evening was winding down and only a few guests were lingering about, we did some dancing. Dan G twirled me around the living room. "You're a dream!" he exclaimed. Those thousands of dollars in dance lessons at Arthur Murray have definitely paid off, and I must admit that I'm pretty darn good at following anyone who leads well. And if they can't lead, I improvise. We all had a grand time and finally fell into bed about 4:00 Sunday morning.

October 3, Sunday

We decided to hang out in Central Park this afternoon since it was such a gorgeous day. We took the subway up to Eighty-sixth Street and walked over to the park. We spread some blankets on the ground and lay down to relax. I had on pants and a large sweater so that the harmful rays of the sun would not touch my skin. I lay down with my face in the shade but allowed my protected torso and legs sun exposure because the warm rays felt so fantastic.

We had to leave around 3:30 p.m. because Carlos had a plane to catch. Beckie and I made a detour to get a cake for Karen B because we were planning to celebrate her birthday, which is October 7, later in the evening. After Carlos departed, we dined at an Indian restaurant. Back at the apartment, we ate cake and ice cream, and Karen B opened her gifts.

October 4, Monday

I had a Pilates class with Beckie this morning. It was so good for me but definitely not easy. It was a challenge focusing on the whole mind-body connection while struggling to get into and maintain a position. But Beckie is an excellent coach, and I felt I did pretty well for my first attempt working with the Pilates machines.

Joseph called. It's been forever since I heard from him. I discovered he has been in Boston taking care of some family issues. He's strong and smart; he'll be fine. However, I will check in on him soon.

October 5, Tuesday

I met Karen B at Joe Allen's for dinner; then we went to the John Golden Theatre to see *Avenue Q*. We laughed through the entire show. When the finale song, "For Now," was sung, it brought tears to my eyes. It seemed so appropriate to my life situation at the moment, and it made me remember that this bout with cancer *is* only for now. Dan G was supposed to go with me. He secured the tickets but at the last minute, was called into a production meeting for a Broadway musical he's working on, so he gave the tickets to me and told me to invite someone else. We had tenth-row seats, stage level with a clear view of the actors and puppets. Karen B and I had considered going out for a drink afterward, but because we were both wiped out from our busy day, we opted instead to head back to the apartment.

October 6, Wednesday

I caught the 1:17 p.m. train out to Far Hills. Barbara was there to pick me up, and Andrew was in his car seat. He had changed so much. He was much more alert than he had been eight days earlier, and his skin now had such beautiful coloring.

About two or three days into my stay in New York City, Nelson asked me if I missed the kids. At that point, I didn't. However, around day 5, I did start missing them. It's curious how those little creatures get under your skin. You miss their smell, their smiles, their cuteness, and even their tantrums. I have treasured this time being a part of their lives. Watching the children grow and evolve has been an extraordinary gift.

October 8, Friday

I've been back in Basking Ridge since Wednesday afternoon. Yesterday was Barbara and Dan's fourth wedding anniversary and Karen B's birthday.

I had a doctor's appointment yesterday. My platelets were 242,000; hemoglobin was 11.2, which is a good result, but my white blood cell count was down to 1.3. The white blood count kind of freaked me out. Dr. Goldberg told me not to be too concerned about it because I'm probably fighting an infection of some sort. However, there was one white blood cell type, eosinophils (there are five different types of white blood cells), that he is going to keep an eye on because it's a little on the high side. A high eosinophil count is common in people with allergies, but it could also be indicative of GVHD. I know that my blood counts are going to bounce around for a while, so I'm resigned to being patient and not fret about it.

I feel great, I have abundant energy, and my bowel movements are starting to normalize. My stay in the city was a much-needed break for me, and I'm sure Barbara and Dan enjoyed the time alone with the boys. Barbara told me that one night, Aidan was mad at both Dan and her, so he was crying out, "Debbie, Debbie." (He knows I'm Deborah, but it's easier for him to say "Debbie.") It's wonderful to be needed.

October 14, Thursday

I received an amazing gift from Aunt Addie and Uncle Al yesterday. Tucked inside the lovely card they sent was a check for $500. I was stunned by their generosity. I will definitely have to make an effort to see them while I'm in Cincinnati.

My casting director mailing is complete, and I plan to send it out today. I also had a clinic appointment today. My white blood count is still low but up to 2.6, hemoglobin is 11.7, and platelets are 263,000. I feel good, I have abundant energy, and the diarrhea is nonexistent.

Before going to bed, I prayed and meditated. It feels good to get back into a spiritual routine, and I've been sleeping so much better, six to seven hours straight.

October 25, Monday

Mom, Dad, Karen, and Jeff left this morning about 6:30. The weekend is over. It was one of the best times we've had as a family in a long time. I don't think there was one altercation. Most of the time, even though we love one another fiercely, we have some sort of blowup over something, especially when the discussion turns political. We've always been good fighters, but that's because we're all so darn opinionated and obstinate.

I'll recount the weekend's highlights. I picked Mom and Dad up at the airport Thursday evening. Barbara and I had been running errands from the time we dropped Aidan off at day care in the morning until about 3:00 p.m. This included a huge grocery run, and we still didn't get everything we needed.

Friday, Dad carved a pumpkin with Aidan. Aidan loves his pumpkin. He says "big pumpkin" with a smile on his face. I caught him many times throughout the weekend standing by the dining room window, gazing at his pumpkin out on the porch.

Unfortunately, Aidan was sick with a sore throat Saturday morning, so Dan took him to the doctor. It's a good thing I'm taking antiviral and antibacterial medications. I know at the moment, they are protecting me from infections, but I hope they're not making my immune system weak. I've always prided myself on rarely being sick.

Later that afternoon, we presented Mom and Dad with their anniversary gift—the video. (October 17 was their fortieth wedding anniversary.) They really enjoyed it though Barbara was a bit disappointed because she expected more of a "wow" reaction. I understand her disappointment because she put so much effort into this project: sifting through photos, organizing them into the correct order, and painstakingly coordinating them with the songs she'd selected. The video is a photo montage set to music. The photos span the forty years that my parents have been married. The first part of the video is set to Kenny Rogers's "Through the Years," then proceeds with "I Could Not Ask for More" by Edwin McCain, and closes with Louis Armstrong's rendition of "What a Wonderful World." The second part is a Christmas segment containing only Christmas photos from the past forty years, which are accompanied by Judy Garland's rendition of "The Christmas Song." The video wraps up with photos of Mom and Dad to the last refrain of "Through the Years." The final image is their wedding photo. Watching the video (and I've viewed it several times) always makes me cry—it's so full of lovely memories.

After watching the video, we played a game of Gender Gap, not a full game because we had to stop to make dinner. When we stopped, the women were defeating the men. Gender Gap is a board game that pits men against women. Women answer questions that men would typically know and vice versa. The questions cover topics such as sports, home improvement, cooking, family, etc. It's quite entertaining.

Barbara, Mom, Karen, and I made our way to the kitchen. We proceeded to make the salads and the broccoli-cauliflower toss while Dan and Jeff tended to the steaks out on the grill. This was an intimate family anniversary celebration dinner. The menu consisted of pear-walnut salad with slivers of parmesan cheese, marinated steaks, crab-stuffed flounder, baked potatoes, a tangy broccoli-cauliflower toss, and bread. For dessert, there was a small chocolate cake with white icing and red roses (fortieth anniversary is the ruby anniversary) and a small cheesecake. We served wine, water, and iced tea with the meal and coffee with dessert.

Barbara created a gorgeous tablescape. She loves entertaining and is quite adept at creating a beautiful spread. A cream-colored lace tablecloth was draped over the dining room table. In the center, she had placed small pumpkins and gourds surrounded by white candles in glass candleholders. She pulled out her china, crystal goblets, and the good utensils. Dark green napkins tied with sheer orange ribbons were placed on our salad plates.

The meal was delicious, and the conversation lively. We didn't finish dinner until almost 11:00 p.m., and by the time we had cleaned up and gotten into bed, it was a little past midnight.

Sunday was Andrew's day—his baptism and party. We were up early, had breakfast, showered, and were off to church. Aidan was still feeling under the weather, and Jeff now had a sore throat and was feeling ill. Dan and Aidan stayed at home during the service but arrived right afterward, in time for the christening ceremony. Jeff dropped off Mom, Dad, and Karen at the church and returned home to get ready for the christening. I drove with Barbara and Andrew to the church.

Immediately following the service, four different families (of the four babies being christened) gathered at the back of the church where the baptismal font is located. Many family members and friends arrived, and once everyone was settled in their seats, the ceremony began. Karen and Jeff are Andrew's godparents. I tried snapping as many photos as possible. This proved to be challenging because the placement of the parents, godparents, and babies around the priest and the baptismal font was neither conducive to taking good pictures nor many pictures. But I did my best.

Afterward, everyone ended up at Eleonore and Russ's home. They had the party catered. It was great to see and catch up with so many people, all of whom are Dan's family and friends who have also become my family and friends. My short hair was a real hit. Donna called it "sexy and sassy."

Aidan seemed to be feeling better because he was running around playing with Zachary (Alyssa's other little brother, Amy and Dave's son) who's a year older than Aidan. The highlight of my day was when Zachary, whom I'd been playing with earlier, walked up to me, motioned for me to bend down to his level, and kissed my cheek. I love little kids—they can be as sweet as they are terrors. We returned home around 6:00 p.m. and spent the evening relaxing.

Oh, my headshots were mailed last Monday, but I haven't heard from any casting directors yet. I really don't expect to be contacted, but one never knows. I remain hopeful . . .

October 26, Tuesday

Rick at *City Beat* has made two complimentary tickets available to me for the Cincinnati Entertainment Awards ceremony, which takes place November 22. He wrote that it might be a good way for me to see many of my Cincinnati theater colleagues and friends. I definitely want to go. Now I have to figure out whom to take with me.

October 28, Thursday

I had a very successful doctor's appointment today. My white blood count is 5.6, hemoglobin is 11.8, and platelets are at 230,000. Dr. Goldberg told me that if he saw these blood counts and didn't know my history, he would not know that I'd had leukemia. He also instructed me to get on with my life. I was walking on air as I left the clinic.

Driving home, I felt a freedom from illness and experienced everything with more intensity—colors, sounds, textures. A sense of well-being and joy flooded over me. It was a gorgeous day, a bit on the cool side; but the sky was a lucid bright blue, and the leaves on the trees were drenched in vibrant autumn colors. It was stunning; the beauty of it all, along with the emotions swelling up inside of me, brought tears to my eyes. I am so grateful for being given a second chance at life. I thank God all the time. It's really quite extraordinary to reflect back on all I've experienced and learned this year. It's not only been difficult for me, but also for my family and friends. I told Barbara today that I don't know what I would've done without her and Dan. She thinks my being around the boys has really helped me. I agree.

October 30, Saturday

Last night, I did metta meditation before climbing into bed. I should do metta more often. It is such a wonderful way to extend love and positive energy out into the world. In today's turbulent world environment, we need more people sending out good vibes and positive energy to everyone inhabiting this planet—especially to political, religious, and military leaders and educators. If more people sent positive thoughts and love out into the world, I'm sure it would be a more pleasant place to live, and there would be far less fear and anger in our hearts. This fear and anger has done nothing but perpetuate violence. There seems to be excessive violence in the world today though from an historical perspective, this violence is hardly unique to our time. However, due to television, the Internet, and the 24/7 reporting of global news events, the planet is a much smaller place than in previous centuries, even previous decades.

Still, it appears that the world community is dangerously spiraling out of control, with fear, ignorance, and hatred inciting people to commit destructive and brutal acts against one another. I know that most people are good, but I find that even civility on the basic level of human interaction is disappearing. People are quite rude and impatient with one another, and I constantly see examples of this unsavory behavior on the highways and in the subway. I'm not rude—at least never intentionally so; I am impatient. I, at least, am aware of every time my impatience surges. Awareness is the first step. The next step is to learn to be calm even when my temper starts to flare up. These are important realizations for me. I must know my weaknesses and flaws before I can alleviate them or, at the very least, bring them under control so that I may cultivate more compassion toward both myself and others.

November 1, Monday

Tomorrow is election day. Hopefully, regardless of who wins the presidency, it will all be over Wednesday morning, and there will be no challenges to vote counts. I don't think I could stomach another debacle similar to that of the 2000 presidential election. I am so tired of all the bickering and name-calling from both sides. Both the Republicans and Democrats are too easily influenced by, and beholden to, corporate America and special interest groups.

There needs to be some new blood with fresh ideas in Congress. Currently, there is no way an Independent or a Libertarian or a Socialist or a Green party or any other alternate party candidate could win. I would like to see the two-party system and the electoral college eliminated. And I believe the popular vote is what should determine the winner, or if that is unacceptable, then electoral votes should be split in each state based on the percentage of popular vote each candidate receives. For example, currently, in each state, if one candidate gets 51 percent and the other receives 49 percent, all the electoral votes go to the candidate with 51 percent, which I believe is unfair and archaic. It would be more representative if the votes were split along the 51/49 percent popular vote results. If a state has ten electoral votes, then the candidate with 51 percent gets 5.1 electoral votes while the candidate with 49 percent receives 4.9 electoral votes. It's not a perfect solution, but it is definitely more representative of the popular vote. Enough about politics . . .

I had a nice surprise today. Kate Martineau, a casting director for *As the World Turns*, called me. I'm booked to do background work on November 10. I mailed eighteen headshots out two weeks ago and received one phone call, which actually isn't a bad result. I may be there all day, or I may be there for only a few hours. I don't want to do a lot of background work, but it is a way to at least get on the set and meet people. Perhaps if they like my attitude and work ethic, they'll call me in at some point to audition for an "under five" (a role with five or less speaking lines) or a day player role, which is what we actors hope for when getting started in the business.

I'm planning to go into the city the night before because my call time at the studio in Brooklyn is 7:30 a.m. It would be nearly impossible in the morning to get to the studio on time from Basking Ridge. It will be fun to be back on a set and in the world of entertainment.

November 3, Wednesday

It appears that President Bush has won another term. To say I'm disappointed is a gross understatement. Ohio is still undecided, but the state is pretty much leaning toward Bush. The Kerry camp hasn't conceded yet because they want the provisional ballots counted, but Bush has 145,000 votes over Kerry in that state, and I doubt that 250,000 provisional ballots will make a difference.

I am trying not to stew over all this. My hope is that these election results motivate both Democrats and Independents to work to ensure that our values are not dismissed in the future.

November 8, Monday

I have had a tough week since the election. I am trying to overcome feelings of anger, depression, intellectual superiority, disbelief, and grief. I don't want to be bitter about the election results, and I definitely do not want to send negativity out into the world—there is already enough of that. As much as I disagree with many of the issues this president stands for, he needs positive energy directed toward him—an energy of compassion and reason. I hope the president remembers the fifty-five million voters who did not cast their ballots in his favor.

There is this values war going on that is disturbing to me. There are some who feel they have a monopoly on values and that theirs are the only correct ones. I take offense to this because I feel that my values are loving, compassionate, and godlike; I want to see all individuals granted equal rights and respect.

Here is my dilemma: If I hold on to my prejudices toward those with opinions different from mine, no matter how justified I may feel, I am no better than they. I try to understand their logic and remember that it is fear based, based on something they do not understand or care to understand. However, I am going to try to see their views with compassion, not anger and resentment. That doesn't mean I agree with them, but to send hateful vibes out to them is not helpful either. In fact, I am going to attempt this type of thinking throughout the next four years—be compassionate, listen to the other side, and stay well informed of all that is happening. I will hold our elected officials accountable. Unfortunately, since this president doesn't have to worry about being reelected, he really has no reason to care about what the rest of us think. However, his legacy should be important to him.

The principals of Christianity and Buddhism I am currently embracing should help me endure the next few years without being quite so angry. That is my hope anyway. Anger is so futile. When I think of the struggle I've overcome this past year with cancer, there is no reason I should let anger be one of the dominant emotions driving me. I have a new, fresh start in life; I plan to live with as much positive energy, love, and compassion that I can muster, even when confronted with actions and rhetoric from those whom I passionately disagree. I'm really going to make this effort for my own well-being.

Inspiration for the day is taken from a Hero card (seems very timely too):

The welfare of each is bound up in the welfare of all.

—Helen Keller

Now I need to write about a more pleasant topic. I have been spending so much time with Aidan and Andrew. One day last week, Barbara and I had lunch at Red Lobster, ran some errands, then picked Aidan up from day care. Andrew was sleeping when Barbara went into the day care facility to retrieve Aidan, so I stayed in the car. Andrew started crying, so I climbed into the backseat to comfort him.

When Barbara and Aidan arrived at the car, I was still in the back, wedged between the two car seats (fortunately, I'm small enough to do that); and when Aidan saw me, he smiled. I stayed in the backseat to entertain Aidan during the drive home. At one point, he leaned his head over to me, as if giving me a hug, and said, "I love you." My heart melted. "I love you too," I told him as I gave him a kiss. That was the best gift I have received this past week. I am so in love with these children, and if I never have children of my own, I at least have them.

November 10, Wednesday

Today, I worked again as an actor—well, sort of. I was on the set of *As the World Turns* working as an extra. The scene was set in a hospital, and I was a patient milling about the ward. I was only there from 7:30 a.m. to 11:00 a.m., so I made a little over $34 an hour. The studio is quite nice, and I even had a dressing room, which I shared with another actor. It was beneficial having her there with me because she had worked at *ATWT* before and was familiar with the routine, so I followed her lead

It is 10:15 p.m., and I have to get some sleep. I leave for Cincinnati tomorrow.

November 14, Sunday

Karen and I spent Friday together; it was a day of sisterly bonding. In the morning, we sat around leisurely sipping coffee and talking. We ran some errands in the afternoon and later in the evening, took in a movie, *Bridget Jones: The Edge of Reason*. It was so funny. I am usually disappointed in sequels, but this one was just as romantic and silly as the first. Oh, and I'm a huge Colin Firth fan, and Hugh Grant isn't too difficult to look at either.

November 15, Monday

I'm meeting Yvonne, on of my ex-coworkers, for lunch today. We are going to Backstage Deli to get tuna supreme sandwiches. These are the best tuna salad sandwiches *ever*, and when I worked downtown, I used to have one at least once a week.

While I have some time before I leave, I'll write about this past weekend. Karen, Jeff, and I spent Saturday with Cindy, John, and the kids. Jake gave me a big hug when he first saw me and said, "I've missed you."

I responded, "I've missed you too," and gave him a tight squeeze. Jake is taller than me now and possesses quite a sturdy build.

Megan has grown so much too. She is tall for a seven-year-old, and she informed me that she's the second tallest girl in her class. I told her that I had been one of the shortest girls in my class. She's a very pretty little girl who is all legs—I envy that. I haven't seen Cindy, John, or the kids since Karen and Jeff's wedding on September 20, 2003.

Cindy and John are doing well though they've been through a difficult time lately. Among other things, a dear friend of John's, who was only forty-two years old, died a few weeks ago from a brain tumor. They're still reeling from that tragedy. We spent the day eating, drinking, talking, and goofing off. We stayed there until about 9:00 p.m., and the day's activities physically drained Karen.

Karen and Jeff decided they were too tired to make the trips to Centerville and Dayton with me on Sunday, so I drove up by myself. I had lunch with Aunt Addie and Uncle Al and spent about two and a half hours with them. Afterward, I headed over to Mike's home. I spent the rest of the afternoon with him and his family and even joined them for dinner. I played marbles with his children, Jake and Kaitlin. This was the first time I'd ever played marbles. Kaitlin is six, and Jake is eight. They're both very lovable children.

Mike is still thin, but he seems well. He had another checkup in Cleveland this past week. He continues to experience a good deal of pain, resulting from his surgeries and is searching for pain-management options. I can see why he is in so much discomfort. He showed his scars to me; he has two of them. There is a large one extending from his upper chest to his neck where the doctor removed his esophagus. The other scar extends from his naval and curves up around his back; he was literally cut in half. To replace his esophagus, they had to stretch his stomach upward and attach it below the larynx (the voice box). The risk here is that the voice box will be damaged, so once Mike had regained consciousness after surgery, the doctor had to make sure he could still speak. They also had to make sure there was no damage to the pharynx, which both food and air pass through. Of course, this rearrangement of his upper digestive tract took a little getting used to. According to Mike, the internal sensations of swallowing were quite bizarre. I was astounded. It is fascinating the techniques medical professionals can utilize.

When I envision what he has endured, I feel like my experience was a piece of cake. Of course, it wasn't; but compared with Mike's experience, it does not compare with regards to complications and residual pain.

I'm so glad I was able to reconnect with these relatives. Mike is so fortunate to have had his family with him during this difficult period.

11:30 p.m.

I met Yvonne at her office around noon. She looks fabulous. When she walked out to meet me, I did a double take. She's lost seventy pounds! She is a bit irritated with herself because she's regained twenty of them, but she still looks amazing. She told me that she threw out all of her fat clothes because she never plans to get that large again.

I left my car in the parking lot, and she drove us downtown to get our tuna supreme sandwiches. The deli owner and his cashier were pleasantly surprised to see me. I told him that New York City doesn't have a tuna sandwich to compare—at least I've not discovered one yet. After purchasing the food, we went to Yvonne's home where we ate and then talked for much of the afternoon. We chatted about her family, my family, her weight loss, my cancer, and politics.

Before I left, she took a photo of me. She said the guys (meaning her husband, Lance, and sons, Michael and Christopher) wanted to see how I look now. It would've been nice to see the guys. They always put a smile on my face. Yvonne drove me back to my car, and then I headed to Karen's home. Yvonne and Donna C (another former coworker) are planning to be at the Vineyard Wine Bar tomorrow night for the party Karen B has organized, so I will get to see Yvonne again before I leave.

November 16, Tuesday

Karen B really outdid herself. The cocktail party she arranged at the Vineyard Wine Bar was lovely. The bar itself is quite elegant with white French doors that lead to an outdoor patio. Tiny white lights contribute to the ambience, very festive. The place was decorated with balloons and photos of me. Karen B had flowers there as well.

Many of my friends showed up, and I also met quite a few new people. Many of these people had donated money to help with my medical expenses. I met Jeff B, who ran with my name on his jersey during the Flying Pig Marathon.

I felt overwhelmed by and undeserving of people telling me what an inspiration I am. They're very kind to say it, but it embarrasses me a bit. One comment that didn't make me feel self-conscious was from a woman whose sister had died of breast cancer five years ago. She said it was good for her to see someone survive a cancer diagnosis.

Driving home, I was overcome with emotion, not only from the outpouring of love I had received from these people, but also with the love I felt for them. I'm grateful for their thoughts and prayers, and I know these thoughts and prayers have significantly contributed to my recovery. The power of prayer is very powerful indeed.

November 18, Thursday

Ed and I had lunch at Rookwood Pottery up in Mount Adams today. We talked about Cincinnati Playhouse in the Park's Tony Award, its season, the New York shows he and I have seen (we both loved *Avenue Q*), my recovery, and politics. The election has been discussed in almost every visit I've had.

However, I did not discuss politics with Lisa tonight. We're on different sides of the political spectrum, so I avoid political debates with her. She's an amazing friend, so I can look past her politics as I'm sure she looks past mine.

Joshua is adorable; he reminds me of Aidan. Lisa's parents were there, as well as Karen D, another friend from theater; her husband, Andy; and their daughter, Maddie. (It's Maddie's birthday, so Lisa had ordered a cake to celebrate.) Dinner was delicious as usual because Lisa possesses considerable culinary prowess.

I really missed my boys today. It's going to be difficult for me when I move out of Barbara's home. I love her children so much. As challenging as they can be at times, I enjoy holding them and playing with them, seeing their smiles, and comforting them when they're distressed. They are Aunt Deborah's little precious ones.

November 20, Saturday

Susan's big day has arrived. I'm lounging around in the hotel room and watching CNN. I'll start getting ready soon.

The drive up yesterday with Jenny and Marie was enjoyable. Marie and Jenny are friends of Susan's with whom I used to socialize when we would go out on weekends when Susan still lived in Cincinnati. Once she moved, I lost touch with them. Now they are both married and have children.

Once I checked into the hotel and settled into my room, Jenny, Marie, and I hooked up in the lobby to go out for dinner. On my way down, I ran into Doug in the hallway, and he told me where I could find Susan. I popped in briefly to say hi.

I hope today is everything she's ever dreamed her wedding to be.

November 21, Sunday

I was dissatisfied with my performance. We were running very late because Jenny and Marie could not get out of their hotel parking garage, and thus, I did not have a chance to run through the music with the accompanist and had to wing it. We were off tempo on "The Wedding Song." I'm used to slowing down the tempo and singing it with more emotion. He played it at a quicker pace than

I'm used to hearing, and the other vocalist annoyed me because I could see her in my peripheral vision trying to direct me to speed up to the music. Well, I've always been told a good accompanist follows the singer. Also, it didn't help that there were so many pages of sheet music, and he had difficulty turning the pages. "The Prayer of St. Francis" was sung beautifully until I got to the "Oh, Master, grant . . ." section. I was nervous and failed to have sufficient breath support, so I know I was off-key on a couple notes. I was so mad. That's what happens when I don't have sufficient rehearsal time.

However, I did receive many compliments. And what matters more than anything else is that Susan loved it. To the untrained ear, I was probably fine; but if Karen (who has heard me sing often and when relaxed) had been there, she would have noticed my vocal weaknesses. I decided my days of singing at weddings are over.

Although I felt badly about my performance, Susan's wedding and reception were beautiful. She looked stunning. Her wedding dress was strapless and slim cut, and she wore a long veil.

The reception was at the hotel, which was convenient. I left around 8:30 p.m. because I was very tired; plus Jenny and Marie were leaving. Receptions are always more fun when you have a date, or at least someone with whom to dance. Watching Susan dance with her father and then with Doug made me want to get married. I'd like that experience at some point in my life, but sometimes, I feel it's just not in the cards for me.

Susan and Doug looked so happy. I hope that happiness lasts throughout their years together.

November 22, Monday

I attempted to talk to Aidan on the phone last night, but he was more interested in pushing the buttons on the receiver. He did manage to say, "Hi, Debbie." Dan was playing the role of Dad and berating me for not checking in with them before now. I think he might actually miss me a little.

I met Karen B's parents today. They had invited me over for lunch. Her mom made a delicious chicken salad that included grapes, which added such freshness to the dish. Karen B definitely inherited her sentimentality from her father. As he talked about his heart transplant and other heart-transplant patients he's counseled, tears welled up in his eyes. He's a minister, so he is also a very spiritual person. I like knowing my friends' parents because it provides more insight into my friends.

Later in the day, I picked up Michael D, and we headed to the Old St. George where the Cincinnati Entertainment Awards were being held. I saw

Rick and thanked him for making the tickets available to me. I didn't know many other people in attendance. Corrine and Sunshine (two women I worked with and befriended in Cincinnati) were nominated as Best Local Actor and Best Local Supporting Actor, respectively, for Ovation's production of Noël Coward's *Fallen Angels*. Both won their categories. Joe, artistic director of Ovation Theatre Company and the director of *Fallen Angels*, will be pleased. No one from Ovation was there representing the company, so I felt like I was the one doing it.

When the Visiting Actor award was announced, it was presented to Marni who was there to accept it. I was so surprised; I had no idea she was going to be there. Her acceptance speech was well prepared, and I was most touched by it. At the end, she said, "I want to dedicate this award to two women who have inspired me this year: my sixteen-year-old cousin who is performing in a show tonight and my good friend Deborah Ludwig, cofounder of Ovation. Both these women beat leukemia this year."

A bit later, I found Marni standing in the crowded lobby (the show was still going on, but people were mingling about). She was surprised to see me too. We hugged. She asked, "You heard the speech?"

"Yes," I replied, "it made me cry."

Michael D and I stayed for all but the last two awards. We blew off the after-party because we were both tired.

November 24, Wednesday

Robin visited last night. I met Robin in an on-camera acting class. We didn't interact much throughout the six-week class period; however, one day, shortly after the class had ended, she and I were attending the same commercial audition. There was a long line of actors in front of us, so we struck up a conversation. We exchanged phone numbers; a couple days later, she called me, and a friendship quickly developed. Robin is married; her husband's name is Mark.

Robin definitely does not look forty—actually, more like twenty-five. She possesses a youthful appearance, and she's small in stature like me. She seems to be making progress in her personal growth. Ever since I've known her, she has dealt with the scars from her past and battled insecurities. She told me that reading my blog has helped her, especially the entry in which I talk about the book *The Four Agreements*. She bought the book, read it, then gave it to her therapist to read so they could discuss it. It's so fulfilling to me when my insights or suggested resources are beneficial to someone. That's what it's all about, helping others.

November 25, Thursday, Thanksgiving Day

Karen, Jeff, and I drove to Tell City this morning. Mom prepared a delicious feast of turkey, dressing, sweet potatoes, green bean casserole, cranberry sauce, broccoli, and rolls. Of course, pumpkin pie filled our dessert plates.

Grandpa joined us for dinner, and when he first walked in the door, he smiled and said to me, "You look really good for what you've been through," and then added, "You look about sixteen years old." I smiled and told him that I really loved him.

Later that day, when Dad and I were decorating the Christmas tree in the sunroom, he hugged me and said, "I love you. I'm so glad you're well." I returned the hug.

Lynn dropped by with Kyle and Kara, who really enjoyed playing with Dante. And of course, I always treasure spending time with Lynn. I'm spending my time here truly enjoying every moment, absorbing every nuance, and giving thanks for all the love that has been bestowed upon me.

November 29, Monday

Saturday, Diane and I had a phone conversation. She started crying a couple of times and apologized for this. I told her that she was allowed to cry and that no apology was necessary. My hope is to visit with her in December before she goes into the hospital for her stem cell collection. Diane's treatment includes two autologous stem cell transplants. Her own stem cells will be extracted, cleaned, and transfused back into her. She faces a very difficult road, so I will keep her in my thoughts and prayers.

Saturday evening, we watched *It's a Wonderful Life*. It's one of those holiday classics I watch annually. My favorite moment comes at the end of the movie when George receives Clarence's copy of *Tom Sawyer* as a gift, and Clarence has written the following message in it: "Dear, George, remember no man is a failure who has friends. Thanks for the wings! Love, Clarence." I love that sentiment, and it so applies to me. I'm nearly penniless, but I am wealthy and successful in my relationships.

December 1, Wednesday

I've been back in New Jersey since Monday. Andrew is smiling constantly these days, and Aidan is speaking so well—I can engage him in conversation. Aidan has actually been calling me Deborah as often as he calls me Debbie. My body can tell I've been away from the kids for a while because my leg, arm, and back muscles ache from picking them up and playing with them. Living with them is as good for my physical well-being as it is for my emotional well-being.

Of all the Christmas decorations in the house, Aidan is quite taken with the manger. He constantly wants to look at and then hold the baby Jesus figurine. He says, "Baby Jesus." It sounds so sweet when he says it. Barbara bought the boys a Little People manger of their own. It's placed under the tree, and the angel that sits atop the manger serves a dual purpose—decorative and musical. When the angel is pressed down, the star illuminates, and music to "Away in a Manger" plays.

I have a doctor's appointment tomorrow. Hopefully, my blood work will come back fine. I have experienced some slight pain in my torso area in various places but nothing tremendously uncomfortable. I used to think nothing of little aches and pains, but nowadays, I am suspicious of anything that seems out of the ordinary.

December 2, Thursday

This morning, I was doing a bit of catch-up reading in *God Calling*, *365 Tao*, and *Latin Sayings for Spiritual Growth*. As I have gotten better and able to take on more responsibilities here at the house and the sun doesn't rouse me from sleep quite as early this time of year, I have found myself straying from my morning spiritual rituals—reading, meditating, praying. My challenge is to continue these practices and carve out the time for them when my life gets back to normal and everyday tasks and goals require more of my attention.

These spiritual practices have inspired me and given me strength and courage during the most grueling times of my illness. I began to trust that "all will be well" if I let go of fear and allowed God to do his work. My meditation practice produced a sense of calm. I found an appreciation for living in the present moment that had been absent from my life. Affirmations and guided imagery techniques fostered positive energy and optimism. I felt a peace and contentment that had been missing for a long time.

I am feeling energized these days and am making plans for the future, yet I find myself anxious again. My biggest concerns are money and housing. I need a job, but I can't work out here in New Jersey because I need a car, and I don't have one. I could work in the city and commute by train for a while, but commuting would eat up money I should be saving, around $95 per week. I'd love to move into the city, but I have no money to put toward a deposit and the first month's rent. I'm stuck between a rock and a hard place. I need to get out of Barbara and Dan's home—not because I want to leave, but because I feel they need their privacy. It's been almost a year that I've lived here. I am doing better and am ready to move on, but I need to figure out a workable financial strategy.

My doctor's appointment went well. The white blood count is 4.5, hemoglobin is 11.7 (same as the last visit), and platelets are 205,000 (down about twenty thousand but still well within the normal range). Dr. Goldberg told me that I can stop taking the magnesium. He also advised me to stay on the folic acid until my red blood cells get smaller; they're still a little large. I didn't tell him of the minor aches I've been experiencing in my torso, but I will continue monitoring the pain. He asked me questions about dry mouth, gritty-feeling eyes, dry skin (which I've had this entire year), tightness of the skin, and arthritis, particularly upon waking. All were negatives except for the dry skin. He was pleased with my negative responses because these symptoms can all be indicative of chronic GVHD. Chronic GVHD occurs after the third month posttransplant; acute GVHD happens during the first three months posttransplant. My next appointment isn't scheduled until January 6.

December 4, Saturday

Yesterday, Barbara and I went to the Mall at Short Hills. We had lunch there, and Barbara finished almost all of her Christmas shopping. I still have many gifts to buy and on a very tight budget.

Later that evening, while Dan was out picking up the pizza and a few groceries, Barbara was carrying Andrew and walking around the living room, Aidan was playing on the floor, and I was browsing through the latest issue of the *One Spirit* catalogue. Barbara walked over to me, leaned down, and kissed me on the cheek, then put Andrew to my face and made a kissing sound as if the kiss were coming from him. I looked up and smiled. "What was that for?" I asked.

"Because we love Aunt Deborah," Barbara replied. "She helps out with so much, and we kiss the people we love." That simple gesture meant the world to me.

December 6, Monday

Yesterday's *God Calling* passage made me think differently about the act of giving.

> *Law of Supply* (December 5)
> THE first law of giving is of the spirit world. Give to all you meet, or whose lives touch yours, or your prayers, your time, yourselves, your love, your thought. You must practice this giving first.

Then give of this world's goods and money, as you have them given to you. To give money and material things without having first made the habit daily, hourly, ever increasingly, of giving on the higher plane, is wrong.

Give, give, give all your best to all who need it. Be great givers—great givers. Remember, as I have told you before, give according to need, never according to desert. In giving, with the thought of supplying a real need you must closely resemble that Father in Heaven, the Great Giver.[50]

The most important act of giving is the giving of ourselves. I have often lamented the fact that I don't have sufficient funds to donate to charities or friends and family members who may be in need of financial assistance. However, if you do not have the means to give money, then you can certainly give time and love and say prayers, which are all precious gifts. And best of all, anyone can give of these things regardless of one's economic situation. The above instruction for giving removes the guilt of not being able to be monetarily generous. As a line in the Prayer of St. Francis reads, "It's in giving of ourselves that we receive."

It's going to be a busy week of shopping, party planning, and completing last-minute tasks before I leave on Sunday. Last night, Barbara, Dan, Alyssa, Aidan, and I went to the PNC Bank Arts Center Holiday Light Spectacular. It was quite elaborate and impressive; it *was* spectacular. Millions of lights, intricately woven together, created displays of Santa, snowmen, elves, reindeer, Santa's workshop, a whole area set up for the Twelve Days of Christmas, a manger scene, and a Hanukkah display. Guests drove through the park, surrounded by these stunning holiday light displays. Afterward, we went to Chili's for dinner before taking Alyssa home.

December 10, Friday

I have been trying to figure out what I need to do come January. Dan suggested that, after the holiday, I bring my car back from Tell City. (I'd signed the lien over to my parents shortly after moving to the Northeast.) This would help facilitate transportation to and from a place of employment here in New Jersey or the train station, should I work in the city. I'll discuss it with Mom and Dad. My biggest concern is driving the car from Indiana to New Jersey in January because of the condition of the car—it's almost eleven years old. Having my own transportation would definitely make all of our lives easier.

I am still vacillating between continuing to pursue an acting career or not. I am envious of actors; I'm not envious of people in other careers. This envy is a sign to me that acting is the path I need to follow—at least for a while longer. I sometimes wonder if I truly love acting, or is it the idea of fame and fortune with which I'm enamored? If my ambition is achieving fame and fortune, then that is unfortunate because so few actors accomplish this goal. Still, even though I've lost a year and I'm not getting any younger, I'm not ready to relinquish the dream. I'm thirty-eight years old, yet I believe in myself regardless of my age. I just need to be more aggressive and confident.

I keep praying and listening for answers. My gut feeling and intuition are guiding forces for me. This is how God speaks to me I'm convinced. I'm taking my time and really waiting for answers. But then, as life changes, so do those intuitions and feelings; I have to go with what I feel is best. I believe by asking, listening, and being in sync with intuition, God helps us make right decisions. We just have to be open and receptive to whatever messages are being sent to us.

December 13, Monday

I arrived at the Louisville airport yesterday afternoon, and Mom and Dad were there to meet me. This morning, I meditated, read a couple more sections of the Sunday *New York Times*, called Diane and left a message on her answering machine, started reading *Word 2002 for Dummies*, and prepared lunch for Mom and me. This afternoon, I am focusing on some writing, checking e-mails, and practicing Word applications. I'm attempting to refresh my Word processing skills so that when I take the skills tests at temp agencies, I will achieve a high score, thus commanding higher compensation for my work. Of course, once the rest of the family arrives, I will want to join them for all the merriment and not be planted in front of a computer screen. I should be disciplined and carve out a few hours to work each day, but family is more important to me at this moment than improving my computer proficiency.

Saturday was the Christmas celebration with the New Jersey relatives and friends. Santa Claus arrived after dinner. Bob dressed up as the merry old gentleman in the Santa suit that Donna had bought him last Christmas. After donning the costume with Donna's assistance in the secrecy of the basement, Bob sneaked around to the back of the house and knocked on the door. Zachary was the one who answered the door, and I wish I had seen his face because Bob said it was priceless. Santa entered, greeting everyone with a jovial "Merry Christmas!"

Santa sat down in a chair placed in the middle of the living room as everyone gathered around. Zachary was the first child to sit on his lap. Aidan, curious yet a bit afraid and hesitant to approach the jolly old man, was clinging to Barbara; so I yelled, "I'll sit on Santa's lap!" I jumped up and plopped myself on Bob. Everyone howled with laughter and snapped photos.

Santa said, "You can tell who the actor is here."

Barbara finally persuaded Aidan to sit on Santa's lap. After all the photos were taken, it was gift time. Santa passed out the presents. Each boy received a box with the following: two plastic shovels (a huge hit with Aidan), a plastic garden claw, a metal slinky, a small car, and a clear rubber ball with a picture of Elmo inside. Santa said good-bye; then Bob reappeared.

The kids finished opening their other presents, assisted by the grown-ups; then it was time for the adults to open their gifts. This was not the elaborate and painfully slow Ludwig method but rather everyone simultaneously ripping open their packages. I received $50 from Eleonore and Russ and as a joke, a sixty-four-ounce bottle of ketchup. Regardless of its joke value, it is definitely a good gift for me, being the ketchup lover that I am.

Once the packages were exchanged, it was dessert time. While the adults talked, Aidan, Zachary, and Luke scurried around the house—screaming, chasing one another, and having a blast. Later, I walked into the sitting room and spied all three of them crouched in front of the fireplace. "This has to be trouble," I chuckled to myself. I knew they were dying to touch the glass.

I snuck up behind them and asked in a low, menacing voice, "What are you boys doing?"

They looked up at me as if caught doing something mischievous, and then Aidan piped up, "Touch, fire, hot."

I laughed, saying, "You shouldn't touch it. It could be hot."

Zachary replied, "I'm not touching it."

Aidan, the little rebel, was compelled to touch it out of defiance. I laughed and shook my head. I felt the glass, and it wasn't hot. The fireplace is purely decorative, so it doesn't emit heat; however, because of the flame, there is potential for parts of the glass to get hot. It was adorable seeing those three little munchkins gathered around the fire, contemplating mischief.

The evening was quite enjoyable, and it's wonderful to be accepted as part of Dan's family.

December 15, Wednesday

Mom and I went Christmas shopping in Evansville yesterday. I found a Hokey Pokey Elmo and a play Home Depot drill at Toys "R" Us for Aidan. The drill comes with screws, bits, and a small plastic board in which Aidan can drill the screws. All the pieces are oversized. The toy is designed for kids ages three and above, but Aidan loves toys that are very similar to adult items, especially tools and phones. I think he'll really like these gifts.

Today's inspiration is from December 13's *God Calling*:

> *Perpetual Guidance*
> Wait for Guidance in every step. Wait to be shown My way. The thought of this loving leading should give you great joy. All the responsibility of life taken off your shoulders. All its business worry taken off your shoulders. It is indeed a joy for you to feel so free and yet so planned for.[51]

Currently, in my life, I am waiting for guidance, watching for signs, and working toward goals in the hope that those goals are what I am meant to accomplish. If they're not, then they will be abandoned at some point. The interests and activities we keep returning to are the very things we should be pursuing, learning, and cultivating. I will continue to have faith and listen for clues as to how my future should unfold. I am not going to fret—though I will strategize—over money, jobs, and housing. In the end, all will be well. I continue to believe this.

December 18, Saturday

A year ago today, devastating news was delivered to me. I had leukemia, and my first thought was, "I'm going to die." I woke up this morning with Aidan sleeping next to me. I looked at his angelic little face and smiled. I thanked God for this moment. It was a halcyon moment, not one full of fear and anxiety like that morning last year when I awoke in the hospital, still guessing at what lay ahead. What a difference a year makes. As I write this, I feel tears welling up in my eyes. So far, I've beaten my cancer; I feel well, I'm energetic, and I'm ready to reenter the work world. Yet as I'm healing, others are sick.

I visited with Diane yesterday and let her talk about her experience. I answered questions she asked about my ordeal and treatment. She is scared and anxious about being away from home for so long and at such a distance. She is concerned about her five-year-old daughter and how her husband will be able to handle taking care of the little girl in her absence. She is fearful that neither of her siblings will be a match though she is hopeful.

I pray my visit with her was helpful. I left her with a small bag of gifts—a journal, some bath products with which to pamper herself, and a small book of inspirational sayings for mind, body, and spirit. She seemed appreciative of my time, and I requested that she give me her address and phone number once she is settled into the hospital. The transplant phase was the second scariest part of my experience; the scariest was hearing I had cancer. What a dreadful word. However, it is only a word and one that can be viewed as a death sentence or as a means to discover one's strength. I feel that I have discovered how much inner strength and resolve I possess, and surprisingly, it's more than I ever could have imagined.

December 23, Thursday

Joseph called this morning, and he's finally set up online. I'll need to check my e-mail later because he told me he had sent a message. We talked for about twenty minutes. He believes 2005 is going to be a good year for both of us. I hope so.

Much has happened over the course of the past few days. Karen and Jeff were supposed to depart for Tampa today to spend Christmas with Jeff's family, but that was delayed due to a huge snowstorm that hit the area. It has been snowing since yesterday morning, and there is an accumulation of about eighteen inches, higher where there are snowdrifts. Parts of Interstate 64 were closed, which made it impossible for Karen and Jeff to get to the Louisville airport. This area of the country doesn't have the capability to deal with this amount of snowfall because it rarely gets this much accumulation. The last time I recall this large amount of snow was in 1978, and maybe there was a foot of it. However, it is gorgeous how the snow sparkles in the sunlight. I don't mind snow when I don't have to get out in it. When I can snuggle by a warm fire in a cozy house, especially when it is still overcast and snowing, I am quite content.

Karen and Jeff are now scheduled to depart from Louisville on Christmas Eve. Mom is calling around to see if there is anyone who can plow their long driveway because shoveling it is a backbreaking option.

Let's see if I can recall some highlights of the past few days. Tuesday, at Dan's suggestion and because he thought Aidan would enjoy it, we took Aidan to Grandpa's farm to show him the cows and guinea hens. While we were there, Uncle Lloyd arrived on his tractor. This was thrilling for Aidan because Lloyd let him sit on the huge piece of machinery and showed him how to honk the horn. Lloyd was telling us about a baby calf that had been born two days ago at his farm and asked if we'd like to take Aidan there.

When we got there, Linda, Lloyd's wife, showed us the calf in the barn. The calf was so young that it couldn't walk yet. Aidan loved the little animal, and he also enjoyed the horses and dogs. Next, Linda took him to see the kittens in the cellar. The kittens were so small; I could have held one of them in the palm of my hand. They were adorable white fur balls. Aidan really liked the kittens, but he was more captivated by their little plastic balls with bells inside. He wanted to keep the balls, but we told him that the kittens would be sad without their toys, so he gave them back. It was wonderful watching Aidan's reaction to these animals. I experience the world through his eyes, and it all looks new again.

After the farm adventure on Tuesday, Aidan had the prison adventure on Wednesday. Although the snow was coming down quite heavily, Dad wanted to take Aidan to the prison and show him off to his coworkers. Dad said some of them would like to see me too; they all know my health situation, and many have asked about me from time to time.

We only stayed a brief while, then headed back to town to pick up some groceries. Dad had driven Mom to her office earlier that morning, so I called Mom and told her to call my cell phone when she was ready to be picked up from work. We bought the groceries and picked Mom up at 1:00 p.m. On the way home, Mom told me a story about when I was seven or eight months old. She had gotten off work, and it was snowing, which prevented her from getting up the hill to the babysitter's house; so she had someone put chains on the tires. She knew Dad would not like this, but she told me, "I had to pick up my Deborah." I love that story. I envision a pretty dark-haired twenty-one-year-old woman snuggling her baby girl close to her, trudging through the snow from the babysitter's front door to a black '61 Ford.

Last night was Christmas gift opening with Karen and Jeff since they were supposed to leave today. Aidan had a blast ripping open the packages. Barbara said that when he went to bed last night, he was lying there and wistfully said, "Santa Claus." Then he looked out the open blind and saw the trees lit up in the front yard. Dad had constructed a large tree with strands of lights, and he had also decorated a little bush for Aidan. When Aidan saw these, he said "Papa's tree" and "Aidan's tree."

So far, this has been the best Christmas ever. The whole family is here, we're all in good health, and it snowed. Usually, my father is either bemoaning the fact it didn't snow on Christmas or loving life because it did. This year, before it snowed, he told me he didn't care if it snowed or not; he was just glad that I was well. I'm definitely glad I'm healthy, but I'm also glad Dad got his snow.

December 24, Friday, Christmas Eve

Last December 24, I was experiencing a good deal of bone pain and was sick after having performed a grueling pulmonary function test. We began chemotherapy that evening, and I was given morphine to alleviate the pain. That was an agonizing day. However, as I've said before, what a difference a year makes. I'm so grateful to be here with my family and in good health.

Karen and Jeff left around 9:00 a.m. for the Louisville airport. The rest of the day, we hung out here at the house. In the evening hours, Dad turned on his video recorder, and we began the gift-opening ritual. Aidan loved his Hokey Pokey Elmo. He eventually discovered that if Elmo falls over, the doll says, "Ooopsy. Can you help Elmo up?" So after hearing that, all he wanted to do was knock Elmo over. Poor Elmo!

There were so many gifts he treasured, which included the following: the Home Depot toolbox from Mom and Dad (he especially likes the hammer), books, building blocks, plastic play food, and, of course, the Home Depot drill. Christmas is a very different experience when small children are involved; the focus is on them and their joy. It was a very special Christmas indeed.

December 31, Friday

The last hours of 2004 are waning. We are back in New Jersey, having arrived yesterday after a two-day journey.

I was sad to leave Tell City on Wednesday. Since I was driving back, I decided it would be best to return when Barbara and Dan did, just in case there happened to be inclement weather or the Lumina had mechanical problems. I took my parents' car instead of my Cavalier, which I'd signed over to them when I moved to the Northeast. Their car is in better condition even though it's older than mine.

Now the year is ending, and what a year it was. I've grown so much spiritually and mentally. I received a lovely e-mail message from Joseph on the twenty-eighth but didn't read it until today because I've been off-line. He wrote,

> What a lucky person I am to have met you. You constantly remind me of the power of strength, faith, and love. I don't always have a handle on any of them—but I try. You, however, live them every day. I was reading your journey [Joseph is referring to my blog], and I believe you have to follow your dream to be an actor. I know you are an actor—but you can be so successful! Trust me; go to LA and become the new—no—become the first Debbie Ludwig. That's my new name for ya.
>
> Okay, now I'm getting too mushy. You're a pro and don't need sweet words—you need work. So come take it.

> Love you,
> Joseph

At 11:00 p.m., Barbara, Dan, and I made a toast to our surviving the past year; I also toasted them and their generosity. After drinking their champagne, they retired for the night. It is now 11:15 p.m., forty-five minutes to go, and I'm watching *New Year's Eve Live with Anderson Cooper* on CNN (I know, I'm a wild and crazy gal!).

As I wait for the ball to drop in Times Square to herald in the coming year, I thank God for my life. I would never have asked to be given cancer; yet somehow, reflecting on the experience and all I gained from it, I feel the suffering was necessary in order to receive the gifts.

But what possible gifts could there be from the tsunami disaster that happened in Southeast Asia on Sunday? The answer is very difficult. The devastation is incomprehensible. Right now, the death toll is 135,000 and rising. The Aceh province of Indonesia was completely wiped out. It looks like an atomic bomb exploded there. My heart breaks for these people. The United States has pledged $350 million in aid. I plan to give a donation, which unfortunately won't be much—maybe $50, maybe $100. But if everyone gave $50 to the relief effort, it would add up to a sizable worldwide contribution. So perhaps the gift from this disaster will be that the world's inhabitants—regardless of cultural, political, and religious differences—will come together to give aid and comfort to the victims and help restore the region. This disaster is a reminder that life is fragile and that it can be gone in an instant.

This year has been one of much suffering for me, my family, and my friends; it has also been one of tremendous discoveries and growth. I will never take my life for granted again or think that I have decades yet to live. No one is guaranteed tomorrow, so live for today. Live and love as if it were your last day. When you live and love in this way, you will truly discover what your priorities are in life, your relationships will thrive, and you will not wait to pursue dreams and goals—you will be brave enough to start reaching for them now.

I continue to practice all that I've learned this year. There is much work yet to do because it is not easy to change lifelong habits. The key is to be aware of the habits and characteristics that are unattractive in order to change those behaviors in the future. I'm not always consistent. I may still yell or honk at a driver who cuts me off in traffic, but these days I notice my behavior more. This awareness allows me to calm down and take some long, deep breaths, and then send loving-kindness to that person. I'm not perfect nor do I ever expect to be nor do I want to be, but I am working to be the best human being I can.

This year was one of physical, mental, and spiritual rebirth. So much of this past year has been about reflecting on my life, appreciating what I have as opposed to bemoaning what I don't, finding trust in God, cherishing the people in my life, realizing the value of my own life, and living in the present more fully than I ever have before. Life is a journey with many peaks and valleys. Most of life is lived between these two extremes, but to enjoy the emotional high of the peaks, one must experience the valley's lows. It's the way in which we deal with our misfortunes in the valley that truly define our character and increase our personal power.

Life is tremendously precious—treasure every moment of it. So here's to life. Here's to rebirth. Let the New Year begin. Cheers!

Epilogue

It has been four years since my bone marrow transplant, and I remain in remission. I moved into my own place in June of 2006 after having lived with Barbara and Dan for two and half years. Leaving the children was heartbreaking, and there were three of them by 2006 as Alexa had been born May 1. But it was time for me to resume life on my own. Of course, I visit them often.

I celebrated my fortieth birthday May 7, 2006. I never thought I'd be happy to see forty, but from where I sit, forty looks pretty darn good. And now forty-two looks even better! I am also going through early menopause, which I was told would happen. But I am dealing with it, and more importantly, I am healthy.

Some of my creative goals have been met in the past couple of years. I've worked on three commercials and one industrial, performed a reenactment on *Maury*, was cast in a supporting role in a SAG short film that is currently being submitted to film festivals, and my biggest acting coup was costarring in an independent feature last summer titled *Twists of Fate*, which had its premiere here in Manhattan on August 16, 2008, and will now be submitted to film festivals. I have to admit it was quite exciting to see my name flash across the screen during the opening credits. However, I feel that writing and publishing this book is my biggest achievement because it was a labor of love that has taken four years to complete.

I am working on a second book that deals with remembering the lessons learned during my fight with cancer because unfortunately, there are still moments of weakness—more than I care to admit—when I'm frustrated that I fall back on negative behavioral patterns. Still, I continue to work on patience and perspective, and I venture to guess I will do so until the day I die.

The most important lesson that came out of my cancer experience was learning how to keep everything in perspective—well, again, for the most part. For example, a while back, I was walking up Park Avenue, and rain was pouring down from the heavens. I was grumbling to myself because it was cold and miserable. Then I stopped and thought, *Would you rather be out in this crappy weather or in a hospital bed receiving chemotherapy?* The answer was a no-brainer. My mind-set swiftly shifted, and a smile formed on my face as I unsuccessfully jumped over a huge puddle, soaking my feet in the process. I was out in the world living my life. How exhilarating is that?

I am confident that I will be around for many years, yet lingering distantly in the recesses of my psyche resides the possibility that I could relapse or somewhere down the road, develop a secondary cancer, a result of the chemotherapy and radiation treatments I received. However, I try to keep pessimistic thinking to a minimum.

Family, friends, and God are held dear to my heart while love, compassion, awareness, relaxation, and trust are practiced daily. As the years pass, I do not know what other health problems, grief, or challenges will confront me; but I know they will occur. When they do, hopefully, I will face them with the same energy and grace with which I tackled leukemia. The strength and courage I found was not just within me, but also aided by many hands—visible and invisible—supporting, nurturing, and guiding me along the way. For this loving assistance, I will be forever grateful.

ACKNOWLEDGMENTS

This acknowledgment will be inadequate, despite its length, due to the many people who should be thanked—not only in getting this book published, but more importantly, in supporting and loving me before, during, and after my cancer diagnosis.

A big thank-you goes to Dr. Stuart Goldberg for writing the foreword to my book as well as for checking the medical facts. I owe a huge debt of gratitude to Kelsey Kester, a very special and intelligent young lady, who painstakingly went through the entire manuscript, making excellent suggestions as to what could be deleted, what additional information might enhance the story, and suggestions to increase clarity and reduce redundancies. Because of the time she spent with the manuscript, it is so much better than it would have been. Katie Rice and Maggie Hemphill also read the manuscript and offered constructive feedback.

I want to thank all the medical professionals who took care of me: Dr. Alita Dizon, my primary care physician, who suspected leukemia and took it upon herself to ensure that I was diagnosed immediately; Dr. Stuart Goldberg, my oncologist, who was instrumental in my recovery and was always forthcoming, approachable, and compassionate—the kind of physician all patients should be so fortunate to have caring for them; Dr. Scott Rowley, who was in charge of the bone marrow transplant phase of my treatment and was always available for questions, and I am especially grateful for the excellent care he gave my sister during the bone marrow donor process; and Phyllis McKiernan, who always had a smile for me and took care of all issues that arose during my treatment. I also want to extend a warm thank-you to all the nurses, aides, and staff at HUMC for making my hospital stays comfortable, offering kindness and compassion when I needed it, and making a terrible situation bearable.

The Leukemia & Lymphoma Society granted me two $500 reimbursement grants, which helped cover transportation costs to and from outpatient visits and some chemotherapy medications. These grants were so appreciated. I have since become a volunteer with the Society, starting in the fall of 2005 when I was trained as a first connection volunteer. I am also active in their advocacy network.

My New York City friends deserve thanks—their phone calls, gifts, prayers, and visits all helped tremendously. These special people include Lani Ford, Marni Penning, Bobbi Kravis, Jennifer Jiles, Dan Gallagher, Karen Culp, and Deb Rabbai. Also, a thank-you to Terry Schreiber, Carol Reynolds, and all the staff and students at the T. Schreiber Studio for being so kind and keeping me in their thoughts and prayers, especially to fellow students Joseph Rodriguez and Cristina Doikos.

Other friends that deserve acknowledgment: Geralynn Schneider and Kimberly Barbour, two college friends that have remained in my life throughout the years, and Cincinnati friends who remain a constant—Lisa Breithaupt, Yvonne Telander, Michael Drake, Robin Crawford, and Joe Stollenwerk, and even though they do not live there anymore, Susan Campbell, Lori Phillips, Mark Sumpter, Scott Sponsler, and everyone in the Cincinnati theater community who reached out to me.

A great debt of thanks to those who drove me to and from the hospital and the Cancer Center: Russ McCabe, Shelley Devine, who became a dear friend, and Mary Evelyn Morris, a neighbor on Princeton Court. These days could be very long, and Russ and Shelley endured the longest ones.

To those friends who gave above and beyond what was ever expected from them: Natalie Bauman, who spent five days with me in March 2004, and Katie Rice, who spent five days with me, away from her husband, in February 2004; Nelson Miranda and Beckie Wilson were in constant contact with me—e-mailing, calling, and visiting me at the hospital and at home. They opened their home to me when I wanted to escape to the city; Karen Burke not only visited for a week in February 2004, but also was with me in the hospital the day of transplant and returned a week later. She also organized a fund-raiser to help with my medical expenses and acted as liaison throughout my treatment by reporting my progress via e-mail to family and friends.

Lynn Varble, Cindy Liebenow, and Maria Brooks are my oldest and dearest friends. We went through grade school and high school together, and Maria and I continued our education together at Indiana University. These women have been there for me nearly my entire life. Thank you for thirty-six years of friendship and love. We have endured!

Then there is my family . . . thank you to Sister Bernardine Ludwig who kept me in her prayers and allowed me to spend time with her at the convent in May 2005; thank you to aunts, uncles, and cousins who gave money, said prayers, and spent time with me when I visited Tell City and Cincinnati, as well as to Donna and Bob Rooney for giving Barbara, Dan, and me love and support—they are family; thank you to Russ and Eleonore McCabe, whom I've grown to love so dearly—they have welcomed me into their family, they are unbelievably generous, and they take excellent care of all of us; and to Michael Krumnauer, my dear cousin, for all his encouragement; he is an inspiration to me for having survived his own cancer battle.

Words are woefully inadequate for expressing my thanks and love to my immediate family, but I'll try. Karen Ludwig-Purvis made several trips to New Jersey to be with me, and Jeff did not begrudge her this time. Thanks, Jeff, I love you and Karen so much. Also, Karen was with Karen Burke the day of the bone marrow transplant, and she stayed with me in the hospital the following week.

Thank you to my parents, Bill and Nancy Ludwig, who are the foundation of everything I am and ever will be. Their love has sustained me through every trial in my life. We often disagree, but I know their love is unconditional; I feel extremely blessed. I love you—you are the best parents in the world.

Three children have come into my life since 2005: Grace, Karen's daughter; Nathaniel, Karen's son; and Alexa, Barbara's little girl. Little children, you've added even more joy to my world. Much love from your auntie.

Then there is Aidan and Andrew McCabe . . . these special little boys made me smile and gave me a reason to continue fighting for my life: I did not want them to grow up without me. Aidan is one of my godchildren (as are Alexa and Nathaniel), but Andrew is my angel. Andrew will always hold a very dear place in my heart for the very reason that he went through all of this with his mother—her stress, her worry, her bone marrow aspiration, her strength. Andrew is a part of me. It'll be many years before he can understand what his role in this whole ordeal was, but it was extraordinary. Aidan and Andrew, I love you so much, sometimes so much so that it makes my heart ache. You will always be "my boys."

And last, but most certainly not least, thank you to Barbara and Dan McCabe for taking me into their home for two and a half years. They not only shared their home, but also their money, their time, and their hearts without expecting anything in return. I can't imagine what my existence would have been like had they not been there for me. Their generosity, kindness, and love overwhelm me.

And, Barbara, thank you most of all for giving me back my life. I can't imagine the struggle of making the decision to be my donor was for you. You had the courage to give me back my life that spring, and then later that summer, you had the joy of giving life to your precious baby Andrew. Many people that Barbara has shared her story with say "how heroic she was" and "what an amazing thing to do." But she doesn't see it as heroic or amazing; she simply replies, "I'm a mother and a sister. That's just what we do."

I am so grateful that everything went well, and Andrew is now a gorgeous healthy four-year-old child. I am so rich in the family and friends that have appeared and remain in my life. Barbara and Dan bore the burden of my care, my finances, and my life; so it is to them, with much love, that this book is dedicated.

Cancer Resources

American Cancer Society
1599 Clifton Road, NE
Atlanta, GA 30329
800-ACS-2345 or 866-228-4327
http://www.cancer.org

Cancer Care, Inc.
275 Seventh Avenue
New York, NY 10001
800-813-HOPE or 212-712-8400
http://www.cancercare.org
E-mail: info@cancercare.org

National Coalition for Cancer
Survivorship
1010 Wayne Avenue, Suite 770
Silver Spring, MD 20910
877-NCCS-YES or 301-650-9127
http://www.canceradvocacy.org
E-mail: info@canceradvocacy.org

Leukemia & Lymphoma Society
1311 Mamaroneck Avenue
White Plains, NY 10605
800-955-4572 or 914-949-0084
http://www.lls.org
E-mail: infocenter@leukemia-lymphma.org

National Marrow Donor Program
(NMDP)
3001 Broadway, NE, Suite 100
Minneapolis, MN 55413
800-MARROW2 or 800-627-7692
http://www.marrow.org

Blood and Marrow Transplant
Information Network
2310 Skokie Valley Road, Suite 104
Highland Park, IL 60035
888-597-7674 or 847-433-3313
http://www.bmtinfonet.org
E-mail: help@bmtinfonet.org

Lance Armstrong Foundation
PO Box 161150
Austin, TX 78716-1150
866-467-7205
http://www.livestrong.org

Partnership for Prescription Assistance
888-4PPA-NOW or 888-477-2669
http://www.pparx.org

BIBLIOGRAPHY

Frankl, Viktor. *Man's Search for Meaning*. New York: Simon & Schuster/ Touchstone Book, Third Edition, 1984.

Thich Naht Hahn, *The Miracle of Mindfulness*, (Boston: Beacon Press, 1987)

Deng Ming-Dao, *Tao 365 Daily Meditations* (San Francisco: Harper, 1992)

Caroline, Myss, and Norman C. Shealy. *The Creation of Health* (New York: Three Rivers Press 1988, 1993)

Belleruth Naparstek, *Chemotherapy, Guided Imagery Tape* (Akron, OH: Image Paths, Inc, 1991)

Catherine Ponder, *Healing Secrets of the Ages*, (DeVorss & Company, Marina Del Ray, CA, 1967, Revised and updated by the author 1985)

Catherine Ponder, *The Dynamic Laws of Healing*, (DeVorss & Company, Marina Del Ray, CA, 1966, Revised and updated by author, 1985)

Sharon Salzberg and Joseph Goldberg, *Insight Meditation* (Boulder, CO: Sounds True, 2001)

Susan K. Stewart, *Bone Marrow and Blood Stem Cell Transplants*, (Highland Park, IL: BMT Info Network, 2002)

Elizabeth K. Stratton, *Seeds of Light*, (New York: Fireside, Simon & Schuster, Inc.,1997)

Suggestions for Further Reading

Armstrong, Lance. *It's Not about the Bike: My Journey Back to Life*. New York: Berkley Books, 2000, 2001.

Chödrön, Pema, *When Things Fall Apart: Heart Advice for Difficult Times*, (Boston: Shambala, 2000)

Coelho, Paul, *The Alchemist*, (Harper San Francisco, 1993)

Cousins, Norman, *Head First: The Biology of Hope*, (New York: E.P. Dutton, 1989)

Drescher, Fran, *Cancer Schmancer*,(New York: Warner Books, Inc, 2002)

Epstein, MD, Gerald, *Healing Visualizations: Creating Health through Imagery*, (New York: Bantam Books, 1989)

Ruiz, Don Miguel, *The Four Agreements*, (San Rafael, CA: Amber-Allen Publishing, 1997)

Siegel, MD, Bernie S., *Love, Medicine, and Miracles*, (New York: Harper & Row Publishers, 1986, Reissued 1998; reprinted in Quill 2002)

Sprague, Stephen, *Life After Leukemia . . . The Continuing Story of One Man's Cord Blood Miracle*, 2003 (Complimentary copies may be requested at: P.O. Box 140676, Staten Island, NY 10314-0676 or e-mail: spraguecml@aol.com)

Tolle, Eckhart, *The Power of NOW: A Guide to Spiritual Enlightenment*, (Novato, CA: New World Library, 1999)

ENDNOTES

[1] Eastern Cooperative Oncology Group Study: Phase II Randomized Trial of Autologous and Allogeneic Bone Marrow Transplantation versus Intensive Conventional Chemotherapy in Acute Lymphoblastic Leukemia in First remission. Consent Form Version II Dec. 2002 CD, 06/03.

[2] Used with permission of the Helen Steiner Rice Foundation, Cincinnati, Ohio. ©1965 The Helen Steiner Rice Foundation—All Rights Reserved.

[3] Hagop M. Kantarjian and others, eds. *Results of Treatment With Hyper-CVAD, a Dose-Intensive Regimen, in Adult Acute Lymphocytic Leukemia*, Journal of Clinical Oncology, Vol. 18, No. 3 (February), 2000, p. 547

[4] Definition from Healthy NJ—Information for Healthy Living: *http://www.healthynj. org/dis-con/bells/main.htm*, July 2006.

[5] Catherine Ponder, *The Dynamic Laws of Healing*, (DeVorss & Company, Marina Del Ray, CA, 1966, Revised and updated by author, 1985), 149-163.

[6] Ibid., 164-180.

[7] Ibid., 179-196.

[8] Catherine Ponder, *Healing Secrets of the Ages*, (DeVorss & Company, Marina Del Ray, CA, 1967, Revised and updated by the author 1985), 72.

[9] Ibid., 165.

[10] Ibid., 249.

[11] Ibid., 268.

[12] Ibid., 259

[13] Caroline, Myss PhD & Norman C. Shealy, MD, PhD, *The Creation of Health* (New York: Three Rivers Press 1988, 1993), 131

[14] Ibid., 132-133.

[15] Ibid., 135.

[16] See January 2 entry for normal hemoglobin range.

[17] See December 17 entry for normal platelet range.

[18] Deng Ming-Dao, *Tao 365 Daily Meditations* (San Francisco: Harper, 1992), 44.

[19] Partnership for Prescription Assistance is another good resource for affordable medications. I did not know about this until 2006. Web site: https://www.pparx.org.

[20] A.J. Russell, ed., *God Calling* (Used with permission by John Hunt Publishing, Ltd., 46a West Street, New Alresford, Hants S024 9A, United Kingdom, 1978), 44-45.

[21] Catherine Sebban and others, eds. Allogeneic Bone Marrow Transplantation in Adult Lymphoblastic Leukemia in First Complete Remission: A Comparative Study, Journal of Clinical Oncology, vol. 12, no. 12 (December) 1994: pp 2580

[22] Belleruth Naparstek, *Chemotherapy, Guided Imagery Tape* (Akron, OH: Image Paths, Inc, 1991).

[23] Op cit, A.J. Russell, ed., 50.

[24] Note: I cannot reveal what the "four agreements" are because I would be giving away the entire book, and I'm sure I would not be granted permission to reprint them. It is a book I highly recommend, so if you are curious as to what the four agreements are, I suggest buying the book or checking it out of the library.

[25] Op cit, A.J. Russell, ed., 52-53.

[26] Chakras are energy centers in the body. To learn more about chakras, I suggest reading *Chakra Balancing* by Anodea Judith.

[27] Elizabeth K. Stratton, MS, *Seeds of Light*, (New York: Fireside, Simon & Schuster, Inc., 1997), 71-73.

[28] Ibid., 57.

[29] Ibid., 59.

[30] Ibid., 59-60.

[31] Viktor Frankl, *Man's Search for Meaning*, (New York: Simon & Schuster/Touchstone Book, Third Edition, 1984), 109.

[32] Op cit, Deng Ming-Dao, 94.

[33] Thich Naht Hahn, *The Miracle of Mindfulness*, (Boston: Beacon Press, 1987), 107-117 (This is included in chapter 7, "Three Wondrous Questions.")

[34] Op cit, A.J. Russell, ed., 68.

[35] The Flying Pig Marathon is a 26.2-mile race held every spring in Cincinnati, Ohio, so Karen dubbed her fundraising event the EuroK Flying Pig Challenge. EuroK is the name that Nelson bestowed upon Karen B after she'd returned from her European trip, the summer of 2002, when she did and said things totally out of character. The first event that caught Nelson off guard was one evening when he, Natalie, Lori, Karen B, and I had gone out dancing; and Karen B made a comment like, "Yes, I know I'm wearing flip-flops with a dress, and I haven't shaved my legs, so you can see stubble. But hey, I'm here, aren't I?" But the event that solidified Karen B's changed attitude and newfound audaciousness was the evening she pressured Nelson into getting out of bed and accompanying her to the John Cougar concert, which was starting in fifteen minutes. She told Nelson they could try scalping tickets as she didn't have any for admission. There were no scalpers at the venue, so they ended up going salsa dancing at Mad Frog. Nelson looked at her and asked, "Who *are* you? You're not the

same Karen who went to Europe. You're . . . you're . . . you're EuroK!" Thus, her alter ego, EuroK, was born.

36   Op cit, A. J. Russell, ed., 77-78.

37   Ibid., 79.

38   Note: The one-week-only hospital stay must've been because this patient had an autologous stem cell transplant; these patients, because their own stem cells are used, are out of the hospital much sooner than allogeneic transplant patients, who tend to be hospitalized for several weeks.

39   Note: Unfortunately, I am unable to include the specific verse because Hallmark does not grant permission to reprint any images or writings by their artists.

40   Dan G says that I am "defying gravity," which is the name of one of the songs in the Broadway musical *Wicked*. He believes that I am defying gravity by fighting this cancer battle.

41   Dan G writes the word "popular" like "POP-uUUU-larrr" because he is trying to capture Galinda's inflection of how she sings it in the song "Popular" from the Broadway musical *Wicked*.

42   Used with permission by Stephen Schwartz. Stephen Schwartz, "Defying Gravity," *Wicked*, (New York: Universal Classics Group, a Division of BMG Recordings, 2003.)

43   A Randomized Double-Blind Trial of Fluconazole Versus Voriconazole for the Prevention of Invasive Fungal Infections in Allogeneic Blood and Marrow Transplant Patients, BMT Clinical Trials Network; Fungal Prophylaxis Protocol-0101; Version 3.0 dated August 5, 2003.

44   Susan K. Stewart, *Bone Marrow and Blood Stem Cell Transplants*, (Highland Park, IL: BMT Info Network, 2002), 8.

45   Ibid., 81.

46   Op cit, A.J. Russell, ed., 113-114.

47   James C, McKinley, Jr., "A Journey From a Mill Town Ends With a Run for President," *The New York Times*, January 12, 2004.

48   Sharon Salzberg and Joseph Goldberg, *Insight Meditation* (Boulder, CO: Sounds True, 2001), 133

49   "This Day" reprinted with permission from Lani Ford © 2004.

50   Op cit, A.J. Russell, ed., 194.

51   Ibid., 198-199.

Breinigsville, PA USA
28 October 2009
226557BV00002B/3/P